DATE DUE			
Feb29 80			
Mar26'80			
Dec11 '81			

THE DYNAMICS OF THE ARMS RACE

The Dynamics of the Arms Race

EDITED BY DAVID CARLTON AND CARLO SCHAERF

CROOM HELM LONDON

First published 1975
© 1975 International School on Disarmament
and Research on Conflicts Fourth Course

Croom Helm Ltd
2-10 St John's Road London SW11

ISBN: 0–85664–270–3

327. 174
D99
100724
aju. 1977

Set by Red Lion Setters, Holborn, London
Printed by Biddles of Guildford

CONTENTS

Preface

Summary of Proceedings *J. Henk Leurdijk*

Part I The Nuclear Arms Race

Part II Chemical and Biological Warfare

Part III Theory of Conflict and Some Regional Case Studies

PREFACE

The organization of the course and the symposium was made possible by the generous collaboration and financial contributions of different organizations and individuals.

For their financial contributions we wish to express our gratitude to:
UNESCO, in particular Prof. M. Paronetto-Valier;
National Science Foundation (USA);
The Ford Foundation, in particular Mr William B. Bader and Dr Alessandro Silj;
The Italian Ministry of Foreign Affairs;
The Italian Ministry of Public Education;
The Italian National Research Council.

For hospitality in the City of Padua and in the Collegio Carlo Ederle we are indebted to:
The University of Padua, sponsor of the meeting;
The Opera Universitaria of the University of Padua and in particular its Government Commissioner, Prof. Paolo Alghisi to whom we owe the granting of the facilities of Collegio Carlo Ederle;
The Physics Department of the University of Padua and in particular Prof. Antonio Rostagni and Prof. Claudio Villi;
The Laboratori Nazionali di Lègnaro and in particular Prof. Renato Ricci and Dr Paolo Kusstatscher.

Our stay in Padua was made particularly enjoyable by a group of our Paduan friends who volunteered a very large amount of their time to ensure efficient organization. Special thanks are due to Dr Alessandro Pascolini, member of our Board of Directors and Secretary of the School, with his wife Maria Rosa, and Dr Luigi Filippo Donà dalle Rose.

Dr Smeralda Bozzo and Mr Fernando Pacciani collaborated in the preparatory work in Frascati.

We would also like to acknowledge the dedicated collaboration of Mrs and Mr Giorgio Gregori, Miss Viviana Panaccia, Mr Mauro Pascolini and the staff of Collegio Carlo Ederle.

The editors are grateful for technical advice on contributions from Dr Julian Perry Robinson of the University of Sussex and to Dr John Beckman of Queen Mary College, London.

David Carlton
Carlo Schaerf

SUMMARY OF PROCEEDINGS

J. Henk Leurdijk

Introduction

It should be recognised that this summary of the lectures and discussions is biased as to the selection of the items and may be unbalanced in its presentation. This is so for two reasons: first, no written records were made of the discussions so that the summary is a highly personal view of the course and the symposium, and second, the discussions often covered a wide range of subjects occasionally in a rather undisciplined fashion, whereas this summary tries to structure the discussions in a possibly artificially systematic way.

   This summary is organised along the same lines as the presentation of the articles: first, the nuclear arms race in terms of its technological aspects and its political implications; second, biological and chemical weapons; and finally, theory of conflict and some regional case studies.

Nuclear Weapons

The main focus of the school and the symposium was on the nuclear arms race. Any full-scale discussion of this subject has to touch upon a number of interdependent aspects: the technological aspects of strategic and tactical nuclear weapon systems, and their political implications, that is the systematic exposition of ideas of how to use them (strategic and tactical nuclear doctrines) and how to control and eliminate them (nuclear arms control and disarmament). Often these aspects are treated separately, although fully to comprehend the phenomenon of the arms race and its relevance or irrelevance involves studying how they interact. Weapons and strategy interact because it is the quality of nuclear weapons that determines their strategic uses, while at the same time strategic thinking may be an important factor in weapon developments. In addition, it is necessary to consider how the efforts to control the arms race can be understood in terms of some organising principle which relates them with the on-going arms race, thereby making a certain pattern visible instead of treating arms control agreement as unique phenomena.

2

There is ample evidence that at present the nuclear arms race is strongly technologically determined. In his lecture on the origins of Multiple Independently Targetable Re-entry Vehicles (MIRVs), Herbert York explained that in this case almost all decisions were influenced by considerations of technology while the political implications did not enter into the process until it was too late to have any effect. Strategic nuclear weapon systems and their development were described in great detail by three American scientists. Kosta Tsipis dealt with the sea-based deterrent consisting of nuclear missile-carrying submarines (SLBMs) which he described as the ideal deterrent weapons for the future. Their mobility in a water environment makes then invulnerable to a pre-emptive first strike from an opponent and for the same reasons they are unsuitable for delivering a first strike against the enemy weapons. On the other hand, the land-based part of the deterrent (ICBMs) is becoming less important because the fixed position of land-based missiles makes them at the same time vulnerable to a pre-emptive first strike and suitable as a first strike weapon against the opponent as a result of the high accuracy of their delivery. Adopting a launch-on-warning posture would introduce destabilizing elements into the deterrent situation which arms control agreements are trying to prevent. The history of three weapon systems (ICBM, MIRV and ABM) was outlined by Herbert York, who described in great detail the interaction of strategic, political and technological motivations in their development. The most recent destabilizing factor in the offensive missiles race was the introduction and development by the United States of the MIRV. The development of this weapon was described by Herbert York as a result of the coincidence of different motivations held by different groups of people: some gave priority to the maintenance of the American deterrent as a means of dealing with the Soviet ABM system; the Air Force stressed the increase in the number of points that could be targeted with MIRVs in a counter-force posture; while the arms controllers in the American Government saw MIRVs as a device to prevent the building of more missiles.

General and complete disarmament being a rather elusive goal and conventional disarmament not being regarded as of urgent importance, most efforts for arms control and disarmament during the last decade have been concerned with nuclear weapons. But the little progress that was made along this road has been far outdistanced by the developments in the nuclear arms race. Anti-Ballistic Missiles (ABMs), ICBMs and SLBMs are now quantitatively though not qualitatively limited in the SALT Agreements of April 1972, which were evaluated by Jack Ruina as only important when seen as part

3

of a process of negotiating arms limitations. The main justification of the ABM Treaty was the recognition by implication that deterrence should be upheld as the strategic principle of the American-Soviet relationship. The positive effects of the offensive missiles limitation agreement could be found in the spin-off from the negotiation process that both parties went through. As next steps in the arms control process he advocated curbing the qualitative aspects of the arms race and negotiating a complete test-ban treaty and a ban on ASW techniques.

As a result of the development of these highly sophisticated weapon systems, people gradually came to believe that nuclear weapons had the effect of creating a qualitatively new system of international politics. During the 1950s and early 1960s, with perhaps the Cuban missile crisis as the turning point, efforts were made to 'conventionalize' nuclear weapons. This was made possible by miniaturizing the nuclear warheads and improving the accuracy and reliability of their means of delivery. Arguing that nuclear weapons were just another kind of weapon, some strategists had thus sought to establish the political usefulness of nuclear weapons. Hans Morgenthau discussed such concepts as the 'clean bomb', massive retaliation, tactical nuclear warfare and strategic doctrines such as counter-force, population defence, damage limitation and first strike postures. These were, in fact, all 'winning-the-war' strategies whereby superpowers would aim not to go undamaged but, in Hans Morgenthau's words, 'to come out wounded but not dead'. Such thinking still is an important factor stimulating the invention and development of new weapons, such as Herbert York described in the case of MIRVs and Kosta Tsipis in the case of anti-submarine warfare (ASW). Developing MIRVs meant increasing the number of points that could be targeted which was welcomed by those, especially in the Air Force, who advocated a counter-force strategy. The improvement of ASW techniques would degrade the sea-based second strike force. But, in the view of most participants, in the nuclear age the aim should be avoidance rather than the conventionalization of nuclear war. With this objective in mind, two major points emerged from the discussion: first, it was contended that a controlled nuclear war is not possible either in the form of a tactical nuclear war or in the form of a counter-force exchange, and secondly, it was admitted that the concept of deterrence, although generally regarded as the only possible strategic nuclear relationship between the two powers in the present state of technology, has in itself major weaknesses.

The possibility of a controlled nuclear war was discussed in the context of the tactical use of nuclear weapons and of counter-force warfare. Counter-force strategies require the possibility of distinguishing between conventional and military targets, which was regarded as impossible in view of the destructiveness of nuclear weapons, the geographical mix of conventional and military targets and the problem of classification of weapons in either of the two categories.

The concept of tactical nuclear warfare was discussed by David Carlton who stated that, if one started from the assumptions of NATO, one could put forward arguments for a variant of tactical nuclear warfare. This concept emphasises the usefulness of delivering 'teaching strikes' on targets in the enemy's heartland in a situation in which the credibility of the United States as a superpower is at stake or her own survival as an independent state. Most participants, however, discarded the possibility of tactical nuclear warfare if it were based on a distinction between tactical and strategic nuclear warfare, advancing three arguments:

1. the distinction between tactical and strategic nuclear weapons is not relevant in view of the destructiveness of even the smallest nuclear weapons. There are weapons that could, theoretically, be used in a tactical or strategic way but all would bring terrible destruction;

2. as soon as nuclear weapons are used, escalation to all-out strategic war is almost inevitable;

3. especially with regard to Europe where the concept of tactical nuclear war has its greatest applicability, the asymmetric geographical situation makes this concept extremely dangerous. The conventional unbalanced situation will create pressures for an early use of tactical nuclear weapons, while the high density of its population and industry will make it difficult to discriminate between the strategic and tactical uses of nuclear weapons in Western and Central Europe. It was pointed out that although it is often said that the presence of tactical nuclear weapons in Europe may have contributed to the stability of the situation in Europe, this could not be proved or disproved and, in any case, it has done so at the price of creating a dangerous situation: thousands of nuclear weapons are available in a politically fluid situation where, if the threshold between conventional weapons and tactical nuclear weapons were crossed, the crossing of the threshold between tactical and strategic nuclear weapons would be easier.

It was contended, then, that the threshold should be between conventional and nuclear weapons: the choice between a quick death (when strategic nuclear weapons are used) and a slow death (when tactical nuclear weapons are used) is a matter of taste, not of principle.

The general problems of nuclear armament and arms control were introduced from different perspectives of academic disciplines and diplomatic practice. But most participants were agreed that nuclear weapons have had a deep impact on the practice and theory of international politics.

Hans Morgenthau, in his lecture on the political aspects of disarmament, stressed the discontinuity in the evolution of armaments as a result of the development of nuclear weapons that qualitatively changed the nature of international politics. Milan Sahovic, however, who spoke on disarmament and international law, stressed the continuing validity in the nuclear age of basic legal obligations concerning warfare and armaments such as the protection of inhabitants and belligerents under the Hague Conventions, the illegality of the use of weapons that cause unnecessary harm under the Geneva Protocol (1925) and the general obligation of states to observe the territorial integrity and sovereignty of the other states. Both, however, agreed on a number of points. The introduction of nuclear weapons into the international system fundamentally challenged basic concepts of international law and relations. The advent of nuclear weapons resulted in a new kind of relationship between the major powers based on the concept of deterrence, changing forever the notions of offense and defence. In a framework of deterrence defensive weapons may have offensive implications while offensive weapons are regarded as defensive if they threaten the opponent's population. There was agreement, too, on the need for a new approach in which the adoption of new and effective legal rules and obligations and a new kind of politics was suggested. While governments which are in possession of these new weapons emphasize that they are not subject to the legal obligations assumed previously, it is also evident that many statesmen and responsible politicians are still thinking in terms of the old concepts. They base their thinking on traditional notions such as 'defending the country', 'winning a war', 'balance of power' and the relevance of the distinction between victory and defeat, that may weaken and destabilize the relationship of mutual deterrence that is said to guarantee peace. A third point of agreement that emerged from the discussions was that the results of arms control efforts are rather disappointing. According to Hans Morgenthau, there is now objective room for agreements on arms control and disarmament because in the nuclear situation the quantitive relation between the number of possible targets and the number and destructiveness of weapons had changed to the advantage of the latter. While being functional and politically inspired in a conventional system, the arms race in a nuclear international system is disfunctional and technologically inspired. Nevertheless, it was stressed that most agreements on arms control were in fact treaties of non-armament and interpreted as efforts of the

6

armed to disarm the unarmed. Friedhelm Solms, in his lecture on some socio-economic aspects of disarmament, also stressed the close relationship between the arms race and technological innovations.

From this it is evident that the participants in the school regarded the international system as essentially bipolar in nuclear terms and the history of the disarmament negotiations, as reviewed by William Epstein, as an exercise in freezing this structure. William Epstein recognised a clear trend toward a bilateral framework for disarmament negotiations. During much of the history of such negotiations, however, this framework was multilateral in form and Roberto Caracciolo, in dealing with the accomplishments of the CCD (previously the ENCD) evaluated the role of the smaller powers as one of stimulating, mediating and catalyzing issues between the major powers. The co-chairmanship of the United States and the Soviet Union of this Committee testified to the substantially bilateral framework of the disarmament negotiations and Jules Moch emphasized his view that giving up this chairmanship is a fundamental precondition for the return of France to the negotiating table.

Although there are now five countries with nuclear weapns and a number of countries on the threshold of acquiring nuclear weapons, the world is still essentially bipolar. During the progress of the nuclear arms control negotiations, the bipolar nature of the international system became still more pronounced as a result of the nature of the nuclear agreements and the formal framework for the negotiations was accordingly adapted to this situation. The CCD is now running out of work and dealing only with marginal matters, while the Soviet Union and the United States have entered on a course of bilateral negotiations, leaving the other countries out in the cold. The impact of this state of affairs is strongly resented by the smaller countries but no solution to this problem emerged, most of the participants being rather sceptical about the prospects for a world disarmament conference. But at the same time there was much fear of what may be the only possible course that could basically change this situation: the build-up of nuclear armaments by the present small nuclear powers and the proliferation of nuclear weapons to non-nuclear weapon countries. Many voiced strong reservations on the deterrent possibilities of the nuclear forces of France and Great Britain, even combined. One major difficulty which was mentioned, among others, was that the political *raison d'être* of the independent French nuclear force is to sustain an independent French foreign policy which France is not likely to give up in the event of Franco-British nuclear co-operation. Francesco Cavalletti elaborated, in the context of his lecture on the contributions of Western Europe to disarmament, on the prospects for such nuclear collaboration. Reviewing the favourable technological,

7

financial and strategic preconditions for British and French nuclear co-operation which, in his view, far outweighted the obstacles, he nevertheless voiced his fears that collective European nuclear armaments would stimulate the arms race while aggravating global tension. Of major importance would be the outcome of the next stage of SALT because a continuing nuclear arms race between the Soviet Union and the United States would strengthen pressures for nuclear arms for Europe.

Although during the discussions the political value of the recent SALT agreement was recognised, many doubted the substantive value of these agreements with regard to ending the arms race and arms control. But there is clearly a dilemma here, which was reflected in the contrasting opinions of the participants, some favouring the extension of the deterrence principle to at least three and possibly more political entities but most arguing in favour of a continuing bipolar relationship. In these discussions it was also suggested that France and Great Britain might assume a major rôle at the level of tactical nuclear armament, these weapons having a greater deterrent value than the British and French nuclear submarines.

The strategic nuclear forces of the Soviet Union and the United States consist of three weapon systems:
1. the Strategic Air Command (SAC) consisting of long range bombers. Although it was generally recognised that they only have a supplementary role in nuclear strategy because they are vulnerable to a surprise enemy attack and their penetration capability is seriously endangered by the active air defences of the enemy, it was stated that they are not unreliable enough to give up — they can at least complicate the task of the defences — while in the future they may be equipped with long-range missiles that can have a function comparable to the undersea missiles;
2. the land-based ICBMs which may become obsolete as a result of recent technological developments: the increasing accuracy — a 30-metre accuracy was mentioned — makes the fixed land-based missiles increasingly fit for counter-force options and if both superpowers settle on a strategic relationship of mutual deterrence, the ICBMs may become outdated as a result of both their technological superiority and their vulnerability;
3. the sea-based SLBMs which will in the future be the strategic weapon systems both of the major powers and of the minor nuclear powers.
The relevance of these weapon systems is a function of their strategic uses. In a world of two major powers having achieved a

comparable technological development, three symmetrical postures are possible:

1. if both powers adopt a defensive posture (defence, that is, in the traditional meaning of defending the population) their strategic relationship is based on the principle of defence;

2. if both powers adopt a counter-force posture (aiming at eliminating the opponent's nuclear weapons) their strategic relationship is based on mutual first strike capabilities; although there may be differences counter-force, pre-emptive first strike and damage-limiting first strike, the technological requirements are much the same and all are 'winning-the-war' strategies;

3. if both powers adopt a defensive posture by threatening to destroy the opponent's population only if the opponent attacks, their strategic relationship is based on the principle of deterrence.

It can be argued that, among equal nuclear powers exploiting the available nuclear technology, neither a defensive nor a first strike relationship can obtain so that of necessity their strategic relationship has to be based on deterrence. But this picture is more complicated in practice. First, there exist asymmetries in nuclear technology, the United States always having been ahead of the Soviet Union in nuclear weapons technology. Secondly, there are often pressures from the internal bureaucratic organisations in favour of further arms development and even in favour of bids for nuclear superiority. In short, a relevant superiority in defensive or offensive weapons may give one country a choice between all three postures, or a combination of them, placing it in a superior strategic position *vis à vis* its opponent.

Although not structured as presented here, the debate on the relative adequacy of these strategic relationships developed along the following lines:

1. A defensive relationship based on the defence of a superpower's own population rather than on the threatened destruction of the opponent's population is not possible in the nuclear age although the idea is, emotionally and ethically, quite attractive. It was pointed out that, in order to work, the population defence system should provide a 100 per cent reliability because a few out of thousands of missiles in an all-out attack can do unimaginable harm. A country will not dare to trust for its security on defensive weapons alone because it can never be sure that its untested system can handle all kinds of tricks the opponent may devise. There is clear evidence that in the interaction of offensive and defensive nuclear weapons development, offensive weapons always have the advantage. This is why a country will organize its defence in the conviction that it can more easily deter an enemy by making sure that the enemy will suffer than by making sure that his attack will fail. It was concluded that

9

the concept of defence in the nuclear age is a relic from the conventional past.

2. A strategic relationship based on counter-force postures was considered unlikely for the following reasons:

(a) while it is possible to wipe out one missile, it is unthinkable that all of thousands of missiles could be destroyed in a very short time;

(b) it is difficult to think of a scenario that can eliminate in a surprise attack all these components of a nuclear force at the same time without giving adequate warning time to one of them;

(c) it is always possible to adopt a launch-on-warning posture although it would be very dangerous to do so and it was argued that to avoid such an unstable posture should be a major aim of arms control negotiations.

3. According to many interpretations of the SALT agreements, the Soviet Union and the United States have agreed to settle their relationship on the basis of deterrence. But while a deterrent relationship seems to be the inescapable result of the strategic arms race, we have to be aware of the weaknesses of the doctrine of deterrence and of the relative importance of the SALT agreements. Joseph Kashi, for example, discussed loopholes in current theories of deterrence, while George Rathjens, evaluating the SALT agreements, elaborated on the possibility of a limitation on missile testing as an arms control technique.

Joseph Kashi suggested a number of reasons why deterrence can break down during a crisis as so nearly happened during the Cuban missile crisis of 1962, as a result of bureaucratic inertia in large organisations and the serious defects of the rational actor model of decision-making in deterrence theory. During the discussion a broad range of arguments was raised, questioning the stability of a strategic relationship based on mutual deterrence between the two superpowers:

(a) The state of nuclear technology in the two countries has never been equal and a superior nuclear power may try to maintain or, perhaps, exploit its superiority for political purposes by adopting a counter-force posture. It was suggested that the introduction of an element of 'irresponsibility' in deterrence is very dangerous because someone may call the bluff and non-nuclear weapon countries may decide to acquire nuclear weapons to avoid nuclear blackmail. Many political leaders from different countries were quoted to the effect that they would not settle for less than superiority, some of them minimizing the consequences of a nuclear war. But doubt was expressed whether this should be interpreted a rhetoric or as an of counter-force postures

(b) There seems to be an internal inconsistency in the logic of

10

deterrence, interpreted as a game of chicken where both can end up on the losing side by behaving rationally: deterrence means the conscious manipulation of risks because it only works if you can make your opponent believe that you are really determined to use nuclear weapons or you may calculate that your opponent will act 'rationally' by backing down in face of a nuclear catastrophe.

(c)   The technological dynamics behind the arms race, that is the possibility of a technological breakthrough that reduces the confidence of a country in the invulnerability of its forces and the long lead-time for the development and deployment of counter-weapons, may cause the adoption of counter-force postures which may give incentives for a first strike.

(d)   There is a great potential for miscalculations as a result of possible misperception of enemy actions and interactions; the lack of information about how to find the optimal solution to a problem; the overloading of a decision-maker's emotional and intellectual capabilities; and the adoption of rigid postures. Leaders can behave irrationally in a situation where the control of the use of nuclear weapons is highly centralized and they have to act in a situation of stress.

(e)   There is a bureaucratic inertia which can interfere with the smooth operation of deterrence.

During the discussions references were often made to the SALT agreements. It seems possible to evaluate the importance of these agreements on three levels and opinions mainly differed about which level should be regarded as most important. Some emphasized the political relevance of the results of the talks between the two superpowers which involved the first agreed limitations on the further expansion of their own armaments and which may point the way to further agreements. It was pointed out that these agreements were concluded in opposition to strong internal pressures. But at the same time there was a consensus that the two superpowers had only formally fulfilled the conditions of Article VI of the Non-Proliferation Treaty (NPT) to pursue negotiations in good faith on effective measures for nuclear disarmament and had not done so in practice because of the lack of substantive results on other levels. On the strategic level some stressed the importance of the implied agreement on deterrence as the guiding principle of their strategic relationship. But others tended to the conclusion that although both superpowers had given up the option of an ABM defence of the whole population, there remained the threat that the relationship of deterrence may give way to efforts to attain superiority, since the two powers had not addressed themselves to the question of nuclear sufficiency. Least important are the results on the arms race level. As regards the ABM agreement it was mentioned that ABM would not work in any case with the present state of defence technology while the text of the Agreed Interpretations on ABM did not rule out the possibility of a defence based on other physical possibilities and hence the obvious need to negotiate this issue as technology improves will constitute a permanent danger to the ABM treaty. The quantitative freeze of the Offensive Weapons Limitation Agreement was considered hardly more relevant because both powers had only negotiated on what they would have done unilaterally in any case. And as no qualitative limits were agreed upon, it was clear to the participants that pressures would develop for a qualitative arms race that might endanger the relative stability of the deterrence relationship. Especially, as all indications point to a future deterrent, mainly sea-based, the failure to deal with anti-submarine warfare (ASW) techniques may prove to be the major weakness of the SALT agreements. Although ASW may not be able to deny the SLBMs their deterrent value, it may endanger its credibility and so stimulate the arms race. This may be a major negotiating issue for a subsequent phase of SALT. The sea-based deterrent could be stabilized, as Kosta Tsipis suggested, by forbidding the installation of large acoustical arrays capable of tracking missile-carrying submarines and designating areas in the oceans accessible only to submarines of one nation. In this context it was noted that the failure of SALT to limit qualitative improvements in weapons would prevent the conclusion of a complete test ban agreement.

The evident consequence of the offensive missiles limitation part of the SALT agreements is that the qualitative arms race will continue, which may threaten the future stability of the relationship of mutual deterrence. Although it is generally recognised that the ABM Treaty, with its ban on population defence, implies acceptance of the deterrence doctrine by both sides, the qualitative arms race in offensive missiles may lead to 'war fighting' capabilities. To develop a 'war fighting' capability, however, requires extensive missile testing in order to develop the necessary high accuracy, confidence and reliability of the offensive weapons. In his lecture, George Rathjens suggested that an agreement on limiting missile testing to an agreed number could prevent such a development and curb the arms race. He argued that if both countries really wanted to adopt a deterrence relationship such an agreement might be a very good vehicle of arms control because (a) in contrast to a counter-force posture, the deterrence relationship is compatible with a large measure of uncertainty with regard to one's own missiles (there is little difference between retaliation being 90 per cent or 99 per cent effective) and

(b) extensive testing is required to build an effective 'war fighting' capability and this can easily be observed without intrusive inspection. This is why there are important reasons for trying to limit the qualitative arms race which is still going on at the testing stage, an opportunity which was missed in the case of MIRVs.

Arms control agreements, and especially the SALT agreements, which did so little to control the arms race, raise important questions as to why they are negotiated anyway and why the arms race is so important that it cannot be stopped by arms control agreements. Answers to these questions were sought by Thomas Schelling in his lecture on the interest structures that may underlie arms agreements or understandings and by Kosta Tsipis who compared the arms race with the practice of posturing. The SALT agreements had had a quite sceptical reception in many quarters in that they were seen as agreements not to stop the arms race but to channel it into certain other directions and they may even have been designed to have this effect, or as agreements that merely reflected what the Soviet Union and the United States wanted in any case.

Thomas Schelling analyzed several bargaining situations as interest structures underlying arms control agreements between two parties based on the many possible combinations of their preferences and motives and he gave several reasons why it is important to have a treaty even though it only reflects what parties would do anyhow in the absence of a treaty. He recognised that in arms control agreements there may be elements of posturing, a practice which was described by Kosta Tsipis with regard to the arms race as a stable and credible channel of non-combative resolution of conflict between two nations of comparable technological development.

In the discussion, two aspects of Thomas Schelling's thesis received particular attention: the degree of specificity that is desirable in a treaty and the value of the negotiating process itself. Thomas Schelling emphasized that the deliberately vague wording of an agreement might inhibit the participants from challenging or endangering the spirit of the treaty and Herbert Scoville argued that in respect of the complexity of arms control matters this vagueness often is a prerequisite of agreement. Others argued, however, that these views did not take into account the mutual distrust among opponents and their different frames of reference which might require a very specific agreement. It was also pointed out that agreement results from a complicated pattern of internal and international compromises. The negotiating process could also be differently evaluated: positive aspects might be that parties undergo, while negotiating, a learning process, that they resolve differences where they disagree or can find out what is relevant or irrelevant. Others emphasized the negative aspects of the negotiating process. Support for negotiations can be counter-productive because it may be an argument for inaction in the field of arms control while at the same time the arms race continues to create 'bargaining chips'.

As to the arms race as a practice of posturing it was pointed out that it has many dangerous aspects: the arms race is a race in nuclear weapons which in itself makes all the difference between this and earlier examples of posturing; the element of bluff and counter-bluff in a deterrence relationship; the American-Soviet rivalry outside the framework of the arms race can interfere with the process of posturing; and, finally, posturing requires a common frame of reference. It was recognised that the arms race as a practice of posturing does not necessarily imply a judgment in terms of good or bad because it serves as a substitute for war, but it makes us understand what in fact is difficult to comprehend: the senseless accumulation of weapons. And it is definitely not a contribution to the resolution of conflict in terms of its settlement or solution.

A special session was devoted to the question of nuclear-free zones, introduced by Jozef Goldblat and William Epstein. Jozef Goldbalt was rather pessimistic on the prospects of concluding relevant agreements on nuclear-free zones. He pointed to the Treaty of Tlatelolco which, while creating a nuclear-free zone for Latin America, does not bind the two largest countries in Latin America, Argentina and Brazil, which are precisely the two countries in the area with any nuclear weapons potential and aspirations. Moreover, the main arguments in favour of nuclear-free zone arrangements have lost much of their validity:

1. the prevention of the acquisition of nuclear weapons by the threshold countries is now being covered by the Non-Proliferation Treaty (NPT) on a universal basis;

2. the prevention of deployment of nuclear weapons in non-nuclear weapon countries by outside nuclear powers is no longer of urgent importance following the development of long-range missiles and a sea-based deterrent;

3. the removal of existing nuclear weapons from the territory of non-nuclear powers is the only relevant remaining objective but this is the most difficult to achieve. It was, in fact, considered unlikely that a nuclear-free zone arrangement will be the appropriate instrument for the removal of foreign nuclear weapons from the only region where they actually are, namely Central Europe.

Proposals for a nuclear-free zone have been made for many areas in the world and most of the arms control agreements concluded thus far are in fact nuclear-free zone arrangements (Latin America, space, Antarctica and the sea-bed, the last three regions being uninhabited).

William Epstein argued that nuclear-free zone arrangements could be relevant for the prohibition of the *use* of nuclear weapons against non-nuclear weapon countries. The NPT does not deal, to the dismay of the non-nuclear weapon countries, with the use or non-use of nuclear weapons, mainly as a result of opposition from the United States. The most quoted reason for the unwillingness of the United States to forego 'no-use' or 'no-first-use' options is the unbalanced situation at the conventional level in Europe which nuclear weapons are said to balance. The United States, however, had accepted a no-use formula in the context of the Latin America Treaty which the Soviet Union refused to endorse. Jozef Goldbalt pointed out that a universal declaration on the prohibition of the use of nuclear weapons would deal with the above-mentioned third purpose for which a nuclear-free zone might be negotiated.

An issue that come up in most discussions on conventional, biological, chemical, and nuclear disarmament is the problem of verification. This problem has been a major stumbling block in the negotiations since the Second World War and it was thus appropriate that a veteran participant in these negotiations, Jules Moch, introduced the subject. He reviewed the differences between the Western and Soviet positions on verification which diverged on two fundamental issues. First, there was the fact that, while the United States stressed the need for on-site inspections as a fundamental arms control principle, the Soviet Union strongly insisted on the adequacy of national means of verification. Secondly, there was the problem of what should be verified: while the United States emphasized the need to verify what was present before and after disarming, the Soviet Union wished to see the verification restricted to what was being destroyed.

It is appropriate at this point to make a distinction between three forms of inspection: first, self-inspection, meaning verification by a state within its own territory such as is mentioned in the Biological Disarmament Convention as the only means of verification; secondly, national verification, meaning the use of national means of verification by a country to observe another country; and thirdly, international means of verification.

The debate on verification procedures centred very much on the problem of on-site inspection. The debate in the international negotiations during the past twenty-five years has reflected the inadequacy of detection mechanisms; the different social conceptions of the two major powers; and the relative power position of the great and smaller powers. Over the years, however, many things have changed. Detection mechanisms have improved so that we now have available radars, satellites and computers to process information. As a consequence, we can rely on national detection mechanisms which are not regarded as intrusive by the other party, reducing the need for on-site inspection. As a result of this improvement in long-range inspection techniques it was possible, for instance, to conclude the Partial Test Ban Treaty (1963). Both the ABM Treaty (Article 12) and the Offensive Weapons Limitation Agreement (Article 5) recognised the applicability of national means as a way of verifying the observance of these international agreements. Nevertheless, it may be possible for a country to interfere with the opponent's verification mechanisms, sometimes with dangerous international complications as occurred with the shooting down of a U-2 spy plane in 1960 just before the planned Summit Conference and with the shooting down of a U-2 over Cuba at the height of the Cuban missile crisis of 1962. It is, therefore, extremely significant that both the Soviet Union and the United States have now formally recognised the importance of the improvement in detection techniques for arms control agreements in undertaking, in the SALT agreements, not to interfere with the national technical means of verification of the other party.

Although the positions of the Soviet Union and the United States have approached each other, there remains a clear difference of emphasis reflecting different types of social organisation. But it was pointed out during the discussions that inconsistent elements are present in the arguments of both sides. There is a basic contradiction in the Soviet insistence that, on the one hand, a country can place trust in the self-insepction of another country because an agreement is there to honour and, on the other hand, its position that it for its part could not accept international verification because of fear of industrial espionage. In the context of the discussion on chemical weapons, however, the Soviet Union has proposed an international programme to supervise the activities of national verification commissions. As regards the United States's position, it was pointed out that there were limits to what even on-site inspection can achieve. The Mirving of missiles was mentioned as one example and Herbert York took nuclear underground explosions as a further example. He argued that it is not possible to attain 100 per cent reliability of detecting and identifying nuclear explosions below a certain threshold; but that the use of on-site verification will make it possible to introduce the risk of detection and identification of very small nuclear explosions.

It was suggested that, as a result of these considerations, a combination of national and international inspection procedures might be acceptable. In this context, it was noted that at the CCD a change of attitude could be observed: the emphasis was no longer on absolute but rather on adequate verification, the objective no longer being to detect violations but rather to deter violations. What is important is the reduction of the risks of evasions involving programmes of military significance to acceptable levels.

While the positions of the Soviet Union and the United States are obviously approaching each other, the improvement of detection techniques has created uneasiness among the smaller powers. As was pointed out in the debate, these techniques are now so sophisticated that they are the monopoly of the major powers and so the smaller powers are excluded. This is why they emphasize international procedures rather than national means of verification. In the NPT the non-nuclear powers had to agree to international control of their peaceful applications of nuclear energy in order to get assistance from the nuclear weapon countries. In the Latin American Treaty they even accepted a right of transit of nuclear weapons over their territory. The same applies to the sea-bed treaty in which the smaller powers take great interest.

Chemical and Biological Weapons

Substantial attention was devoted to the problem of biological and chemical weapons. While the present agreements in the nuclear field are in fact treaties of non-armament, the Biological Disarmament Convention stands out as the only real disarmament undertaking. Jozef Goldblat showed that this convention, in which parties undertake not to develop, produce, stockpile or otherwise acquire or retain biological agents and toxins, has major deficiencies. Slautcho Neytcheff spoke of the application of micro-organisms in biological warfare.

In the field of chemical disarmament not much progress has been reported although chemical weapons have occasionally been used in war. The problem of definition is a major obstacle. Oleg Reutov discussed the question whether limiting the control of the production and accumulation of chemical weapons to organo-phosphorus substances would not make possible the uncontrolled accumulation of toxic substances belonging to other chemical classes. He concluded that both should be limited as both could be used as warfare agents, favouring as the most rational system of verification a system of self-inspection.

The state of negotiations on chemical weapons was reviewed by Jozef Goldblat who focused on the scope of non-production and non-stockpiling commitments which would be appropriate. He mentioned as the major difficulty the inadequacy of definitions when it comes to determining whether a particular chemical product should be classified as a warfare agent.

17

From the discussion on these subjects four reasons emerged which explain why biological weapons (BW) are effectively banned while chemical weapons (CW) are not:

1. while many countries have the basic material for CW production, this is much less so in the case of BWs; only three countries actually had a stockpile of BWs and all were nuclear weapon countries;

2. while biological warfare agents, with very few exceptions, have no peaceful use, chemical agents can be grouped into three large categories: single-purpose agents, which, like biological warfare agents, have no use other than for warfare (only very small quantities may be employed for scientific and medical purposes); dual-purpose agents, which are commonly used for civilian needs, but which can also be used in war; and intermediates, which may or may not have civilian applications and which do not have immediate significance unless converted into agents;

3. while BWs are essentially uncontrollable and may thus even harm their users, CWs are more controllable and considered militarily useful, while in may countries they are used for internal riot control. In view of the small military utility of BWs, therefore, the Biological Disarmament Convention is only a marginal disarmament measure as compared to the banning of CWs;

4. while the verification of a CW ban can only be made effective by an effort on a gigantic scale, which in practice is likely to be unattainable, in the case of a ban on BWs no provisions for control were made because there was felt to be no need for them.

The Study of Conflict

A number of lectures provided the methodological basic of the study of conflict which is basic for the understanding of the area of disarmament and arms control in which we mostly take the existence of conflict for granted. There is at the present time a wealth of methodologies for conflict study, or international relations in general, but no agreement of the relative importance of these approaches. Albert Chammah gave an introduction to the laboratory-simulated study of conflict, dealing with applications of game theory and, more specifically, with the chicken game, the prisoner's dilemma game and bargaining games. Joseph Ben-Dak dealt with the event data analysis of international conflict, studying the exchanges of actions and responses (activities and behaviour) between nations. International actions consisting of transactions that represent flows of routinized actions and event interactions being single actions of a non-routine character, event data analysis concentrates on these data in order to arrive at the sociometry — the pattern of conflict and co-operation —

of international society. This should assist in constructing operational definitions for testing hypotheses and in analytical diagnosis. Alan Dowty provided the framework for a comparative historical sociology, that is a framwork for the comparison of relations among sovereign political units under widely varying historical and cultural settings. The aim of this particular approach is the identification of patterns basic to all periods and cultures which will help to clarify the influence of both particular features and larger historical changes. He applied this approach to the incidence of foreign-linked factionalism (the alliance of internal factions with an external enemy) identifying it as a 'strategic constant' independent of cultural influences and structural features of the international system and characterized on the dyadic level by a small factionalized state 'sandwiched' between two strong neighbours. A second area of applicability was the systematic analysis of international guarantees which are a typical feature of the relationship between great and small powers.

The relevance of these approaches, deriving from the study of other social and behavioural sciences and stressing the importance of rigorous, scientific methods of study with reliance on strict standards of verification and proof as opposed to the traditional approaches, deriving from history, law and diplomatic practice and relying on the exercise of judgment, is much debated. Some of the participants in the discussions did not hide their deep distrust of what they called physicalist approaches. According to their criticism, these methodologies ignore the essentially unique character of international phenomena, taking the substance out of international conflict in order to process the data. The general view emerged from this discussion that both approaches to the study of international conflict should have their own place. Most participants were able to agree with the view expressed by one of them that those who favour the so-called behavioural approaches do want to keep the substance of international conflict which is in the motives and feelings of the people and decision-makers, but want to exclude the interference of their own prejudices in their analyses.

Against this methodological background attention was paid to two particular conflict-cases: Southern Africa and the Middle East. William Gutteridge dealt with the international aspects of the South African situation, evaluating the factors sustaining the *status quo* and those tending to undermine it. Simha Flapan elaborated on the theme of new options for the Middle East, suggesting a number of factors that justified an optimistic view of the possibilities for peace. Concentrating on the relations between Egypt and Israel, his optimism was based on the decline in the international status of Egypt resulting from the withdrawal of the Soviet presence from Egypt, the decline of

19

Pan-Arabism as a dominant force in Egyptian policies and the economic burdens of armament, and on the process of reorientation among the Palestinians as a result of the failure of guerrilla warfare and the experience of many Palestinians with the Isreali economic and social structure which was inducing them to look for political alternatives. Both conflicts provided much of the reference material for sessions on arms control in developing countries and on the role of peacekeeping forces.

Peter Kodzić concentrated on the problem of the conventional arms race in the Third World which did not differ from the armaments problems elsewhere in both its dynamics and its relation to economic development.

Armaments being endemic in an anarchistic world system of sovereign states, it was suggested that international devices such as arms control (especially nuclear-free zones) and peace-keeping (international guarantees) might be useful in containing the violent aspects of these conflicts. Both Israel and South Africa are among the most advanced of the potential nuclear weapon states and there can be little doubt that both do want to keep their nuclear weapons option open by not signing the Non-Proliferation Treaty. Yet, while this is an obstacle to the creation of nuclear-free zones, these countries are at the same time conventionally in a far superior position *vis-à-vis* their opponents and hence there is no immediate fear of nuclear weapons being introduced into the region from inside. And nuclear intervention on the part of one of the great powers was considered unlikely.

Peace-keeping forces might serve as a second restraint on the possibilities for the violent eruption of these conflicts. In the Middle East unilateral guarantees were not considered feasible unless they are limited to Soviet and American guarantees against each other, but it was suggested by Alan Dowty in his lecture on guarantees that an impartial, multilateral guarantee backed by a peace-keeping force of small and medium powers with no direct interests and with a clear mandate for enforcement might be relevant.

Martin Aitken argued that, since the use of force is inevitably a last resort in the resolution of conflict, the central problem in minimizing the incidence of war is, not how the world should be disarmed, but who should control the world's armaments and to what end. On this premise he discussed the role of peace-keeping forces in general and complete disarmament (GCD). Since GCD would necessitate the establishment of an international force with world-wide capabilities, its permanence can be assumed. International politics being basically anarchic, planned GCD is impossible. For the same reason, disarmament by an individual state lacks permanency. Even if this were not so, on the basis of the initial premise, the successive disarmament of individual states could not of itself constitute progress towards GCD. He contended that such a process could lead to GCD only if it resulted from each state involved receiving an assurance of security from one or more non-aligned and international peace-keeping forces, the generalized responsibility for which would hold out the possibility of their permanence. He concluded that, if GCD were desired as a means of preventing war, it would depend initially on the pragmatic introduction of such forces between states. In the distant future they might be combined into a world-wide force. He met considerable opposition, however, with his suggestion that some peace-keeping forces would require a nuclear capability, both in order to guarantee the security of nuclear states in the process of nuclear disarmament, and to maintain the deterrent effect of nuclear weapons on the conventional use of force.

PART I
THE NUCLEAR ARMS RACE

1. THE ORIGINS OF MIRV

Herbert F. York

MIRV Description

One of the most important military inventions in recent years is MIRV. This acronym stands for Multiple Independently-targetable Re-entry Vehicles. A single ballistic missile with a MIRV capability can deliver one or more warheads with a very high accuracy to each of several different targets. Multiplicities as high as fourteen have been reported. This is accomplished by means of a 'bus', a device sometimes more formally called the Post Boost Control System (PBCS) and sometimes the Sequential Payload Delivery System (SPD).

The MIRV system works as follows: initially, the main rocket booster puts the bus on a course that would cause it to impact somewhat near target number one. The bus contains several re-entry vehicles, a guidance and control system, and some small rocket propulsion units. The guidance system instructs these small rockets to modify the velocity of the bus so that it is aimed as precisely as possible along the orbit leading to target number one. When this has been accomplished, the bus very gently ejects one of the re-entry vehicles (RV). While this first re-entry vehicle continues inexorably on its course to target one, the bus guidance system instructs the propulsion units to modify its course so as to put it on a course orbit leading to target two, and repeats the process until each RV is on route to its prescribed target.

What follows is an attempt to show just how it was that MIRV came to be. We shall see that several independent military requirements led to several different lines of technological developments. As time went on, ideas and personnel were interchanged among the various programmes, resulting in a very complex web of technological developments and inventions. This web could have been cut in a large number of places, and the ultimate result would have remained about the same: MIRVs on ICBMs at the beginning of the 1970s.

The Polaris A-3 MRV

A convenient date to pick up the oldest strand in the web leading to MIRV is 1957. In the autumn of that year the first Sputnik was launched. Shortly after, and at least partially in response, the

23

Department of Defense set up a so-called Re-entry Body Identification Group, a committee to study the question of whether the designers of offensive missiles (ICBMs and Polarises) should take seriously the possibility of defences against missiles (ABMs), and, if so, what they should do about it. The committee was fully informed about the American ABM programme (then the Nike-Zeus) and was aware that the Soviet Union was probably working on something similar. In early 1958, the committee concluded that the possibility of missile defence should be taken seriously, but it described a number of counter-measures for the offense. These included decoys, chaff, reduced radar cross-sections for the RV, blackout, tank fragments, and, most important for our purposes here, multiple warheads. All except the last are designed to confuse the defences; multiple warheads, on the other hand, penetrate defences simply by saturating or exhausting them. Collectively, these counter-measures are called penetration aids.

The committee's report was unusually influential, coming as it did at a rather critical juncture, and eventually its conclusions were widely accepted. The Air Force incorporated several of the deception devices such as decoys in its early penetration aids packages, and the Navy developed a multiple warhead system for the A-3 version of Polaris.

The Polaris A-3 warhead system consists of a cluster of three separate re-entry vehicles each of which contains a nuclear warhead. This type of system is called an MRV, the acronym standing for Multiple Re-entry Vehicle. The cluster of three is launched as a unit, and is aimed as accurately as possible at some particular target. After the boosters burn out, the three re-entry vehicles are mechanically separated from each other and given an additional velocity of some tens of feet per second relative to the velocity of a cluster as a whole. As a result, the three warheads impact in a triangular pattern having dimensions of the order of a mile, and centred more or less on the target. Thus, against soft targets the damage radius of one RV is, very roughly speaking, about the same as their separation, and the destruction caused by such an MRV is about the same as that which would be caused by a single warhead.

The first MRVs were deployed on Polaris A-3s in 1964. It has been estimated that the yield of an individual RV is 200kt.

In the first few years after the decision to deploy these MRVs, considerable progress was made in the design of American ABM systems, and American perceptions of what the Soviets were doing also changed. As a result, it was realised in about 1962 to 1963 that the separation of the re-entry vehicles in the A-3 MRV was too small to cope with any except a first generation ABM, and that by the late 1960s it might become possible in principle to intercept all three RVs with a single ABM. This problem could not be solved by simply increasing the spread of the impact points; doing so would mean making the separation distance bigger than the dimensions of most targets. We will return to this matter later.

Early Multiple Satellites

Following the launch of the first Soviet ICBM in August 1957 and of the first Sputnik in October 1957, there was an outburst of new ideas in the United States about how to make and how to use missiles and satellites. Some of these involved launching multiple satellites with a single booster.

One early multiple satellite idea had missile defence as its goal. The basic design objective was to intercept ballistic missiles during the first few minutes after launch while their booster engines were still operating. Missiles are especially vulnerable during that period because simply puncturing their propellant tanks with shrapnel will cause them to fall thousands of miles short of their targets. In this scheme, the detection and destruction of the missiles was to be accomplished by defensive satellites overhead at the time of launch. Satellite systems designed to achieve these objectives were collectively known as BAMBI, for Ballistic Anti-Missile Boost Interceptor.

One version of the missile defence multiple satellite idea involved a 'mother ship' which housed a number of sub-satellites. Typically, the mother ship was conceived of as having on board some kind of sensors and computer intelligence which could detect and track enemy ICBMs as they rose from the atmosphere. Using this intelligence, it was supposed to orient itself appropriately and to determine when, at what rate, and in what direction to launch its sub-satellites. The sub-satellites were to contain their own propulsion systems, and enough of a guidance and control system so that they could accomplish the final steps of the intercept.

No BAMBI satellite system was ever built, but many versions were studied in depth by the Advanced Research Project Agency (ARPA) of the Department of Defense. During those early years after its founding in February 1958, there was an especially rapid interchange of key technical personnel between ARPA and industry, and among the industrial groups most heavily involved in missile and space technology. As a result, many of the persons involved in working out these paper concepts later turned up in the groups that designed and developed the real hardware to be discussed below.

The first multiple satellite launch, involving real hardware, took place on 22 June 1960. The satellites were Transit IIA and an NRL Solar Radiation Satellite. The first stage booster was a Thor and the second stage was an Able-Star. The booster plus upper stage were first used to place the upper stage with the two satellites still coupled to it on a trajectory with an apogee of 500 miles. The velocity necessary was achieved after the second stage engine had burned about four minutes, and well before apogee was reached.

Then they continued on an altitude-controlled coast for about eighteen minutes, on up to apogee. There the Able-Star engines were restarted and operated for fourteen seconds more, placing the combination on what was intended to be a circular orbit at 500 miles above the earth. The pair of satellites was then decoupled from the Able-Star stage and separated from each other by a compressed spring which gave the smaller one an additional velocity of 1.5 feet per second.

This Able-Star second stage engine was designed and built by Aerojet-General, and used hypergolic propellants, that is propellants which ignite simply on contact. The Able-Star also included a number of sub-systems designed and integrated into it by Space Technology Laboratories, including the restart and the guidance and control units, and a programmer and accelerometer. All of these capabilities, techniques, and sub-systems are essential for the MIRV bus, and the Able-Stars thus represented a major step in the development of MIRV technology.

Another interesting case, involving an additional small step, occurred on 16 October 1963, when the Atlas-Agena combination was used to launch a pair of VELA satellites. In this case the requirement was more complicated than in the case of the Transit launches: the two satellites were to be placed in two very different positions.

The Agena is the oldest American space vehicle with its own propulsion and guidance and control system. It was developed under a contract awarded by the USAF to Lockheed in 1956, well before Sputnik went into orbit. The VELA satellites were designed to detect nuclear explosions in space and in the upper atmosphere. Their purpose was to monitor compliance with the Partial Test Ban Treaty of 1963 which prohibited nuclear tests anywhere except underground.

In the October 1963 flight, the Agena with the two VELAs on board first placed itself on a very elongated equatorial orbit having a perigee near the earth but an apogee at an altitude of 64,000 miles. On first reaching apogee, the Agena oriented and released one of the VELA satellites. The VELA had a solid propellant rocket motor which it fired to give it enough additional velocity to circularize its orbit. The Agena and the second VELA then made a round trip down to perigee and back to apogee. By that time the first VELA was roughly halfway around the earth. The second VELA was then oriented, released, and accelerated like the first. The result was two satellites, launched together from the earth, but now about 180° apart on orbits varying from 62,000 to 72,000 miles above the earth. Lockheed Missiles and Space Division, which was responsible for the Agena stage, later designed the Poseidon MIRV, and the Space Technology Laboratory, which was prime contractor for the VELA system, did the systems engineering and technical direction for the Minuteman programme.

Titan III and Transtage

The Transtage is a highly flexible Post Boost Control System or 'bus', as it is usually called. The origins of Transtage, and the Titan III launch vehicle which are used to boost it into orbit, are to be found in 1961. The first successful launch of a Titan III with Transtage took place on 10 December 1964, and the first fully successful delivery of multiple sub-satellites into multiple orbits took place in 1966. In 1968, when John Foster, the Director of Defense Research and Engineering was being questioned about why he was so confident that the Minuteman III and Poseidon MIRVs would work, he cited the successful operation of Transtage as proof that all the essential engineering problems had been solved.

The technical requirements that led to the development of Titan III and Transtage arose in the first months of Robert McNamara's term as American Secretary of Defense. Shortly after taking office, the new Secretary issued to his various chief subordinates a very long list of questions. One of the questions asked why it was that in the previous three-and-a-half years the Soviets had been so much more successful than the Americans in launching satellites, and what might be done to change that situation. Even while the study was in progress, Yuri Gagarin became the first man to orbit the earth; the importance of the study was re-emphasized, and its due date was moved forward.

The study concluded that part of the answer lay in the fact that the Soviet Union had used the same rocket booster for all their space launches, while the Americans had used a wide variety of rockets, often developing a new launcher for each new satellite. One of the unfortunate results of the Americans' approach was that they seldom got the 'bugs' fully worked out of one system before they moved on and began to use a newer one. The solution proposed was that the DoD and NASA should jointly agree on the development of a very limited family of standardized boosters of different sizes, each with enough flexibility to launch a variety of satellites to different orbits.

It was further recommended that the largest member of this family of 'standardized workhorses' be based on the Titan II, the largest and ruggedest of the missile boosters. The first two stages were to be the two stages of the Titan II. The upper stage was to be a new unit, known as Transtage equipped with the Titan II guidance system and having a propulsion system capable of coasting and restarting as in Able-Star and Agena-B. Further flexibility was to be achieved by making it possible to strap two large solid rocket boosters onto opposite sides of the Titan II first stage, thus giving a much larger initial thrust, and making it possible to launch still heavier payloads.

The Transtage was to be designed so that it could reach the 'stationary' or '24-hour' circular orbit at 19,000 miles above the earth. There was no specific military requirement for such a booster, but it was expected one would develop, so McNamara and James Webb, the Administrator of NASA, concurred in the recommendation. Hardware development was initiated through a contract issued to Martin Marietta on 20 August 1962.

Development of the system proceeded smoothly and rapidly, but the anticipated need for such a vehicle failed to appear. Finally, it was decided to use the Titan IIIC/Transtage to launch the IDCSP (Initial Defense Communication Satellite Program) Satellite.

The question of what kind of satellites should be used in a defence communciation system, how many there should be, what altitudes they should be at, and who should build and control them were all matters of very heated controversy, largely beyond the scope of the present discussion. However, two generalizations are pertinent here. Usually it is held that a military communication satellite system should involve many satellites at very high altitudes. They should be many so that broad coverage of the whole world can be achieved and so that the sudden failure of one or two, accidentally or deliberately, will not seriously degrade the system. They should be very high, again for coverage, but also so that extreme rapid slewing of ground receiving antennas is not necessary. The question of exactly how high was one of the most complicated and heated of the arguments.

The coming into being of the Titan IIIC/Transtage, without a specific mission but with plenty of capacity and flexibility helped to resolve some of these questions. Finally, on 16 June 1966 this new launch vehicle was used to place eight communications satellites in eight different predetermined equatorial orbits, all at an altitude of approximately 21,000 nautical miles.

As has already been stated, the Transtage is a true Post Boost Control System or 'bus'. Using its coast and restart capacity, the Transtage first achieved a very nearly circular orbit varying from 20,913 to 21,051 miles and having a period of 1,334.2 minutes. It then gently nudged off one of the sub-satellites. Then, using its 450-pound thrust vernier motors for controlling pitch and yaw, it added the very small increment of velocity needed, and dropped off the second satellite at essentially the same altitude, but with a period of 1,334.7 minutes. It repeated this manoeuvre on through number eight which was dropped off three minutes later with a period of 1,347.6 minutes. More of these 100-pound IDCSP satellites were added in multiple launches on 18 January 1967, 1 July 1967 and 13 June 1968.

The systems engineering on the Titan III and the Transtage programmes was performed for the space and missile office of the US Air Force by the Aerospace Corporation. The same organisations were involved in the Minuteman III MIRV programme, which was initiated after this Transtage programme was conceived but before it achieved its first flight.

The Poseidon MIRV

In the early sixties, a number of events, developments, and situations brought about the requirements for and the development of the Poseidon MIRV. The most important of these were: the completion of the Polaris A-3 development programme; changing ideas about ABM design and possibilities, particularly changes in American perceptions about Soviet ABM; and further developments in strategic thinking, as exemplified by Secretary McNamara's 'Counter-force' speech.

As the A-3 development programme was nearing its end, the Special Projects Office, then under the direction of Rear Admiral Levering Smith, turned its attention to the next step, then designated the B-3. From the beginning it was clear that the B-3 would be a bigger and more accurate rocket than the A-3. The improved version could be used to deliver a bigger bomb more accurately or, at the other extreme, could be used for making a higher multiplicity MRV, thus further reinforcing its defence penetration ability and enhancing its deterrent or 'counter-value' role.

As mentioned earlier, ABM had moved along steadily since the earlier days when the A-3 MRV was first proposed as a solution to ABM penetration. Similarly, accumulating intelligence information about the Soviet programme, plus Krushchev's famous boast that 'You can say our rocket hits a fly in outer space', plus what the Americans knew about the Soviet nuclear tests at high altitude in 1961 and 1962, led the Americans to ascribe to the Soviet ABM the capabilities which they knew that they could achieve, in principle, on their own. In particular, it was deduced that the explosion of a single large ABM warhead could simultaneously destroy all three of the A-3 MRVs. Thus, it was concluded that the separation of approximately one mile between warheads as in the A-3 MRV was too small, and that separation of tens or even a hundred miles might be necessary. Clearly, simply expanding the size of the triangular pattern of the A-3 MRV would not do. Doing that would simply mean that, even in the case of a large soft target like a city, at the most only one of the RVs would be aimed at the city, and that one RV in theory is the one any defence system would concentrate on. Thus, the simple straightforward 'shotgun' approach to multiple RVs was seen as obsolescent, and so, from an early date, a different approach was sought for the B-3.

The third important factor that influenced the Poseidon/B-3 warhead decision was the counter-force strategic philosophy as enunciated in Secretary McNamara's speech at Ann Arbor in 1962. McNamara did not originate the idea of a counter-force strategy; it had been a natural part of strategic thinking before the advent of nuclear weapons, and had never been entirely forgotten. However, the notion of 'deterrence' by threatening cities and the industrial base ('counter-value' targets) had gained the upper hand everywhere except in Air Force circles in the years before the Ann Arbor speech. Furthermore, McNamara was surprised by the reaction to his speech, especially by the Air Force interpretation of it as justifying their most extreme missile deployment plans. As a result, he soon afterward backed away from the views expressed in his Counter-force speech, much to the disappointment of those who advocated expanded deployments.

But despite their transitory nature, the ideas in that speech put a 'pulse' through the technological community which stimulated the kind of thinking that promoted MIRV-like ideas as a means of expanding the number of points that could be targetted.

From the beginning of the nuclear age there has always been an intense rivalry between the Navy and Air Force over rôles and missions, especially in the realm of strategic warfare. The Polaris and the Minuteman were both part of and involved in that rivalry. When the principal mission of each missile was thought of as deterrence of nuclear war by threatening to destroy cities and industry (i.e. so-called counter-value targets), Polaris and Minuteman could play roughly equivalent roles. Then, the arguments about which was 'better' revolved around such issues as cost-effectiveness and survivability in the face of a pre-emptive attack. But when the mission became an enemy's well-protected missiles and other military forces (i.e. so-called counter-force targets), then the Minuteman with its accurately delivered single bomb was seen as possibly gaining a decisive edge over the Polaris 'shotgun' MRV in the rôles and missions argument.

The transformation of MRV to MIRV neatly solved this last problem. By using a 'bus', or PBCS, as described earlier, it was in principle possible to deliver multiple warheads to one single target, but along trajectories having different apogees. Thus, they could all be aimed at a single (hard) target as accurately as guidance technology would allow, but they would all arrive at different times; being spaced as much as a hundred miles apart. Therefore, they would still have the same potential for exhausting a newer, more powerful ABM as the original MRV had against a smaller, cruder, ABM.

In principle, a bus system providing multiple shots with smaller bombs is more effective against hard targets than a single shot with a larger bomb, provided not too much total yield is sacrificed in dividing the explosive up into smaller pieces and in providing the weight needed for the bus.

This conceptual development deserves to be emphasized because it clearly shows that the PBCSs 'independently targetable' feature was essential for solving the ABM penetration problem alone, independent of whatever other military uses it may also have.

The development of Poseidon MIRV was approved in the autumn of 1964, its deployment was approved in 1966, and the first boatload was deployed at sea on the James Madison SSBN on 1 April 1971. The Poseidon MIRV is usually described as having from ten to fourteen individual warheads of 50kt each.

Minuteman MIRV

The Air Force at first concentrated its missile warhead development programme on single, large, accurately launched warheads protected against interception by the various types of confusion devices described in the Re-entry Body Identification Group's report such as decoys and low radar cross-sections. But in 1962 and 1963, stimulated, like the Navy, by progress in ABM and the Soviet high altitude nuclear test series, the US Air Force began to give serious consideration to installing multiple warheads on Air Force missiles as a means of improving their ability to penetrate defences. At about the same time, a steady growth in the perceived number of vital individual military targets in the Soviet Union stimulated interest in the use of multiple warheads as a means of improving force effectiveness. The Air Force was as usual aided in these considerations by its extensive advisory apparatus (RAND, The Aerospace Corporation, and various *ad hoc* committees of outside experts). In 1968, John Foster, U.S. Director of Defense Research and Engineering, made it clear in Senate testimony that the Air Force had this dual motivation for turning to multiple warheads in the early 1960s and that this was still the case in 1968.

But despite there being two complementary reasons for turning to MIRV, the argument about whether multiple small weapons were preferable to a single large one persisted within the defence

31

establishment for some time. The controversy reached a point where a contract which was about to be let for the development of a large single weapon RV was held up because of the dispute over the question. Since information about commerical contracts is normally in the public domain, news of this struggle thus reached the missile press. *Aviation Week* reported in its issue of 29 July 1963 that 'Selection of a contractor to develop Mark 12 [the RV for Minuteman III] had been stymied over the past six months by the Department of Defense Research and Engineering's criticism of USAF's original development plan ... DDR&E intervened during the Air Force's first competition to pick a contractor ... last Fall, charging that the USAF development plan was insufficiently advanced and lacking in multiple warhead capability. The Air Force's concept of Mark 12 was referred to as just another "rock" '.

While this argument was still going on, two entirely different versions of MIRV were being considered. In one concept, a single missile would launch a cluster of small, one-stage missiles each with its own self-contained propulsion and guidance systems. After the cluster as a whole was placed on an approximately correct trajectory to the target area, the cluster would break up, and the individual sub-missiles would then adjust their velocities so as to get on to precise trajectories to their predetermined targets. The extra weight (and even cost) of the individual guidance and control system made this a rather poor option compared to the 'bus', and its development was never authorized.

The other version given consideration in the period 1962-1964 was the 'bus' or Post Boost Control System (PBCS), virtually identical to the Transtage already being developed at that time under the direction of the same Air Force office.

This really was the better idea, and since the necessary technology was already under development, it was finally selected as the appropriate technological solution in 1964. Full-scale development of the bus-type MIRV followed promptly. The decision actually to deploy MIRV was made in 1966, and the 'first flight' of ten Minuteman III missiles with MIRV was turned over to SAC on 19 June 1970.

In addition to the specific developments discussed above, bits and pieces of MIRV technology were invented independently or re-invented in some other Air Force programmes.

One such programme was the development of a 'Sequential Payload Delivery' System (SPD) whose purpose was to deliver a sequence of RVs from California to Kwajalein Atoll where they were used as test targets in the ABM development programme underway at the latter location. The main stimulus for this SPD development was simply economics; delivering several targets with a single launch was cheaper than providing a separate launcher for each one. This programme was approved in 1964 and the first successful application was in 1966. It was done by the same organisation which was responsible for the Transtage.

Of course, practically all of the technological techniques that make MIRV possible were also eventually developed in the civilian space programme, particularly in the lunar exploration programme. However, emphasis has been placed here only on those that had their origin in some military requirement.

The Decision to Deploy

I think that for all practical purposes the decision to deploy the two MIRVs were made inevitable by the decisions to develop them. Even so, the matter continued to be argued after the development decisions were made, and the matter was not really finally and formally resolved until the deployments actually took place in 1970 and 1971.

The argument had several facets. The basic reasons for supporting MIRV deployment were those already discussed: ABM penetration and increasing the number of points that could be targeted.

The ABM penetration feature of MIRV was most strongly put forward by those in the United States who believed the historic Russian penchant for defensive measures would stimulate the Soviets to press forward rapidly with the development and widespread deployment of ABM systems. The Soviets had indeed followed just such a pattern in the case of defence against bombers. The most extreme form of this argument held that the Soviets might be secretly preparing to modify their very numerous and ubiquitous SAM-2 bomber defence system so as to upgrade them into an ABM system.

The expansion of the number of targets that could be hit was primarily of interest to those who took the counter-force mission most seriously. Counter-force strategies are closely connected to and encourage notions about actually fighting and winning a nuclear war. Such notions in turn lead to requirements for a substantially larger force than is needed for simple deterrence. In their extreme form, these notions lead to essentially open-ended requirements for ever more offensive weapons.

These two ideas obviously reinforce each other, and were often combined into a single argument favouring MIRV. Thus we find John Foster in 1968 defending the need for MIRV by saying that we need enough warheads so that we can 'be sure of exhausting their defence capability, and then being able to deliver enough to provide assured destruction'.

Secretary McNamara had another interest in MIRV. His

Counter-force speech unintentionally gave support to calculations of numbers of offensive weapons needed that were very much bigger than the force he had in mind. Some argued for very substantial increases in the total number of Minuteman and Polarises. In this context, the MIRV development programme became a tool in McNamara's arguments against force expansion. In the continuation of the Foster testimony just cited, he said: 'Now, we could choose, for example, to put in a number of Polaris boats. We could increase the Polaris force by a factor of five or ten. . . . But we can get the same equivalent military capability against the Soviet Union by taking the existing . . . boats and changing . . . to the Poseidon missiles.' Hence, from McNamara's point of view, MIRV was a device with an effective positive arms control feature.

Those directly responsible for American policy in arms control did not see it that way. Officials in the US Arms Control and Disarmament Agency, especially Herbert Scoville and George Rathjens, as early as 1964, foresaw ways in which MIRV deployment could upset the 'balance of terror' and destabilize the arms race. They predicted that the deployment of MIRV by one side would be seen by the other as part of a possible preparation for making a first strike. And indeed, an anticipated deployment of MIRV by the Soviets on their large SS-9 ICBMs was seen exactly in that light by Secretary Melvin Laird and his associates in 1969. The Arms Control Agency people therefore opposed MIRV deployment from the start of the development programme.

These important controversies were not known to the public, nor even to any but a selected few in the Congress, until the 1968 Presidential Campaign. Then, Eugene McCarthy echoed the ACDA point of view and said: 'The introduction of sophisticated anti-ballistic missile systems and new missiles equipped with multiple warheads threaten to make the situation unstable. With the deployment of such weapons systems, each side will become concerned as to whether in the event of a pre-emptive attack it will be able to inflict sufficient damage in retaliation — if not its deterrent will not be credible. The arms race will thus be impelled to a new intensity. In crises, there could be an incentive to launch a first strike.'

Later, Senator Brooke introduced a resolution calling for a suspension of MIRV testing, and some other Senators and a number of former officials supported him, but to no avail; the first deployment of MIRV took place while the issue was still being debated.

In summary, the MIRV programme had many roots and branches. Important decisions were made by many persons only loosely connected with each other, and over a period of more than a decade. Of all the stimuli that gave rise to MIRV, the most important was the perceived need to penetrate with assurance ABM systems whose theoretical capability was slowly improving with time. However, all the technologies needed for MIRV had other reasons underlying their development, and so MIRV would very likely have emerged at about the same time even if the need for ABM penetration had not been perceived until much later, and possibly even if it had not arisen at all.

Almost all the important decisions were technologically determined. Economics entered mainly as an added stimulus to the development of the capability for making multiple satellite launches. Strategic analysis entered only fairly late (and indecisively) in a relatively narrow argument over the relationship of MIRV to the arms race. More general strategic thinking, and political considerations did not enter into the process until it was too late for them to have any effect.

2. ANTI-SUBMARINE WARFARE AND MISSILE SUBMARINES

Kosta Tsipis

Introduction

In this paper I intend to examine in some detail the performance characteristics of nuclear missile-carrying submarines, the various uses this weapons system admits, and the type of hostile action it may encounter during war or during periods of international crisis. On the basis of these facts, I will attempt to assess the present and future rôle of the missile-carrying submarine in the strategic arsenals of the United States, the Soviet Union, and other nuclear countries. Although most of my examples and detailed discussion will refer to the United States Polaris/Poseidon system, the arguments about the utility of missile-carrying submarines are exactly symmetrical and apply to the Soviet Yankee-class submarines. I hope to convince the reader that nuclear missile-carrying submarines are an ideal deterrence weapon since they ensure the national security of countries that possess them without destabilizing world peace. Finally, I hope to draw attention to certain components of the arms race now under way that can threaten the deterrence value of missile submarines and thereby plunge us into another spiral of an accelerated arms race.

Submarine-Launched Ballistic Missile Systems

It was evident to strategic planners in the early 1950s (as is evident now) that land-based intercontinental ballistic missiles (ICBMs) are a weapons system unsuitable for deterrence. The central attribute of a deterrent force is its ability to survive a first strike aimed pre-emptively against it. The fixed-targetable location of land-based missiles and the great accuracy that modern inertial guidance-systems afford, combine to deny this primary deterrence feature to land-based missiles. It is commonly accepted that silo superhardening cannot counter the contemplated accuracies of 30 metres that warheads with terminal guidance will be capable of by the end of this decade. Therefore, the credibility, if not the actual performance, of land-based missiles as vectors of deterrence is already seriously eroded and rapidly becoming conjectural. By comparison, the submarine-launched ballistic missile (SLBM) is the 'ideal weapon' for deterrence. The ballistic-missile-carrying submarines have no tactical capability either against surface shipping or against other submarines. Their object is not to attack other vessels but to provide, by remaining invisible and immobile, a non-targetable missile-launching platform, invulnerable to a first strike.

The first ballistic missile submarine, the USS *George Washington*, became operational in November 1960. It was armed with 16 A-1 Polaris missiles which had a range of 1,200 miles and a one megaton warhead and which could be fired while the submarine remained submerged at the rate of one a minute. The Polaris missiles use solid fuel, are expelled from the launch tube by compressed gas, and their rockets ignite once the missiles break through the surface of the sea. By 1966, 41 such submarines were operational. Each submarine *sans* missiles costs about $100 million, is powered by a nuclear reactor, has a length of about 140 metres, a beam of 11 metres, and when submerged displaces 8,250 tons. It has two crews, each consisting of 14 officers and 126 enlisted men, who go on alternate patrols. Each submarine remains on station 60 days and in port 30 days. The submarine's capability to remain submerged is limited only by crew endurance, the amount of provisions they carry and the need for servicing and maintenance. Polaris are swift ships, probably capable of more than 20 knots when submerged. They can descend to 300 to 400 metres but probably not twice that. When cruising at a fraction of their maximum speed, they are practically noiseless. It is said that a Polaris cruising on station emits into the ocean less than a milliwatt of acoustical power, caused mainly by unbalanced rotatory machinery on board. In 1966, of the 41 operational submarines, 8 were carrying A-2 missiles with a range of 1,500 miles and the rest A-3 missiles with a range of 2,500 miles on a 'triplet' warhead which was *not* MIRVed. Since no point on land is further than 1,700 miles from the sea, a Polaris submarine with A-3 missiles can operate in 15 million square miles of ocean covering its targets. Presently, three-fourths of the 41 Polaris submarines are scheduled to undergo changes that will allow them to be equipped with new Poseidon missiles. The cost of conversion is about $30 million per submarine and takes about one year to complete. The new Poseidon missile is twice as heavy as the Polaris A-3 and carries a payload four times as large. Its nominal range is 2,500 miles, but it can be increased by a trade-off between payload and range. Each Poseidon missile carries 10 independently-targetable warheads, each equivalent to 50kt. of TNT, which is roughly more than twice the size of the nuclear bomb that destroyed Hiroshima. All 10 warheads can be aimed at the same target or independently at a separate target. These separate targets, however, must lie in a corridor roughly 50 miles down range and 30 miles wide. The accuracy of these warheads (CEP) is about one-eighth of a mile. The first Poseidon missile was tested in 1968. The first Poseidon-equipped submarine went on duty in March 1971. When the refitting programme is completed, the U.S. submarine force will be able to launch 5,440 warheads against 5,120 separate targets.

Each Polaris submarine has on board three Inertial Navigation Systems (SINS). With the aid of an on-board computer, SINS provides accurate navigation data needed not only for the navigation of the vessel, but also for the preparation of the missiles for launching. The intrinsic precision of SINS is probably extremely good. However, intertial-measurement-unit errors are cumulative, and after days of cruising, SINS needs updating with accurate position information provided by external sources such as satellites, and underwater transponders. With such updating, the position of the submarine at the instant of a missile launch can be known to one or two hundred metres. Updating of SINS while the submarine remains cruising underwater is quite difficult, because electromagnetic waves, the most convenient and efficient carriers of information, are completely attenuated after travelling a few feet in sea-water.

Although the Soviet Union had missile-carrying submarines, both nuclear and diesel-powered in the late 1950s, it was not until 1966 that it launched the first Y-class submarine which is comparable in size and missile complement to the A-1 equipped Polaris craft. Y-class submarines carry 16 single-warhead missiles with a range of 1,300 miles which use storable liquid fuel. Under the Moscow agreement the Soviet Union can possess 62 such submarines if they dismantle up to 210 of their obsolete SS-7 and SS-8 land-based missiles. By 1975, when the present programme of Y-class submarine construction will be completed, the Soviet Union will possess 672 sea-based warheads. I do not know the accuracy of these weapons, but I will assume in the ensuing analysis that it is not better than the accuracy of the Poseidon missile.

First Strike v Deterrence

The opaqueness of the oceans to electromagnetic waves gives the submarine its great advantage as a deterrent, but also makes it a weapon system unsuitable for the first strike against an opponent's land-based strategic weapons.

The strong attenuation of electromagnetic waves by sea-water renders the submerged submarine not only practically incommunicado but also invisible. It combines very tightly invulnerability with uncertain position and, therefore, reduced missile accuracy. The submarine cannot be detected by means of electromagnetic radiation, and therefore it is immune to surprise attack. But its inability to communicate with other submarines or with its national command centre while invisible makes it unfit for a first strike for two reasons. The first reason is that the uncertainty in its position at missile-launch time is rather large. Added in quadrature to the CEP of the Poseidon warhead, the uncertainty results at the present time in an overall accuracy of the submarine-launched ballistic missile which is unsuitable for a first strike attempt, particularly since the Poseidon warhead has only a 50kt. yield. The second reason is even more serious: to possess first strike capability, a submarine fleet must have the ability to carry out a highly co-ordinated and rapid attack. This, however, requires a highly reliable and secure, high-rate, two-way communications link between the command centres and the submarines. In addition, the high degree of reliability necessary for a first strike requires that the missile-launchings have reprogrammable capability that allows for a quick replacement of a missile that has malfunctioned by another one directed at the same target. Neither of these two requirements can be met by the submarines because communication with them is at best laborious and at worst impossible, and because it is almost impossible for the submarine commander to ascertain while submerged whether a given Poseidon warhead has malfunctioned or not, to say nothing of the difficulty of trying to replace it by another one directed on the same target.

Unable to threaten the vectors of deterrence of an opponent, immune to a surprise attack, yet quite capable of completely devastating the urban and industrial centres of a nation, the nuclear submarine appears to be the perfect vehicle of deterrence.

Anti-Submarine Warfare

From time to time, the deterrent value of missile-carrying submarines has been challenged on the basis of claims that strategic submarines are vulnerable to a concerted anti-submarine warfare effort against them. Before I discuss ASW in some detail, I would like to examine with some care the meaning of the term 'vulnerable' in the context of a deterrent force. To threaten SLBMs as a component of strategic deterrence means to be able to destroy in a surprise attack simultaneously, and upon command, all the Polaris (or Yankee) submarines at port or on station in the oceans. If only two Poseidon-equipped submarines escaped, their combined complement of 320 warheads could

39

destroy 50 large cities of the Soviet Union containing 30 per cent of that country's population and 50 per cent of its industry. A similar number would assuredly demolish 75 per cent of the industrial capability of the People's Republic of China. Therefore, even two submarines can inflict politically unacceptable damage and thereby constitute credible deterrence. So to threaten the Polaris fleet as a deterrent force, an opponent's ASW forces must be capable of destroying within a few minutes *all* the Polaris submarines while his offensive missiles attempt to wipe out the land-based Minuteman ICBMs, the SAC bombers, which are dispersed over one hundred airfields, and all the aircraft-carrier-based bombers capable of delivering nuclear weapons. But we do not have to consider such a grandiose attack to find out whether the SLBM force is vulnerable. Let us consider what it takes to destroy only *one* Polaris submarine, and whether current ASW systems have even that limited capability.

Anti-submarine warfare tactical submarines involves four broad operations: intelligence, detection, localization and destruction. In the case of a missile-carrying submarine, the fourth operation cannot be destruction, because to destroy a Polaris is like attacking a field of Minuteman ICBMs. It is an attempt against one's strategic offensive weapons and therefore cannot be carried out in a random unco-ordinated fashion, because it will provoke a nuclear attack against the perpetrator. So in the case of strategic submarines, instead of destruction the fourth operation is tracking. It is quite conceivable that once an opponent manages to track all thirty Polaris submarines on the high seas, he may then attempt to sink them all at once. To sink one or two at a time is meaningless and dangerous for his own safety.

Intelligence includes information about the force levels, number and range of missiles, speed, cruising endurance and noise level of the opponent's SLBM or tactical submarines.

Since the oceans are opaque to electromagnetic waves, high search rate devices aimed at detecting submarines have to employ acoustical methods, either passive or active. Passive methods rely on detecting the presence of a submarine from the noise it produces as it moves in the ocean. Dispersed or concentrated arrays of hydrophones, sonobuoys, or hydrophones mounted on moving platforms (destroyers, helicopters and attack submarines) are all designed to listen for the characteristic noise of a moving submarine. Active techniques utilize a sound generator and a listening system (hydrophones) to receive the portion of the generated sound reflected by a submarine. Thus active systems can in principle detect the presence of an immobile submarine. The sea, however, in which these systems have to perform, is a noisy,

40

inhomogeneous and dissipative medium. The velocity of sound in the ocean varies with temperature, pressure and salinity of the waters, and therefore it varies both as a function of space and time. These variations often bend sound waves. Sound waves are also reflected both from the air-water interface of the surface and from the bottom of the oceans. Thus the paths of underwater sound waves are not straight lines. They converge and diverge, creating 'shadow zones' near the surface of the ocean where submarines can remain undetected even by the most sensitive passive systems. If in addition one recalls that even the noisiest submarine moving at full speed in the ocean generates less than one watt of acoustical power, the nuclear submarines loitering on station are perhaps a thousand times quieter, and that a signal travelling in water loses strength in proportion to the distance it travels, one can gain an impression of the difficulty of merely detecting a submarine a few kilometres away. In general, the effective range of passive detection does not exceed 100 kilometres from a listening array of hydrophones. In general, active systems are more effective for detecting a submarine. Once again, however, the range of sonar systems deployed on submarines, destroyers or even helicopters, is limited to a few tens of miles. By deploying arrays of listening hydrophones utilizing narrow beams of sound in the optimum frequency, and taking advantage of the Doppler shift of the sonar echo reflected from a moving submarine, active systems possess enough processing gain to discriminate submarine echoes from those reflected off a whale or a school of sardines. The use of such mobile systems, however, is to 'sanitize' an area a few hundred square miles around a convoy or a task force of surface vessels, by detecting tactical submarines which try to approach the surface ships for an attack with torpedoes or cruise surface-to-surface missiles. Clearly these systems are not capable of detecting a Polaris submarine that can hear the propeller of surface ships thrashing the ocean hundreds of miles away and take evasive action so that it will remain undetected.

After a submarine has been detected in an area, say 10 kilometres on either side, aircraft, surface craft, or submarines can be employed to localize it. Localization from the air involves dropping directional sonobuoys that can determine the bearing of the submarine with respect to the sonobuoy. By dropping consecutive sonobuoys, an aircraft can locate a submarine within a circle of one kilometre radius. Exact localization is then achieved by a Magnetic Anomaly Device (MAD) that can sense the presence of a large mass of steel underwater. Localization from surface or submarine vessels utilizes sonars and is hampered both by the noise of the hunter vessels and their speed.

Once the submarine is localized, it can be sunk by a torpedo or a depth charge carried by the hunter craft. The active search range of a modern homing torpedo is about a kilometre. Destruction, however, is the expected reaction in the case of tactical submarines. In the case of a strategic submarine, the procedure would be to track it indefinitely.

So far, the procedure for detection, localization and destruction cannot affect the safety of a missile-carrying submarine precisely because they are not designed to do so. They are ASW measures aimed against tactical submarines and therefore their efficacy against missile-carrying submarines is very small if not completely nil. One can therefore conclude that tactical ASW operations, both present and future, do not and cannot threaten the sea-based deterrent.

Counter-SLBM ASW Systems

It is now appropriate to examine two ASW systems which, if built, could generate doubts about the invulnerability of SLBM forces; in addition, I will discuss counter-ASW measures aimed against these systems as an indication of the type of underwater arms race that can be animated by the construction of these systems. I will conclude by suggesting certain arms limitation agreements that can safeguard the invulnerability of the missile-carrying submarines and therefore avoid another spiral in the arms race that can rekindle the familiar 'strategic' and 'crisis' instabilities first induced by the appearance of ABM systems: just like the ABM, counter-SLBM ASW threatens the vectors of deterrence of an opponent, provoking a destabilizing escalation.

The two possible ASW systems that might possess the capability of detecting and localizing simultaneously twenty or thirty nuclear missile-carrying submarines are fixed large underwater acoustical arrays and special trailing vessels. Neither of these systems exists as yet. Both of them have flaws that *a priori* cast doubts on their potential efficacy. But they are often quoted as future threats to an SLBM force. Therefore, I will discuss them in some detail.

The arrays can be either passive or active. Passive arrays can be either dispersed or concentrated. Active arrays can be monostatic or bistatic.

Extensive arrays are favoured over individual sonars, or even small arrays mounted on the sides of hunter-killer submarines, because they possess high processing gain, that is to say they can discriminate in the immense background of ocean noise the signature of a submarine. Let us consider these arrays one at a time.

    1. *Disperse Passive Arrays* consists of hundreds of thousands of hydrophones distributed over millions of square miles of ocean and tied to a central processing centre either by cables or by radio buoys

which transmit the signals received by the hydrophones. The signals detected by the hydrophones are fed into a large computer. The programme of the computer assumes that the signals received by the hydrophones are generated by a submarine moving somewhere in the ocean, successively occupying a continuous line of points. For each such possible point, the programme introduces an appropriate time delay in the output of each hydrophone and adds the delayed signals. Clearly the signals which have the proper delays for the point the submarine actually occupies emerge coherently from the background noise, while all the other signals emerge incoherently and therefore do not give the characteristic signature of a submarine. Thus the computer can pin-point the location of a submarine and track it unobtrusively for indefinite periods of time. (The system actually can work quite well, because once the location and speed of the submarine is known, the computer can 'anticipate' at which point in the ocean the submarine will be at any instant of time and switch to the appropriate processing programme that yields even better resolution.)

2. *Fixed Concentrated Passive Arrays* consist of hydrophones spread in a dense array a few hundred feet long and somewhat less high. Since the water drag prevents the array from having the actual sweeping motion characteristics of radar antennae, the computer simulates this by integrating the signals received by the array after inserting different time delays for each row or column of hydrophones. Each set of consecutively altered delays allows the array to look at a different point of a 360° arc, thereby 'sweeping' the ocean with a 'listening beam'. If the computer is large enough, one can arrange for beams from a number of distinct directions to form simultaneously; this increases the search rate of the array. Since submarines are known to be at most a few hundred metres below the surface of the ocean, vertical directivity of these concentrated arrays enhances their discrimination power.

3. *Monostatic Active Arrays.* Imagine a system consisting of underwater loudspeakers (known as 'emitters') emitting megawatts of acoustical power into the oceans in the form of low frequency sound waves, and arrays of hydrophones listening at the same frequency for the echoes which return after the waves have been reflected by an object in the water. The system utilizes sound of a few hundred Hertz, since these wavelengths are long enough not to be attenuated rapidly or disturbed by local medium inhomogeneities, but short enough to be reflected coherently by an object a few hundred feet long. With the necessary beam-forming capabilities, this system can have resolution in range, azimuth and bearing, such that it can divide the ocean for hundreds of miles around into cells

the size of a submarine, interrogate each one for the presence of reflecting object in it, and thereby be able to localize simultaneously a large number of submerged objects. With enough logic and memory storage, the computer of the system can discriminate submarines from other submerged objects.

4. *Bistatic Systems* differ from the above only in the fact that in this case the emitters are physically removed from the listening hydrophone arrays. Such an arrangement allows for large amounts of emitted acoustical power (by placing the emitters deep in the ocean thereby minimizing power-limiting cavitation effects) and makes the jamming of the system harder.

To what extent any of the above systems can really overcome the noise and inhomogeneities of the ocean medium is not known. It is certain, however, that these sytems can be built (the technology exists); it is equally certain that they can be effectively countered. Active systems advertise both their location and their frequency characteristics. An opponent can either jam them or spoof return signals in the same frequency or, in the case of war, destroy the emitters. Passive systems are harder to detect, but a submarine that suspects that it is being tracked by such a system has a whole spectrum of counter-measures, ranging from decoys to jamming, that can confuse the array and render it useless. Although potentially formidable underwater arrays cannot actually threaten the indefinite viability of the sea-based deterrent; what they can do is cause alarm by creating doubt in the minds of strategic planners as to the invulnerability of missile-carrying submarines.

Let us consider now the threat that overt tracking presents to the submarine-based deterrent. Suppose a country decides to acquire the ability to destroy simultaneously all the missile submarines of an opponent the moment they appear to initiate their missile-firing routine. To do that one needs small swift specialized tracking ships equipped with a few homing torpedoes, manned by a small crew, capable of refueling in the high seas, and equipped with a megahertz sonar that would provide 30-centimetre resolution at 300 metres from its intended quarry. At this distance and with such resolution, the hunter (be it a surface vessel or a hunter-killer submarine) can have a clear pictorial view of the attitude fins of the hunted submarine, and therefore could simply sail in formation with it. Such close overt tracking lacks of course the element of surprise essential in a first strike against an offensive ballistic-missile system, yet it does threaten its efficacy. There is a large number of difficulties associated with being able to tag all the submarines of the opponent, assign trackers to them and maintain the track uninterruptedly, but they do not alter the outcome of the situation drastically.

44

None of the surface or submarine vessels deployed today is capable of such tracking since it has no application to tactical situations and no country has yet launched a programme to acquire this tracking capability. Once again, it is difficult to imagine a completely efficient counter-SLBM tracking system that can deny the missile-carrying submarine its deterrent capabilities. Yet such a system can certainly damage the *credibility* of the SLBM force as an invulnerable deterrent weapon. Such an ASW system would constitute a first strike since it threatens the vectors of deterrence of the opponent without protecting one's own.

How to Safeguard Sea-based Deterrent Systems

The invulnerability of the sea-based deterrent forces of the United States and the Soviet Union cannot be safeguarded with the addition of new weapons systems or any technological advances, but by international arms control agreements. The agreements which I propose are easy to implement and to monitor unilaterally.

The first measure would be to forbid the installation in the oceans of the world of large acoustical active or passive arrays capable of tracking missile-carrying submarines at large distances. Exact technical specifications of power levels and acoustical element distribution can differentiate between arrays designed to monitor the approaches to a country's territorial waters from arrays capable of tracking submarines anywhere in the oceans. Such prohibition is a relatively easy measure to implement since no country has such arrays today, their susceptibility to jamming or spoofing is demonstrable, and their potential cost astronomically high. Because of their size and easy detectability, such arrays cannot be installed or operated clandestinely; therefore unilateral means of inspection can monitor the continuing enforcement of any agreement to ban them.

The threat to SLBM forces from tracking can be removed by any number of bilateral or international agreements. The simplest one, but perhaps not the easiest to verify, is to ban the vehicle and the practice of tracking. Any coherent effort to built a fleet of these highly specialized vehicles can certainly be detected at its nascent stage by satellite inspection. Moreover, since covert tracking is not possible as a counter-SLBM force measure, a nuclear submarine would know immediately if it were tracked.

Another even more reassuring measure would be to designate, by international agreement, areas in the oceans accessible only to submarines of one nation. Each country with submarine-based nuclear weapons could have allocated to her submarine fleet several such areas which would of course be large compared to the search and kill radii of tactical ASW vessel. These areas would have to be away from the lanes of maritime traffic, yet within missile range of the opponent's land mass. Intrusion in these areas by tracking submarines or surface vessels of another country would be declared a hostile act. This measure also would be readily enforced and unilaterally verifiable. It would not degrade the efficiency of the sea-based deterrent, but would remove any visible threat against it with one exception. The exception is, however, important. Suppose during periods of declared non-nuclear war, one country establishes minefields against the tactical submarines of another. How are the missile-carrying submarines to be protected by such a non-discriminating weapon as a bottom-moored mine? A third agreement is needed here to avoid escalation of such a war to nuclear conflict kindled by the destruction of one or more missile-carrying submarines by mines. This agreement should allow missile-carrying submarines to surface, identify themselves and be guided through the minefield at which point they can submerge and disappear once again in the opaque ocean. Once again no elaborate verification procedure is needed to maintain enforcement.

In concluding I wish to stress that SALT I did not address itself to the problem of the invulnerability of the sea-based deterrent, probably an ominous omission, since initiation of counter-SLBM ASW programmes by either the Soviet Union or the United States will threaten the strategic stability which SALT I so laboriously sought to establish.

3. THE ARMS RACE AND SALT

Jack Ruina

The subject of this paper is SALT, what has happened, what the situation is now and what the likely future is of the SALT negotiations in the very narrow sense of the negotiations *per se*. I must warn that my perspective is very limited; it is that of a person from the United States who has been rather deeply involved in some of the technical details of what has been going on at SALT and the pre-SALT situation.

Although there was a lot of enthusiasm at first when the SALT treaty was announced, it did not come as a surprise. There had been a great deal of commitment on the part of both governments for years before this to the fact that there would be an agreement. We really knew when the President of the United States went to Moscow in 1972 that this was going to emerge. Since the treaty was announced, however, there has been a lot of concern expressed that perhaps this agreement does not do very much. In fact the first indications are that after the SALT agreements the arms race accelerated a little, and at any rate talk about the arms race has increased. In my view, one should not look at the agreements — there were actually two agreements, one called a treaty and one called an agreement — except as part of a process. For unless the agreement is viewed as part of a process, the accomplishments must seem very megre indeed.

My very positive feeling about the agreement is based on a negative. If we had not had an agreement, I think it would have been a very sad situation indeed. In short, one of the most significant accomplishments of having a treaty is that failure would have been disastrous for arms control for many years. There was such great commitment on both the Soviet and the American sides to having an agreement, it would have been disastrous if we had failed to reach some agreement in the two or three years of negotiations.

What are the positive results? What did the agreement do? Let us go through the provisions of the agreement. On ABM, which is the key matter since we have an actual treaty, it is agreed that both sides can have only two ABM sites, one site to protect its capital and one site to protect some of its offensive forces, in fact a missile site, not near the capital. What is the significance of that? This means essentially in terms of the superpowers themselves that they are restricted to two ABM sites, and each site is limited in size. Mainly the limitation rests on the number of interceptors at each site. This means as far as the superpowers are concerned that it is the same as zero ABM. It is not a measurable amount of defence. For each interceptor, even if it worked perfectly, could only shoot down one incoming warhead, and each side has many thousands of warheads while the number of interceptors is limited to two hundred. In short, two hundred measured against many thousand is nothing, so essentially it is no defence (I will show later how we got into that trap of having even that little bit). Moreover, even against a missile force of another country, not a superpower, it does not constitute very much of a defence. True, it is not zero but it is an epsilon even against another power for the simple reason that no cities are defended except the capitals. So anyone with any missile force is not facing very much defence.

Another important part of the ABM agreement which must be recognised is that after years and years of discussion, starting with Pugwash meetings as early as 1963, through official meetings between the United States and the Soviet Union in 1967, and the Glassboro meetings when Kosygin came to the United States, we have been discussing with the Soviet Union the possibility of limiting defence. Finally, after all these years, both parties agree that we are not going to have any defence whatsoever and that the populations of both countries are to remain hostages essentially. This has been done by formal agreement, and thus it is legal that there will be no defence. This might imply, although it does not prove, that both countries are accepting the fact that deterrence is the only strategy for the day and that nuclear weapons are not considered to be for war fighting but only for use as a deterrent force. On the other hand, one can be a little more cynical — and people have been — and argue that perhaps this is not proved at all. It just demonstrates that since both the superpowers recognised that technically defence is impossible, they accepted that they might as well have a treaty about it. They do not, however, necessarily accept the deterrent strategy at all. Indeed, some of the building-up and some of the thoughts about build-up of nuclear forces at this time indicate that deterrence is not the accepted strategy. For with such limited ABM, essentially zero ABM for practical purposes, one can have a credible deterrent force with very low levels of weapons. Much of the build-up in the past of weaponry, at least in the United States, has been justified, has been rationalised on the basis of the fact that we have had to escalate the arms race because the other fellow looks as if he is building an ABM or he might be thinking about building the ABM. Once the ABM business is ruled out, the need and the justification for further build-up is very much reduced. I cannot say eliminated, but it has been very much reduced. In short, one can argue to have a credible deterrent one can have a very, very small force, a small fraction of what we now have.

Another significant implication of the ABM Treaty is that some of the military arguments for continued nuclear testing have disappeared. The strongest argument for continued nuclear testing has been that we have to measure the effects of weapons in case we have to penetrate an ABM. Without the ABM issue involved at all, I think the important military arguments for continued testing have disappeared. So this opens the way for a comprehensive test ban.

There was also an agreement, which was not called a treaty on offensive weapons. The limit on offensive weapons is not much of a limit; it is a light limit and it was intended to last for five years. It limits only the numbers of the offensive missile force; it does not limit bombers. It is not clear at all that either superpower would have gone beyond or even up to that limit anyway even without a treaty. Indeed, it might be argued that now that a certain number is permitted people will tend to build up to that number. On the other hand, what it does accomplish, and I think this should not be minimized, is that there was a fear on the part of some that the build-up of missiles would exceed the limit we had in mind, and it was that fear that was a great stimulant to the arms race. It is not that anybody actually had plans to go above that limit, but there was always the fear that they would. It is of course a very asymmetrical situation that we are talking about, for much is known about American planning and the American debate but very little about the internal Soviet debates. Nevertheless, we have always tended to assume that the debates inside the Soviet Union are not that different from those inside the United States. In the United States there have always been fears that the Soviet Union is building so many missiles or so many submarines each year, and if they should continue for ten years or five years, you get enormous numbers from linear extrapolation. This agreement indicates that very high numbers will not be reached; quite high numbers, but not those tremendous numbers resulting from linear extrapolation of what has happened in the previous year.

The cynical view of the offensive agreement is that it really has done nothing; in fact, maybe it has really stimulated the arms race because people might be building to a level they might not have before. On the other hand, on the positive side, it has either reduced the fear of the extremists; or, more probably, if it has not reduced the fear of the extremists, it has reduced the credibility of the extremists' view.

Another vital aspect of the agreement concerns the question of verification. There are provisions in the agreement which say that neither side can interfere with the national means of verification of the

the other side. This is left rather vague: what does interference mean? And what are national means of verification? I think the agreement spoke of legal means of obtaining information, that is not contrary to international law — and international law probably does not allow spying. The way I interpret it, such things are permitted as receiving all forms of electromagnetic radiation outside the boundaries of the country — one may fly an aeroplane around the boundary and pick up all the electromagnetic radiation you want. One may sit on the moon with an antenna and listen to the electromagnetic radiation, and anything one picks up that way is a national means of vertification. Again, if the other fellow prints things in the newspapers and one reads it, that also is a permitted national means of verification. What, then is the significance of the provision that one does not interfere with national means of verification? First of all, it indicates acceptance on both sides that all these national means of verification are legitimate, and the other party is entitled to get this information. Another point relates to the difficulty which has long existed between the United States and the Soviet Union on the question of on-site inspection. There was a feeling for a long time that we cannot have any decent agreement on the arms control without on-site inspection, but here there is a demonstration that you can have a very meaningful agreement without requiring on-site inspection. So we have escaped from the obsession about on-site inspection, which in itself is terribly significant.

Another aspect of the agreement which is implicit rather than explicit is the fact that the United States and the Soviet Union talked about arms levels and so forth as peers. In the past the Americans had enjoyed a tremendous superiority in weapons, and in about 1963 or 1964 started talking about freezes. There was Soviet reluctance to go along with it for quite understandable political reasons; they said, we cannot freeze a position where you have so much more than we have. But now we have talked as peers in the sense that numbers should be the same, and the acceptance of this fact, particularly on the American side, I think eliminates another issue, another stimulant, in the arms race. There should no longer be a concern about who is ahead and who is behind, superiority and inferiority, and getting political advantages from having more or less. The fact that we are dealing as peers, that the two superpowers talk as if they have the same numbers and that it does not really much matter, is I think an important step towards further arms control.

Lastly, I think an important bonus from the total SALT negotiation is that in the process of the negotiation, there has developed now a much more widespread knowledge about nuclear issues in both countries. It is no longer limited to a very small group.

50

Certainly that is true in the United States; I think the knowledge about what we have, and its significance and so on is now much more widespread than it was before, and there are indications that this is certainly true in the Soviet Union as well. I think this in itself is a very important and healthy development.

What SALT did not do, and was somewhat inconsistent about, was on the question of how parity should be defined. Now I think those of us who have been involved in this business recognise that the quest for exact parity is nonsense. What difference does it make if someone has more or less, a hundred more missiles or a hundred less, more interceptors or less, larger weapons or somewhat smaller weapons? Nevertheless, I think in terms of the official agreements between both countries there is an inconsistency. On the one hand we find tremendous concern about being precise in measurements as regards the ABM. In ABM the Soviets have a small ABM system around Moscow, a small number of interceptors, and the United States had at the time of the agreements nothing. The Soviet ABM system, as I mentioned earlier, is essentially of no military consequence whatsoever, as far as the United States is concerned. Yet there were indications that the Russians were unwilling to take it down. Perhaps they have an internal political problem about taking an ABM system down; after all, if one invests so much money and if one has a constituency that wanted this thing, it is very hard to say no now. In the circumstances, then, one would have thought that the United States could be big enough to let the Russians have their ABM and agree to have nothing themselves — but there was concern about asymmetry. Of course from the military's point of view, the whole thing is nonsense. It is of no consequences. Nevertheless the Americans said they had to have something and hence they have started building a missile defence site out in the West somewhere. Then the scholars in this business looked at it and said that the American one is defending missile sites and the Soviet one is defending the capital, and that looks asymmetrical. And so the agreement finally emerged where both sides had to match each other almost precisely. We had a useless ABM site started on the West Coast and the Soviets had a useless ABM site defending Moscow, and the agreement now permits both sides to have two useless ABM sites. What caused that was the concern about symmetry. So symmetry, parity, equality was measured with an extremely fine microscope. Yet from a military point of view it is of absolutely no consequence.

On the offensive weapons issue the parity question seems to have been measured rather sloppily. The negotiators did not worry too much about numbers and it seemed at the last minute that numbers were juggled and the Russians were allowed more submarines and more

51

land-based missiles than the Americans; but the Americans are ahead in the number of multiple warheads and so on. There was a last-minute agreement, put together hastily, to have an agreement, it seems, and no great concern about numbers. As a consequence of the negotiations it is therefore not at all clear whether we are accepting precision measurements or willing to be very sloppy about it. This is an area where SALT has not given us any significant precedent.

Another thing which the first set of agreements by itself did not do, was of course to stop the arms race. In many ways one may argue that perhaps SALT has accelerated the arms race a little, even if hopefully only temporarily. For example, SALT put no limits on modernizing weapons or on replacing weapons. Without limits on modernisation and replacement an enormous arms race is possible, since one can take everything one has and replace it, and keep doing that again and again, thereby improving what one has. There is, in fact, enough in the arsenals of both powers to demand lots of defence dollars for modernisation and replacement. SALT did not address the issue of heavy bombers at all so that there is no limit, no restraint whatsoever, on them, on numbers, on quality, on anything at all. SALT allows the Soviet Union to build more submarines than they now have by a substantial number, 50 per cent more. SALT allows more ABMs to be built on both sides than now exists. So to look at it technically, it hardly seems to have put a brake on the arms race at all.

What is the next step in SALT, or a reasonable menu for the next round of negotiations? Perhaps at the next round we can really look at the ABM issue with a little less emotion, a little less scholarship about equality, and reduce the thing to zero. It would be I think a tremendous step towards arms control if we could just eliminate ABM from the nuclear equation entirely, so that nobody could even confuse the issue about what that small amount of ABM might mean or might not mean. It should be an easy thing to do, and it should present no political problems, at least in the United States (the position in the Soviet Union is less clear); since from the military point of view the current level is not significant. It would be symbolic and an elimination of possible confusion at a later point. I want to point out, however, that there is a difference in point of view. Many American experts in arms control say that it would be a mistake to put any emphasis on the ABM problem; since it is not significant, why not put your energies and your thoughts into other and more significant areas.

Another thing that can be done in SALT II is to put a limit, a real limit, on offensive weapons, which would include bombers and would be much more comprehensive than we now have. As was mentioned earlier, the current limits are hardly limits at all in a sense, and putting some comprehensive limits on offensive arms is probably the most important single step that can occur in the next round of SALT. Here again because of the great asymmetries between the United States and the Soviet Union, the entirely different geographies, different population concentrations, different technologies, different political and technical backgrounds, one has to deal not in terms of matching every element of the offensive force against every other element of the offensive force but in some kind of total aggregates. Say the total number of things you are permitted is so much. As is well known, there is a great thorn in this agreement, and that is that the Soviets are deeply concerned about the American nuclear forces in Europe, and the Soviet argument has been with some justification that any nuclear weapon that can reach the Soviet Union is a strategic weapon; whether we have it in the United States or in a submarine or in an aircraft carrier or in England, it is all the same. We cannot, therefore, have a limit which excludes that. The American position has been that once we start dealing with the American nuclear forces in Europe, then it no longer can be a bipolar discussion. We would have to include NATO. It is probably that difficulty that has kept us from going ahead with discussions on a comprehensive agreement on offensive forces.

There is a clear willingness on both sides to overcome what are probably rather small political problems. One can compromise this issue quite easily. It is true that the United States has large number of nuclear forces in Europe; the number that is quoted all the time is 7,000. Most of these have nothing to do with reaching the Soviet Union; they are things like anti-tank weapons, anti-aircraft weapons, and so on. On the other hand, there is a substantial number of weapons that can, and those should be included in the numbers dealt with by SALT. For example, the Americans have a fleet of F-111s. They can be considered tactical weapons on the one hand by some people; on the other hand, they have a very long range and carry nuclear weapons and can reach the Soviet Union very easily. Those should be included in the count. Moreover, without defence the precise size of the forces on both sides is inconsequential. The Americans could easily throw in the F-111s and maybe a few more weapons and say that is part of the count. This should cause no great difficulty when dealing with NATO or our allies in Europe, while at the same time the Soviet Union would be allowed to say that anything which reaches the Soviet Union is included in the count. I think that would be an easy and ready compromise one could make. In other words, there is no basic stumbling block in that issue at all if there is a true willingness to reach a comprehensive agreement.

Another vital thing which must be reached at SALT II, if SALT II is really to represent an important step forward in this process of arms control, is to put some controls on modernisation and replacement.

This business of being able to modernise and replace weapons is something that means we can have one continued arms race at any pace we wish. If we are going to have any nuclear arms control, we have got to deal with this somehow. One of the difficulties, of course, is that there is a verification problem. How does one know that the other fellow is not modernising? He may be taking those aluminium screws out and putting in titanium screws, and that is modernising and it has to be prevented.

Another issue for the next round of SALT, and this is not strictly SALT, is the comprehensive test ban.[1] Technically, I believe that the comprehensive test ban is an issue for Geneva, not an issue for SALT. Nevertheless, in terms of the next step of agreement between the United States and the Soviet Union there should be very few obstacles to a comprehensive test ban. As I read the speeches made in Geneva by both the American and the Soviet delegates, I have the impression that neither of them have had new instructions since 1963. We still talk about on-site inspections, and the discussions at Geneva have not changed in content since 1963, but in fact a great deal has changed. First, one of the main military reasons for wanting nuclear tests is that you may want to build an ABM or you may want to penetrate an ABM. If that is gone, so goes that reason. Another reason for continuing nuclear testing is the unwillingness to give up the option of developing peaceful uses of nuclear explosions. I think in the many experiments and the many analyses that have been done since about 1963, all the indications are that the potential usefulness of peaceful nuclear explosions is very small indeed, and that this does not look like a very exciting technology anyway. At any rate it would be hard to justify not going ahead with a comprehensive test ban on the basis of trying to keep that option open. So we are in an excellent position to go ahead with a comprehensive test ban. The reasons for not doing it would seem to be political, with the military or civilian applications reasons dwarfed in comparison,

The foregoing points, then, would be a reasonable menu for SALT II. But that is hardly the end of arms control. One has to think in terms of what might be happening or hopefully would be happening over a longer future. The obvious kinds of things that we must look forward to is to vast reductions in arms; reductions by 50 per cent, maybe by factors of four, would be something that would seem totally realistic and not difficult at all. We want very tight controls on modernisation and replacement. But I prefer to advocate tight controls and selective controls, rather than a total ban on modernisation and replacement. There is something inconsistent about trying to get very large reductions and at the same time saying no modernisation is possible, because as one works on greater and greater reductions, there

54

will obviously be fears about the vulnerability of the small force, and to eliminate those fears some degree of modernization would have to be permitted. There is a reciprocity there I cannot think through very clearly myself at this point but I think you cannot simultaneously try to put a total stop on modernisation and replacement and have large reductions as well. The larger the reduction, the more sloppy you have got to be in allowing modernization and replacement.

Sooner or later we shall have to put limits on Anti-Submarine Warfare (ASW) so that a small submarine force would be quite adequate for deterrence. At present, however, there are no limits whatsoever in ASW; it has not been addressed at SALT at all. But there are some internal discussions in the United States starting on that subject. In fact the whole question of ASW bears some resemblance to ABM in the sense that if you have no limits then each side fears what the other would be doing in ASW, and hence there is a tremendous incentive to build more submarines or want better submarines or faster submarines or quieter submarines, and to reduce that incentive there have got to be limits on ASW. The ASW question is far more complicated than the ABM question for several reasons. One is that in ABM both sides had essentially zero or very little and so it was easy to start from that and propose limits on something we do not have much of. In ASW both the Americans and the Soviet Union already have substantial forces, maybe not very effective ones but very substantial ones, and there is a large technical community on this in both countries. Not only that, many other countries, any country that has a submarine, that has a boat, has some ASW. If somebody has some sonar on a boat, already there is some ASW. So you are dealing with something that many countries are involved in as well. Also, the ABM has a role only in nuclear warfare considerations, whereas ASW has a role in all kinds of things. The number of countries that have submarines, and the prospects of using submarines for the more traditional role of sinking ships and the like, are such that there is a legitimate use for ASW and hence separating the legitimate use from the nuclear use is going to be very hard indeed. But sooner or later we shall have to address that question, though I do not see it as something that will come up in the next round of SALT or even the round after. There is no urgency about it either, although sooner or later we shall have to face this problem.

Another question that has not been addressed at all in SALT and has not even been thought about I think in regard to SALT is limiting air defence. Although both the United States and the Soviet Union have large expenditures in this field, the Soviet expenditures are far greater than the Americans. The American expenditure is merely a billion or so dollars a year, and it is evident from looking at the size of the Soviet air defence that the expenditure in Moscow is substantially greater. Here, then, is one outlet for arms racing that can be easily plugged also, and again sooner or later that will have to be faced.

NOTE

1. This paper was prepared before President Nixon's Summit meeting in Moscow in 1974.

4. SOME POLITICAL ASPECTS OF DISARMAMENT

Hans J. Morgenthau

Before going into the substance of what I want to say, I wish to make a few conceptual distinctions which are not the result of academic whims but which, while generally overlooked in both theoretical and practical approaches to disarmament, are absolutely necessary for the understanding of the problems with which we are dealing.

We have to make two basic distinctions: a distinction between disarmament and arms control; and a distinction between the conventional and nuclear forms of disarmament and arms control. Arms control is not disarmament at all, it is a mere regulation of the arms race. It is an understanding between two or more nations engaged in an arms race to pursue that race within certain agreed-upon limits. In other words, it is a competition which operates under the control, under the limitations, of a cartel; it is a cartel agreement, you may say. And very typically when one has an arms control agreement, the nations concerned agree to what they would have done anyhow. One of the classic examples is the agreement between the United States and the Soviet Union concerning the arms race in offensive nuclear missiles. The United States said to the Soviet Union, 'We want to build in the next five years so many missiles of this particular kind – do you agree to that?'; and the Soviet Union said, 'Yes.' The Soviet Union said to the United States, 'We will build during the next five years so many missiles of this particular kind – are you agreeable to that?'. And the United States answered in the affirmative. What they agreed upon was essentially, within the existing technological limits, what the nations concerned would have done anyhow.

I am not saying that this is worthless. It has a great deal of value within itself because it gives a certain security to the nations concerned. What formerly would have been the result of guesswork and of more or less reliable intelligence is now put on paper and rationalised and formalised in legal terms. But the point I want to make is that this is not disarmament. This is something quite different.

Disarmament, on the other hand, is the actual reduction or abolition of certain or all types of arms. Again to refer to the SALT agreement: the agreement to forego for all practical purposes the development of anti-ballistic missile systems and to dismantle, partly at least, the existing ones, is disarmament. For the nations concerned limit, if not for all purposes abolish, a particular type of military weapon.

Even more important is the distinction between conventional and nuclear disarmament. The history of conventional disarmament has by and large been a history of failure. I shall try presently to show that those failures have not been accidental. They are intimately related to the very structure of international politics. Hence I would guess, and again I shall elaborate on this, that as long as political conflicts remain among sovereign nation states, we are going to have arms races. For the arms race is a mere particular manifestation of the political conflict. On the other hand, in the field of nuclear disarmament and arms control you have a real chance to achieve genuine results because of the different relationship that exists between the political struggle and nuclear armaments. So it is essential, however pedantic this may sound, to make these distinctions between disarmament and arms control and between nuclear and conventional forms of disarmament and arms control.

The attempts at conventional disarmament started immediately after the Napoleonic Wars. It was in 1816 that Czar Alexander I of Russia sent a message to the British Government suggesting a disarmament agreement. Scores of other attempts have been made since then. Of those attempts only two have been successful; one permanently and the other temporarily. The permanently successful one has been the disarmament between Great Britain and the United States concerning the disarmament of the American-Canadian frontier and the naval disarmament of the Great Lakes bordering on the United States and Canada. The other — temporary — success has been the Washington Treaty on the limitation of naval armaments of 1922.

What is characteristic and illuminating in these two agreements is the fact that they followed a political settlement among the contracting powers. That is to say, after the War of 1812 the United States recognised the territorial *status quo* on its northern frontiers — it gave up the half-hearted attempts to annex or at least to penetrate Canada, and from this time onward it became unnecessary for either nation, one of which was then a possession of the British crown, to arm against each other, because there was nothing to arm about. In other words, the political function which the conventional arms race has traditionally performed did not need to be performed in American-Canadian relations.

Concerning the Washington Treaty of 1922, it was the result of a complex settlement of naval competition between the United States and Great Britain. Until then the United States and Great Britain were involved in a rather fierce and, of course, extremely expensive naval competition in both oceans, with Japan being an ally of Great Britain and therefore adding to the British weight in the competition in the Pacific. Great Britain and the United States agreed upon a division of the two oceans into spheres of influence — Great Britain being predominant in the Atlantic and the United States being predominant in the Pacific; and furthermore they agreed upon the severance of the British-Japanese Alliance. Once this political settlement between Great Britain and the United States was reached there was no longer any reason for naval competition between the two major naval powers, and they were then able to impose their will upon the second-rate naval powers, that is to say, primarily Japan, then France and Italy. Through a ratio into which I shall not go here, they imposed a settlement upon the minor naval powers which limited their naval armaments at a level which would not be risky for the two major naval powers — the United States and Great Britain.

Furthermore, the terms of the Washington Treaty performed the function of the legal ratification of changes in military technology, which are frequently the motivating force of arms control agreements and even disarmament agreements. In this case the First World War had shown dreadnoughts, big capital ships, to be obsolescent.

Since neither Great Britain nor the United States were willing to spend enormous amounts for floating monuments to their national pride, which had no military significance expect to provide enormous targets for naval artillery and submarine torpedoes, they gave them up and concluded a disarmament agreement to that effect, thereby lifting from them the burden of extremely expensive and essentially useless military expenditure. What is interesting in considering this organic functional relationship between disarmament and political settlement is that at the very moment Japan dared to challenge the political settlement of 1922, they is to say, in 1934, after it had invaded Manchuria, it also denounced the Washington Treaty of 1922. That is to say, once the distribution of political power was challenged, the competition for naval armaments again acquired a positive political and military function. So it is not by accident, it is not by virtue of the subjective stubbornness or unenlightenedness of individual governments that the history of conventional disarmament has been by and large a failure; for those nations which were most keen on recognising the need for disarmament — that is to say, the great powers — were also the ones who needed armaments in order to continue, with improved chances for success, their political and military competition.

When you look at the nuclear field you have an entirely different situation. The conventional arms race is fundamentally the result of the discrepancy between available targets and available weapons. In the conventional field the number of, actual and potential targets, by far exceeds the number of available weapons. It is for this reason that you cannot have enough machine guns or enough pieces of artillery in the conventional field. In other words, an uneluctable dynamism moves towards more and more weapons because there are always more targets, if I may use a somewhat euphemistic term, than you can accommodate with the available weapons.

You have an entirely different situation in the nuclear field. For here you are able to reach an optimum beyond which it would be completely irrational to go. Once you are capable of destroying your potential enemy ten times over with nuclear weapons, it obviously becomes absurd to increase that capability to the point where you are able to destroy him twelve or fifteen times over. And your enemy, who is only capable of destroying you six times over, is for this reason not inferior to you. In other words, once you have the nuclear capability to destroy your prospective enemy you have reached the optimum beyond which to go is utterly irrational.

This difference between conventional and nuclear weapons is obviously the result of the enormous, unprecedented, and virtually unimaginable destructiveness of nuclear weapons. When we refer to conventional weapons, we refer to a military economy of scarcity, which is expressed by the discrepancy of the number of targets and the number of available weapons. When you refer to the nuclear field, you refer to a military economy of abundance where the destructiveness of the available weapons by far exceeds the availability of targets. It has been figured out, and I do not vouch for the exactness of the figures, that the United States has approximately the nuclear equivalent of two tons of TNT for each man, woman and child living on this earth.

The magnitude of this utter discrepancy between the destructiveness of the available weapons and available targets, even if you consider all of humanity as a target, points up the utter irrationality of the nuclear arms race. So when we deal with nuclear weapons, in the field of disarmament and arms control, we are dealing not with something quantitively different but with something so qualitatively different that it requires new modes of thought and action appropriate to the novelty of nuclear weapons, that is to say, a radical break with those ways of thinking and acting to which we have been accustomed, since the beginning of history.

It is exactly for this reason that the confusion between the conventional and nuclear forms of disarmament and arms control is not only theoretically untenable but also practically so dangerous. For it is a particular example of a general tendency in our modes of thought and action, which is to apply obsolescent modes of thought and action, hallowed by all of historic experience, to a new field, for which those modes of thought and action are completely inadequate. What we have here is a kind of cultural lag.

We still subjectively live in a world which objectively has been rendered obsolete by the enormous transformation which modern weapons technology has brought about.

I am optimistic about the objective possibility of nuclear disarmament and arms control, and I am pessimistic about the objective possibility of conventional disarmament and arms control, as long as the political issues which have given rise to the armaments race in the first place remain unsettled. In my view the priority in the conventional field is not disarmament *per se* but political settlements. Once there have been political settlements after the model of – to give a radical example – the transformation of the relations between the United States and Great Britain after the War of 1812, then states may safely disarm because the arms race no longer performs a political function. With regard to conventional armaments the point is that the unsucessful attempts in this field have not been the result of technical failures – one has only to take a look at the volumes which were produced by the Geneva Disarmament Conference of 1931 and 1932 in order to see how much intelligence and thought has gone into the prepartion for conventional disarmament – but the utter lack of success of those attempts is due to a reversal of the priorities which ought to have been followed in the conventional field.

Instead of attacking the technical problems of the arms race and searching for means to bring it under control, we ought to have dealt with the political problems of which the conventional arms race is a mere surface manifestation. Take again the example of the United States and Great Britain which were enemies for a long time; one has only to take a look at the history of the American Civil War in order to realise how close the United States came to war with Great Britain over the Trent and Alabama affairs. Today nobody in either Great Britain or the United States would think of engaging in an arms race between the United States and Great Britain. It would be completely senseless, and if there were need for an arms control or disarmament agreement between the United States and Great Britain, it would be an easy matter to put into effect the technical factors which would lead to such agreement. But the very absence of political conflict which could give rise to an arms race has made it unnecessary to make such agreements. In other words, the disappearance of political conflict, which under certain conditions might be supported by force of arms, has in itself eliminated the arms race and has made disarmament between the United States and Great Britain unnecessary. One may choose one's own examples, which abound in history, and I think one is bound then to arrive at the conclusion that genuine disarmament on the conventional level, say, between the United States and the Soviet Union, would be possible only if and when the political conflicts have been eliminated in support of which the conventional arms race between the United States and the Soviet Union has taken place to begin with.

In the field of the nuclear arms race you have an entirely different situation. Here it is not primarily — if it is at all — the presence or absence of political conflict which is the decisive factor. It is primarily the rational insight in the unprecedented novelty of nuclear weapons which require an utterly different approach, commensurate with their novelty, to the solution of the problems they pose. In other words, even though the United States and the Soviet Union are still engaged in political conflict — and the fact that it is no longer justified, at least on the American side, primarily in ideological terms, does not eliminate those conflicts — the United States and the Soviet Union have been capable of recognising, at least in the abstract, that an unlimited continuation of the nuclear arms race after the model of the conventional arms race is an utter absurdity from a rational point of view, and is likely to lead to disastrous practical consequences.

The fact that we have lived with the nuclear arms race for more than twenty years by now is no reason to assume that we can live forever in this kind of semi-orderly and peaceful world. First of all, the nuclear arms race is, of course, economically ruinous. One has only to look at the budget of the United States Government which is relatively open and see to what extent the scarce economic resources of the United States, already strained by the Vietnam adventure, are continuously strained by ever new military expenditures.

There is in the nuclear arms race a dynamism which is different from the dynamism of the conventional arms race. While the latter is politically motivated, the former is technologically conditioned. There is in these technological developments a kind of inner logic — which is technologically rational but politically and militarily irrational — a technological dynamism which leads to ever more novelties, ever more improvements regardless of the military need and of the political consequences. In other words, what seems to be technologically possible is put into practice for no better reason but because it can be done. This dynamism in a sense is more dangerous than the dynamism of the conventional arms race, because it threatens not just one more war after all the others which humanity has survived, but it threatens the destruction of humanity itself.

If not the subjective, then certainly the objective result of a continuing nuclear arms race is potentially destabilizing. And this is what again objectively, if not subjectively, the technological élites of the two superpowers are aiming at. When we Americans speak of damage-limiting capability what we mean is that we can inflict greater damage upon the Soviet Union than the Soviet Union can inflict upon us, and that this may mean the difference between what is still — quite mistakenly — called victory and defeat. You have only to look at the discussions in the American Senate concerning the SALT I agreements in order to realise how persistent those obsolete concepts are which have come into the nuclear age from our previous historical experience. The simple fact is that once you have this ability on both sides to inflict upon the other side unacceptable damage, anything going beyond this, making it 'more' unacceptable, is sheer surplus, is sheer irrationality. So, in other words, what was necessary and could be rationally defended for conventional weapons becomes an utter absurdity when we deal with nuclear weapons.

But those simple changes in our thinking and in our actions, while theoretically acknowledged as legitimate and necessary, are very difficult to put into practice by the same men who theoretically are fully aware of those rational factors I am discussing here. You have only to take a look at the unease with which the military, openly in the United States and probably surreptitiously in the Soviet Union, look at the SALT I agreements. If you take the SALT I agreements, especially by projecting them into the future, at their face value, then the SALT II agreements are intended to make an end to the nuclear arms race altogether. By doing this they will throw overboard the idea of victory and defeat which, of course, is the very essence of conventional military thinking. The basic problem before us, therefore, is to get rid of obsolete conceptions, of obsolete modes of thought and action, when we deal with nuclear weapons. We must realise that to speak of 'weapons' in the nuclear sense is in itself a misnomer which has come to us from the pre-nuclear age, for when we speak of a weapon, we imply a rational relationship between means and ends. I can take an ashtray and throw it at somebody who seems to be not convinced by my argument, and that would be a weapon which performs a somewhat primitive but still a rational purpose, if this is what I want. A nuclear weapon, and I make here no distinction between tactical and strategic nuclear weapons, is in its essence, in spite of what has been said in justification of tactical nuclear weapons, an instrument of indiscriminate destruction. It is not a rational means which you can use for a particular rational purpose. If you have set your mind to wiping your enemy off the face of the earth, you can do it with nuclear weapons. Provided this is a rational purpose, then this is the only rational purpose nuclear weapons, in the strategic sense, perform. So the limitation and the reduction of nuclear weapons, bringing the total process of the nuclear arms race under control, is the fundamental, the most vital problem which people interested in

63

disarmament have to face. When they deal with conventional armaments, they must be aware of the priority of political settlements over technical measures. And if they face those two issues squarely and consistently, they may finally achieve results in the fields of disarmament and arms control — conventional and nuclear.

5. THE IMPORTANCE OF AGREEMENTS

Thomas Schelling

Most of this presentation has to do with identifying the motivational structures that might underlie arms agreements or arms understanding. Some of it has to do with figuring out what the purpose of an agreement is, what we would want to call an agreement, what kinds of agreements there are and how to evaluate them.[1]

We can identify a number of interest structures. There is a variety of ways that two participants can view the outcomes of a possible arms negotiation, and maybe at least classify and somewhat clarify the different kind of situations in which it may be said that both parties want an agreement or one party wants an agreement or neither party wants an agreement. Let us take a question like deciding whether or not to have ABM with the over-simplified assumption that no ABM will be pretty close to zero and some ABM will mean unrestricted ABM. We want ABM if the Russians have it, we want ABM if the Russians do not have it; they want ABM if we have it, they want ABM if we do not have it. But we both prefer that neither have it to both having it. In game theory this has the structure that is familiarly known as Prisoner's Dilemma. In other words, if our behaviour had no influence on their behaviour and if there were no bargain, we would choose to have ABM irrespective of what they did, which is what they also would choose, and yet our desire to have it ourselves being less than our desire that they do not have it, and similarly on their side, means that we can both prefer that both not have it and reach an agreement, the agreement being basically that I will not if you do not. Notice that this agreement requires some kind of enforcement because even if he does not, we would still independently prefer to have ABM, unless our having it will induce him to break his side of the agreement, or unless there is some penalty on violation. I think this is what usually people have in mind when they talk about genuine necessary agreements, agreements that have to be monitored and enforced. It is getting both parties to do what they otherwise would not do, but doing it conditionally with both sides benefiting.

Then there is a second, very different structure, which arises if we want ABM if they have it but not if they do not, and equally they may want it if we have it but not if we do not. If we decide first, we determine their choice. If we have it, they will; if we do not, they will

65

not. If we know that their interest corresponds to ours, we know that if we do not, they will not; that if we do, they will. Since we prefer not to have it if they do not and to have it if they will, we decide whether we would rather both have it or both not have it, and if the hypothesis is that arms control in this circumstance makes sense, then we decide not to have it. That is sufficient to determine that they do not have it. At least it is if they know our decision, if they can observe our action, and if they can respond to it. In this case it does not matter who goes first. Whoever commits himself not to have it — if he can do it visibily and reliably — takes care of the other person's decision. Notice that in this case there is no incentive to violate or cheat; as long as he does not we do not want it. There may be a lot of instances of this, and it is possible that during some periods of the 1960s, to the extent that governments can be said to have had preferences or interest structures rather than simply a multitude of agency and individual positions, this was the situation with respect to ABM. At least one can find endless testimony before American Congressional Committees to the effect that ABM might not be worth having if the Soviets did not have it, but if they have it for a variety of reasons, usually vague psychological reasons, we cannot not have it. I would guess that there are any number of exotic weapons systems that have the characteristic that if they have it we cannot afford not to also for very ill-specified reasons, such as that somebody will think we do not know how. If they have a FOBS, we have to have a FOBS. If they have a nuclear-powered aeroplane, we have to have a nuclear-powered aeroplane. If they build an aeroplane that flies sideways, we have to have an aeroplane that flies sideways, just in case somebody will think that we are lying down on the job or do not know how to build one or will think that they know something we do not.

We can combine those two interest structures by supposing that we want it whether or not they do and they want it only if we do. In other words, if our interest structure is of the first kind I mentioned, and if their interest structure is of the second kind, so that in effect they would follow our lead but that if we had no influence on them we would go ahead and have it, we can determine the situation by voluntarily not having it; they cannot. If they decide not to unconditionally, we would go ahead and have it. We want it even if they do not; they want it only if we do. If we do not perceive that they will respond to us, we will have it and they will have it. On the other hand, if we can abstain unilaterally, we take advantage of the fact that they do not want it unless we do. So we do not, and they do not. Again in this case if they are not afraid that we will surprise them by changing our mind, if they are not afraid that we can do it clandestinely and they will not know it, if it is all open and above-board, there is no need for any enforcement. The abstention is enforced on us by the knowledge that if we buy it, they will. Compared with both having it we prefer that both do not. As long as we understand that their reaction will be not to have it if we do not have it, we can unilaterally have the agreement, have the mutually observed restraint. Here again one can say this is only getting what we both want, but of course what they want depends on whether we have it. What we want is the opposite of what we got in terms of wanting it independently for our side, but the joint outcome, both not having it, we prefer. So in a sense viewing the two decisions of the two sides jointly, we get the best we can get. But we would still rather have it. That is, we are still abstaining from something that we would proceed with except for the notion that if we did they would too.

There are a lot more cases, and one can pair the motives on both sides. Then there are the interesting cases in which one does not quite know what the other side's interest is. For example, suppose that under no circumstances would we build ABM. We have decided that it is not worth the money, that it will scare the population, accelerate the arms race, give aid and comfort to the militarists, and we are against it. Suppose that on the other side they like ABM, they would like it if we do not have it, but they might be willing to do without it if that were the only way to get us to do without it. If they know our motives, they know that no matter what they do we will not waste money on the contraption. They may freely go ahead and have their ABM because they want it, and it looks as though there is nothing we can do about it. On the other hand, if we pretend successfully that we would want it if they had it, then to keep us from having it they may have to abstain. This is one version of the bargaining chip notion.

There is the particularly interesting case, and this probably does sometimes arise — it could, for example, have arisen with ABM — in which each side believes the other wants it but neither side does. Each hopes to negotiate a limitation. Each feels that it has nothing to negotiate with unless it is believed ready to go ahead with it. Both sides simulate strong interest, both sides negotiate arduously. They finally reach an agreement. Each feels satisfaction in having successfully forestalled the other's pursuit of, let us say, ABM. But if they had only known to begin with that both sides were posturing with respect to their interest in ABM, they could have relaxed; they would not have needed an agreement.

Another important interest structure deserves mention. Suppose it is the case, as it may be, that with respect to something like ABM the other side prefers both that we do have it and if we do not have it. In this case it looks as though there is no possible basis on which to appeal to them for an agreement. Suppose we prefer not to have it or at least not to have it if they do not. If the only item on the agenda is ABM, there is nothing we can offer. If we threaten to build it if they do, they still would do it. If we offer not to build it if they do not, they still would do it. On the other hand, if we can find another item, a new bomber, let us say, which has the same interest structure in reverse, namely we want it whether or not they have it, they do not want it, but we prefer both to have it to neither having it because we want it so badly. There again there is no basis for agreement on the bomber. But if one couples the two together, it may be that while we want the bomber badly enough to accept whatever they do about bombers, we more strongly prefer that they not have ABM; and it is possible that though they would prefer ABM independently of what we did about ABM, they even more strongly prefer that we should not have bombers. If the two are put on the same agenda together, one can then find a basis for both agreeing on neither having ABM nor bombers which is a state preferred by both parties to what they would get if the two were kept on separate agendas and in each case no agreement was reached.

There is yet another possibility. Let us suppose that we both prefer no ABM and that if it was an independent item on the agenda it would be easy to agree. On the other hand, we want that bomber very badly, and in the discussion restricted to bombers there is no way that the other side can appeal to us to have a restriction. We do not care that much whether or not they have a bomber. They can still say no ABM, no bomber. No bomber treaty, no ABM treaty. In other words, they can couple together not two things that are asymmetrical — we want one, they want the other — but two things, one of which is symmetrical — we both want it — the other asymmetrical — only one wants it. And if we want badly.enough the thing that we both want, maybe they can hold us up and obtain a bomber treaty by saying they will not go along with the ABM treaty. Then we say that if you have a perfectly good ABM treaty, why jeopardize it by tying it together with, let us say, an offensive missile agreement or with anything else. I think the answer there is that one calculates one's interests, and the other party's interests, one thinks about bargaining tactics, one runs the risk, and then one says that this is the price of that. One can even say that this ought to have been the American policy over the ABM treaty, namely that we should have held out for zero, which is precisely the same as saying that we should have held out for a better offensive weapon agreement. That is to say, in the abstract it is holding up an agreement acceptable on its own merits, mutually desirable, perfectly satisfactory, as leverage on the other side to go along with another agreement that may be harder to get, either because he does not want it or because it is simply too hard to negotiate. And indeed if we were more careful about our language, we might say that we got a zero agreement, a perfect zero agreement, on ABM population defense. But the real question is whether we ought to have held it up in order to get zero agreement on ABM command centre defense and whether we would then have wished to hold that one up in order to get zero agreement on ABM strategic forces defence. It may be a very correct judgement to answer in the affirmative but I think it is important to realise that in principle one is simply saying we have an agreement, and by a certain definition it is a zero ABM defence, or zero defence of particular well-specified important kinds of targets, and whether one holds it up to get an exchange of ballerinas, a wheat sale, a vote in the UN, or zero ABM defence of Moscow and Washington, the fact is one is using it as what one might call a bargaining chip. Indeed, the term 'bargaining chip', which we use so often, ought also to be written down very carefully in order to see precisely what is meant by it. One kind of bargaining chip, and I attribute this to Henry Kissinger because he is quoted as having used it with respect to ABM and, I believe even more recently, with respect perhaps to Trident systems, is either to pretend one wants or commit oneself to get a weapon one does not really want in order to trade it away. This incidentally is a tactic that has a long tradition, not entirely successful, in tariff bargaining. It has always been customary in most governments, at least in most Western governments, that before going off to a big tariff negotiation one makes sure that all possible tariffs are on the books and will go into effect unless a general agreement on tariffs and trade is reached. One does not go empty-handed into a tariff negotiation with no tariff on chickens, tobacco, or automobiles. One at least goes through the motions of getting them. This is what is supposed to be the bargaining chip approach to at least the nominal financing of ABM, and it takes two forms. One is pretence and the other is commitment. If it was pretence in the United States, it probably fooled nobody. One cannot tell a hundred Senators, who will blab it to the newspapers, that we would not touch ABM with a ten-foot pole but we would like to make the Russians think we are thirsting for it so that they will come to the bargaining table and trade it away, because the Russians can read the same newspapers I read, and if I get the impression that ABM is the last thing Henry Kissinger wants but he is pretending to go ahead to fool the Russians, the Russians can also get the impression that he is pretending only to fool them, and they are not fooled. The other form, though, is more deadly serious, and it is to commit oneself to go ahead even though one would rather not. One says, I am not going to kid you that I want this; I do not. But since I will have no leverage on you unless I get it, I will pay for the leverage by running the risk that if the negotiation fails I am stuck with it. I will spend the money on something I do not want. And then if the other side calls our bluff and insists that if the negotiation fails we will not spend the money, the answer may be yes we will, we have ways of making ourselves spend the money. There are legal legislative ways, and there is the more dangerous way of generating such elaborate domestic expectations that we would do it, so much confusion as to whether this was a bargaining tactic or a genuine decision to go ahead if the other side did that we end by having cultivated a desire for it by the bargaining tactic itself. Cultivating a desire is a metaphor; what I particularly having in mind that we probably increase within the government the bargaining power of those who want it by going through the motions of pretending we do so. In short, the likelihood that we feel obliged, the likelihood that we will reach a decision to go ahead, is increased merely by going through the otherwise transparent bargaining chip technique.

The second kind of bargaining chip is one referred to earlier, namely the acceptable agreement that is made part of the bargain. We can either commit ourselves to get ABM as a bargaining chip to reach an agreement or we can commit ourselves to refuse an ABM agreement in order to get an offensive weapons agreement. I mention this because it seems to me that a very common kind of bargaining chip is the one in which one takes an otherwise acceptable agreement and puts it at risk in order to couple it to something else, which is not altogether different from the bargaining chip which takes the form of committing oneself to buy a weapon. And indeed if we think of the same weapon involved in both cases, one is the bargaining chip that says we will get ABM unless something, and the other says we will not have an ABM agreement and therefore get ABM unless something else happens.

The reason why I have presented the foregoing analysis in such detail is that I often find it convenient when I try to think about what we are doing with ABM, submarines, bombers, or whatever it may be, to see if I can identify not just for the two parties but for different elements perhaps within the American Government how they rank their different outcomes. In the ABM case there are four outcomes: we both have it, neither has it, they have it and we do not, we have it and they do not. Just to try to rank these outcomes in order to see what kind of bargaining situation we have, what the motivational structure is, and then to superimpose on top of that what the other side probably perceives our motivational structure to be. One can go a little further: what they think we perceive theirs to be. At some stage one has to stop the gyrations of listing what each misperceives the other's misperceptions to be, but I think in the case of, say, a MIRV test ban, a lot of confusion in the US Government in 1969 may have been due to the fact that nobody was quite clear on what they meant by we want or do not want a MIRV test ban, they want or do not want a MIRV test ban. I even suspect that there was even a brief fleeting moment when both the Soviet Union and the US Governments each thought the other would insist on a MIRV ban of some sort, and I think possibly they both thought wrong. There is an interesting case where one could go quite astray even in characterizing the nature of the bargaining situation unless one had straight whether they really want a MIRV ban or they want it only because they think we want it, or they are pretending to want it, and we are pretending to want it.

I mentioned several different cases, and an interesting question arises with each of them: does any limitation that may be arrived at in any of these interesting structures depend on some kind of enforceable agreement. Here a lot hinges on what we mean by enforcement. Most agreements are enforced by reciprocity. I agree not to burn rubbish in my backyard if you will not burn rubbish in your backyard. I am free to burn rubbish in my back yard anytime I want to, but I expect that you will begin to burn rubbish in your back yard, and we will end up each creating a nuisance for the other that we agreed not to do. Here I think we should distinguish two important things. One is means of observation. With some interest structures there is indeed a motive to cheat. That is to say, you like the agreement, a no ABM agreement, but if you could secretly have it, you would like that even better. Once the Soviet Union and the United States really became interested in a test ban, if they ever did, I think this was probably the result of the excruciating and frustrating dilemma they were in, namely, both might wish it were impossible to test secretly and lament that it is possible and be unable to reach an agreement merely because it is possible to hide tests. Yet if it were impossible to hide tests, impossible not only to hide them but to make them ambiguous; if testing were a well-defined notion as it comes pretty close to being with nuclear explosives, and if testing could not be hidden, then probably a simple moratorium is as durable as a treaty signed in blood by the heads of state.

The interesting question thus arises as to why then they bother with treaties. One answer is that it does not occur to people to do without the treaties: the treaties look good, and they are what diplomats consider to be the money in the game. Enforcement in most of these cases, in important cases at least, is almost solely by reciprocity. Usually there are three broad types of enforcement with agreements. One is based on the analogy of criminal law in which a violation or an unauthorised withdrawal, a renunciation of the treaty, is a bad act to be punished. The second is based on the analogy of civil law in which it is not a bad act but it does open one to a suit for damages; that is to say, one must suitably reimburse the other, and to the extent that he can prove harm take care of him. The third is that one owes him nothing, and is susceptible to no pain or punishment, but he is released from his obligation to one. Not all agreements involve reciprocity of release, but most international agreements do. That is, it is typically construed that if one ratifies a treaty swearing one will never do something, elsewhere in the treaty this is made conditional on the other party's living up to the treaty. Hence an act of violation is in effect a denunciation of the treaty or the agreement by the other party, one's own part of the agreement ceases to exist, and the enforcement on him then is merely the expectation that one will feel free to reciprocate.

If non-compliance can be identified, why should a treaty have anything more than instantaneous duration? That is, why should not the treaty say we hereby inform you that until further notice we will not build ABM, and then set up a teletype system so that it never takes more than five minutes to change one's mind. One could even say, that if we change our mind we will let you know within a week rather than beforehand. In terms of the construction time of ABM, a week before, or a week after is not important. Why should one say five years, twenty-five years, perpetuity? Aside from tradition, a very important reason is to get the subject off the agenda, and not to have to discuss it tomorrow and the day after and next year. Very specifically, this means that nobody has to buy the same agreement twice. If you rent my house, you may want to sign a two-year lease, one reason being that if I ask a certain price for the house wondering whether you will pay it and you accept it, I am not supposed then to raise the price. In other words, once I know that you will accept a treaty, then I may believe that you would accept a treaty slightly less favourable to you, so I may want to back out tomorrow and try again for a higher gain. I think one of the purposes of the treaty is to say no, we settled that. If we have an agreement, this is the agreement. You can break the agreement any time you want to, but the agreement is not automatically open for renegotiation; it is settled. You can break the lease and leave my house, but you cannot argue about lower rent once you are in. Maybe I can throw you out, but as long as you stay I cannot ask for more rent. One of the reasons for a treaty is simply to say that settles it, we do not bargain about it any more; we might wish we had charged a higher price for something we gave away, but there is no chance. In other words, it puts the negotiation beyond easy reach so that what the duration of the treaty really determines is not how long the limit lasts but how long the limit on negotiation lasts, the limit on renegotiation. The duration of the treaty specifies for how long it is in poor taste to suggest renegotiation.

A possible other reason, somewhat related, is that some agreements are better if they are written down. Once one has worked out an agreement in detail it is a shame not to record the details one thinks one has agreed on. One may want to do this merely by an exchange of understandings, but if one does they tend to get printed on both sides and treated virtually as official interpretations of the agreement, so a second purpose of a treaty may simply be to produce a document, and somehow diplomats do not like ephemeral documents, that is, documents with a date which means that when tomorrow comes they cease to be enforced. They like to make them last. Again, if negotiating details is arduous, difficult, even risky in terms of success, it may be nice to put beyond reach the amendment and renegotiation of the terms themselves.

Still another purpose of a treaty which has little to do with the agreement itself is to generate expectations about either the subject of the treaty or other subjects. If the ABM Treaty lasted 365 days, more people would be plotting next year's campaign to get the Senate not to ratify the new treaty. There is something about the formality of a treaty, including making people stand up and vote, twisting their arms if necessary, something even about making it costly to have a treaty, costly in legislative time, that makes a lot of people who otherwise would work to undermine the treaty give up the attempt. This works on one's own populace, it works on agencies of one's own government, and it probably works on allies. Again the treaty is a way of tying your own hands visibly so that others won't importune you to change your mind or attempt to extort from you a change in position through blackmail of some sort, and sometimes it ties the hands of others, or at least seems to. Even if internationally the rules of the game are that when matters of vital interest are at stake the treaty can be forgotten, domestically the existence of a treaty can have powerful effects and inhibit the kind of political action that might otherwise either undermine the treaty or cause various other kinds of nuisance.

An example concerns the partial Test Ban Treaty. It has been claimed that the Test Ban Treaty is an anti-pollution agreement and as such is working well. Somewhat facetiously I would say no, it is an anti-noise agreement: the purpose was to stop all of that endless chatter about test bans which for six years had kept arms control negotiations from getting anywhere. I also think the test ban negotiations were enormously mischievous in getting at least the United States and probably the Soviet Union officially on record with hyprocritical statements of all kinds. It was an inflammatory popular issue, and what the Test Ban Treaty did was to stop test ban negotiations in the best way. I was not one who thought this was a first step; I thought this was a very final terminal step and now we clear the boards and start all over again. I did not think the test ban led directly to anything more: in a literal sense it puts nuclear weapons underground, off the front page. One rarely, since 1963, in the United States has seen in a newspaper a photograph of a mushroom cloud, whereas prior to the test ban treaty a week hardly went by that one did not see one of those traditional photographs of nuclear explosions.

What was the test ban about? In one literal sense the concern was all about fall-out, partly because fall-out became a very simple, human, domestic, homely issue, and a typical housewife or husband, who had no great thoughts about world strategy, could nevertheless be alarmed about the milk he drank or fed his children, that is to say, a sufficient argument to many people against this awful spectre of nuclear warfare was that the testing was bad for children. My personal experience with people who were not in the strategy business was that they almost all thought that somehow nuclear testing was magically associated with the arms race, that it was the only issue of arms control up for decision, and that therefore the best way to put the ogre back in the bottle was to put testing underground or out of existence.

Something else even more important happened with the test ban. Notice that we did not have a ban on the testing of incendiary weapons; we did not have a ban on the testing of means of delivery. The ban was on nuclear weapons, and primarily it said that nuclear weapons are ugly, inhumane, and not like other weapons – they must go underground. The implication was not only do not test them but do not use them or even more do not have them. It was like sending lepers off to a colony; we do not do it with tuberculosis or smallpox but because traditionally leprosy has been considered cursed in spite of the fact that the epidemiology of it makes it comparatively innocuous. The successful effort in the test ban was to continue to put the curse on nuclear weapons, and in that respect it was very ceremonial, very symbolic, and if somebody had discovered a way to eliminate all fall-out from nuclear tests, my guess is that most people would still have wanted a test ban as an almost magical substitute for banning weapons, and that as an expressive act it had a very powerful effect. The willingness of any head of government to use nuclear weapons was reduced by the test ban; perhaps even the willingness of certain governments to possess nuclear weapons was at least temporarily reduced. A slight reaction may set in; once the testing goes underground and the weapons become invisible, the milk gets clean, the geiger counters stop clicking, people may stop worrying, and it may become possible to talk rationally and coolly about nuclear weapons again, just as when the danger of nuclear war seems to recede people lose interest in arms control all over the world. It may be therefore that we should arrange a few dramatic limited nuclear test accidents

74

just to remind people that, as with smallpox, maybe we had better go on vaccinating because the risk of an epidemic is just around the corner. After all, who would ever bother to vaccinate if no one has ever heard of a case of smallpox in the last fifty years?

I have raised a question, why have an agreement? I think there is a lot to be said for unwritten agreements, for understandings arrived at but not written down, for letting the other side know what would and what would not concern one and what one would be prepared to do on certain conditions, but to leave it slightly vague. A reason occasionally for leaving it vague is that if each party wants the agreement badly enough, and if the terms are not written down in fine print, each may bend over backwards to avoid seeming to take advantage of the other or seeming to cheat or violate. One finds this, let us say, in relations between neighbours. If one has an understanding about who mows the lawn up to what line or who shovels snow up to what point or who parks his car where, if one writes it out in fine print one's neighbourly relations become like commercial relations and one does everything right up to the line and one haggles if one thinks he has violated the agreement even slightly. If one leaves it all on a matter of gentlemanly good behaviour, everybody bends over backwards not to seem to be taking advantage of the other or to avoid any possible clash, and very often if there is a vague borderline where genuine altercation may occur, both parties may stay behind the vague borderline to avoid altercation. This often will not work if the subject is so complicated that one has to negotiate out details, but I think one of the reasons why a zero agreement is often so much more viable than any other kind of agreement is that it is typically the one kind that does not have to be written down, and often if one cannot write it down one gets zero; if one can write it down, one gets zero with ninety-nine footnotes of small exceptions.

There is a great advantage in the SALT talks in two respects. First, particularly between the United States and the Soviet Union serious non-posturing conversation between high government officials concerned with arms control was exceedingly difficult until very recently, is still very difficult, and will go on being at least difficult for a long time. Just learning how to converse about these subjects, which is partly learning vocabulary, partly learning concepts, is important. It is equally important to get some appreciation of how the other side values the things you do. It sometimes turns out that the things that concern him most of all are things that one may not think matter terribly much, in which case one can do him lots of favours cheaply. But it may be awfully hard to find that out, and possibly SALT talks, if they go on long enough, will even develop techniques for better discovering the values that each side places on these things. I have to confess that I am on record as not minding if no agreement ever came out of the SALT talks, partly in the belief that the talks themselves were so important that an effort to get written agreements would be disruptive. I now think that was wrong; I think the effort to get an agreement was not altogether disruptive, although there are people who think that the accelerated effort to combine it with a summit visit may have somewhat impeded better agreements than we might have got from SALT I. But most of the interest structures that one can identify will lead to fairly self-enforcing understandings without treaties if there can be a sufficient exploration of where the common interest lies. One might get a lot less arms control as posturing if what one has is private understandings, non-committal understandings, arrived at between two sides, non-binding understandings with merely better appreciation on each side of what the other's behaviour would be.

I think that since about 1967 it has become clearer that either side probably had it in its power to influence the other to take it easy on ABM by simply standing pat himself. There was a kind of implicit moratorium, somewhat disturbed by the bargaining chip notion, which may have been, could have been exceedingly mischievous if the agreement had not been arrived at. But the treaty probably was not required for the no ABM; all that might have been required would have been for Gerard Smith and his counterparts to look each other straight in the eye and say, I cannot bind my government, but for the time being we really would not have any interest unless we thought you were going ahead. In that respect talks on matters that can be monitored and observed may often be as good as and frequently superior to treaties. On the other hand, I have to confess error in that I believe now that the enormous advantage of the ABM Treaty, perhaps like the enormous significance of Nixon's visit to China, is not that it binds the Russians but that it binds the Americans, that it settles an issue internally in a way that it could not have been settled by informal understandings we might have reached with the Russians, and since ABM to Americans became a symbolic issue of the arms race, of militarism, and all of that, I think it is spectacularly good to have the President of the United States indicating that trading with the enemy is not wrong, but that it is the most important kind of trading a country can do. In that respect we have done far more than to settle for the time being the ABM issue in the United States; we have established in a way the legitimacy and the propriety of arms control in a way that it had not been established before. That is to say, SALT is the first genuine recognised effort to try to use an agreement to save money, to slow down the arms race, and to make things a little safer. GCD did not involve any of that; nor was the test ban very much preceived to involve that. An enormous amount of arms negotiation as posturing has discredited arms control all over. But here was a case in which it looked as though a rather stingy Secretary of Defense, Robert McNamara, in effect said I do not want ABM, but if they have it we are bound to have it; let us try not to; and in five years with a treaty succeeded. This probably establishes, particularly with the politically conservative people in the United States, what had already been established with a great many military officers in the United States over the past ten years, namely a belief that really one of the best ways to disarm your enemy is to negotiate.

NOTE

1. This was an impromptu presentation and not a formal paper. The editors, with the kind co-operation of Kosta Tsipis, have prepared it for publication from tapes of Thomas Schelling's talk.

6.   THE ARMS RACE AS POSTURING

Kosta Tsipis

Introduction

It is a highly irregular practice, especially for a natural scientist, to venture the presentation of a thesis that cannot be proven either right or wrong. But let me state at the outset that this is a highly speculative paper based on a number of unstated and unproven assumptions. My intention is not in fact to prove or disprove anything, but to stimulate thinking along a rather unorthodox path about the origins and utilities of the complex phenomenon we are experiencing called the 'strategic arms race'. The thesis I will attempt to develop is that the arms race between the United States and the Soviet Union has common characteristics with the practice of posturing, a phenomenon that is only only readily observable in the animal world, but which has also played an important rôle in resolving conflicts in the time of the recorded history of man. Further, I will try to examine any beneficial traits this commonality of characteristics with posturing may bestow to some forms of the arms race. I will end as the devil's advocate with the suggestion that a modified form of the arms race may indeed be a stable and credible channel of non-combative resolution of conflict between nations of comparable technological development.

Channels for the Resolution of Conflict

Intra-species conflict, to which I will confine the discussion, is considered resolved if the outcome of this resolution persists for a time comparable to a generation of the species in question. Among humans, for example, a conflict will be defined as resolved if it remains in that state for a period of twenty years.

There seem to be only three channels for acceptable resolution of conflicts: combat, negotiation, or posturing. The persistence of the results of posturing seems to be shorter than the other two. Combat provides an easy, unmistakable, and therefore credible way of resolving a conflict by establishing the martial superiority of one or other of the opponents. The right of the mightier to have things his way seems to be generally expected among animal species and therefore once the stronger has been determined the conflict is resolved. Negotiation is a human invention and its acceptance as a viable channel of conflict resolution depends on the belief that a logical process modulated by the imperatives of legitimacy can establish an arrangement that meets the needs and desires of both opponents.

Posturing seems to be based on a mutually held desire to avoid combat while trying to resolve the conflict by the determination of the more competent of the two opponents. Once again, as in the case of combat, the underlying tacit assumption is that the more competent has the right to arrange the outcome of the conflict in accordance with his interests. In its most general form posturing consists of a display of prowess in a pre-agreed field of activities. It may be undertaken by an individual or by a group, but it is always characterized by the non-combativeness of the test that it involves. We have numerous examples of posturing as a means of resolving conflict of interests in the animal world as well as in human societies. From the show of plumage in bird species to the exhibition of 'toughness' among human male adolescents, posturing is readily recognizable as a process through which dominance among members of a species is determined. Sport is certainly a form of posturing, and Olympic competition in which the dominant athletes that have been selected by a process of elimination in each country compete, representing their countries rather than individuals, is certainly a highly organized and modified form of posturing. It is interesting to remember that combat was suspended during the Olympiads in Ancient Greece, emphasizing the rôle of posturing as an alternative to combat, in the peaceful resolution of conflicts.

The intention to avoid combat that is expressed in posturing certainly derives from a desire to avoid elimination of the species through internecine strife. This desire has manifested itself throughout the recorded history of mankind in efforts of varying success to limit actual conflict to a minimum by accepting posturing in its stead. The story of David and Goliath is, I suppose, the oldest account of conflict resolution by posturing: rather than a catholic battle between the two camps, the outcome of the conflict is settled by a duel between only two individuals representing the camps. Although actual combat is not completely eliminated, it is confined to two members of the opposing groups and becomes ritualized in a fashion that can be defined as posturing in the sense that it avoids combat but resolves conflict by establishing the stronger of two opposing groups. In medieval times we see posturing in action once again not only in duels between knights that serve to decide the outcome of a battle, but also in the use of mercenaries. The stronger side is again decided without threatening the survival or even the welfare of the combating camps. It is decided on the basis of their economic strength. Lethal combat once again is not avoided completely, but it is confined to a small group of individuals who do not necessarily belong to the feuding social or political aggregates, and who resolve the conflict in combat by proxy. It is only the universal conscription of the Napoleonic Wars and contemporary warfare that has replaced posturing with large-scale combat among individuals who actually belong to the opposing national or ideological aggregates. Furthermore, nuclear armaments coupled with the concept of total war have for the first time in the history of the human race raised the possibility of complete extinction of the species through intra-species combat. Up until the possibility of nuclear holocaust, military defeat on the battlefield left a nation as an organized society intact and viable. It was a defeat in a symbolic, posturing context that resolved the existing conflict not by testing the might of all members of a nation but of a small representative group. It is an unfortunate historical event that first one and then more nations, impelled by the need to preserve their integrity, introduced universal conscription and total warfare, slowly eroding and finally eliminating posturing as a channel for the resolution of conflict.

Or have they? The United States and the Soviet Union have been engaged for the last quarter of a century in a race to increase and improve the performance of their strategic nuclear weapons. Yet a judicious analysis of the possible uses that these weapons admit will reveal that neither country can make use of its arsenal of nuclear weapons against the other without suffering politically unacceptable damage of its own society, without as a matter of fact facing the threat of annihilation as an organized society. If then these weapons cannot be used, why are they being built at such astronomical cost with such great conviction and national involvement? Is the strategic arms race a new form of posturing between the two countries? It certainly has all the features and characteristics of posturing. It is an effort to display prowess in a mutually agreed upon field of human endeavour. It is in many ways a test of endurance, economic and political, and a test of competence, not physical but technical. But in the century of science one would expect posturing to involve competition along scientific lines. The arms race solves one of the difficulties posturing has had as a channel of conflict resolution: the existence of objective criteria of one's prowess in a given field. It is difficult to assess 'courage' or even endurance but it is quite easy to quantify the explosive yield of a warhead or the accuracy of a missile; the arms race seems to be the perfect posturing vehicle. We have seen other national efforts in both countries assume posturing rôles — the space exploration programme for example — but they do not seem to provide that intangible psychological element implicit in proofs of martial might that makes a lasting resolution of conflict through posturing possible. As the possibility of actual combat between the two countries diminishes because of the threat of total extinction involved, negotiation and posturing assume increasing utility. Since negotiations are not as psychologically gratifying as they should be for large sections of human societies, posturing seems to be of singular importance in resolving future conflicts.

Of course I have led up to the obvious question: since posturing avoids combat, and since the arms race is a contemporary form of posturing, is the arms race a good thing? My qualified answer is that, some forms of arms race may indeed prove to be effective posturing vehicles which will allow the United States and the Soviet Union to assess each other's capabilities, thereby obviating any need to test them by actual combat. Any form of arms race that can lead to strategic or crisis instability (a race at building ABMs, for example, or anti-submarine warfare systems capable of posing a real threat to the missile-carrying submarines) is certainly unfit for posturing purposes because it increases the probability of accidental or deliberate initiation of real conflict. An arms race, however, that would maintain strategic stability and balance between the two countries, may deter actual combat in providing for the satisfaction of those non-quantifiable and little understood psychological factors that lead individuals and nations to aggression. The fact that we do not understand something completely does not mean that it is not important. The fact that we do not understand the psychological dynamics of posturing between nations, or political leaders, or military establishments, does not minimize either their existence or their potential importance in shaping national policies. What we should not forget is that the *esprit de corps* of military establishments is to prove to the opponent the superior might of their weapons. Negotiations cannot achieve that; and in view of the superfluity of nuclear warheads in the arsenals of several nations, it is preferable that attempts at establishing such superiority are non-combative in nature.

Of course I have not proved that posturing is indeed a way of resolving conflict; neither have I established any but the most tenuous resemblance between posturing and the arms race. What I hope I have done is to alert the reader to the possibility that every political, diplomatic or military move is not animated by exclusively rational considerations, and that quantifiable utility and rational justification are not the *sine qua non* of practices designed to avoid a nuclear war.

7. SLOWING DOWN THE ARMS RACE

George Rathjens

The purpose of this paper is to consider the problem of limiting research and development, particularly as it applies to strategic weaponry, the case of limitations on missile testing being taken as a principal example.

At this particular point in history there is a greater interest in limiting development than there was a few years ago, springing from several orgins.

1. There is a widespread belief in the United States, and presumably also elsewhere, that not every technological advance is to mankind's benefit, and that somehow we must control technology more effectively. This is a view that has applied mainly to non-military programmes. Nevertheless, it has had some carry-over into the military area.

2. With some limits having been set on force levels as a result of the strategic arms limitation talks (SALT), there has been much feeling that the effect of SALT I has been not to stop or even slow the arms race, but primarily to channel it into a qualitative direction.

3. It may be further argued that all of the discussion that has surrounded SALT so far has resulted in a more sophisticated dialogue on the whole question of the strategic arms race and on stability in particular, and that one of the consequences is an increased recognition that changes in the qualitative characteristics of weapons are likely to be more destabilizing than increases in force levels.

There is, therefore, an increased interest and perhaps even an increased acceptability of the idea of limiting development. The acceptability has been reinforced by the fact that in the ABM Treaty, if not in the executive agreement relating to offensive systems, there are important provisions that inhibit development.

Much of what follows will be strictly related to the idea that strategic nuclear weapons have their primary role in deterrence of a major attack. That situation is a very different one than the one of 'war fighting', whether with nuclear weapons or conventional ones. If one is concerned with a 'war fighting' situation, marginal changes in weapons' characteristics of one side or the other can really result in substantial advantages. In the deterrent situation, which, in the view of many, characterizes the present strategic balance, this is by no means the case; much larger changes can be tolerated without there being any significant effect on that balance. To the extent one accepts this view, the prospects for limiting development in strategic weaponry ought to be much greater than if we were dealing with conventional arms, or if one goes back to the 1920s, say, in dealing with something like the naval armaments of that time.

The major kinds of changes that could upset the balance ought to be detectable with, in most cases, no need for intrusive kinds of verification, for anything that would be decisive would certainly be apparent with unilateral detection and identification capabilities. For example, in the case of a state developing a nuclear warhead that would really make a dramatic difference, it seems likely that the kind of test required could be detected unilaterally. The same is probably true if one is concerned about new kinds of strategic delivery systems or improvements in delivery systems that would equally make a dramatic difference.

I am going to emphasize greatly the difference in requirements for deterrence and in requirements for war fighting, pre-emptive attacks, or first strike capabilities, for this difference is vitally important in the context in which we find ourselves. I want to throw out a couple of numbers to give you an idea of what I have in mind. Consider the case of a ballistic missile that can be delivered with, say, 99 per cent chance of destroying its target as compared with one that can be delivered with a 90 per cent probability of target destruction. When the concern is about retaliation or deterrence, I submit that there is no significant difference at all between those numbers. Nobody is going to act differently if the number is 99 per cent or if it is 90 per cent. On the other hand, if one is interested in a pre-emptive attack against the other fellow's missiles, whether 99 or 90 percent is destroyed makes an enormous difference. The same kind of an argument can of course be made with respect to one's confidence or assurance that an assumed level of destruction will be achieved. If one is interested in a pre-emptive attack, or in initiating a nuclear war, one may want confidence that approaches 100 per cent that one's weapons systems will perform in the way one has in mind; but for deterrence to be effective, what is really required is that the adversary should not have 100 per cent confidence that one's retaliatory capabilities will not work. Thus, requirements of confidence are dramatically different in these two cases.

Having made these general remarks, I turn to the more specific question of missile testing, improvement in missile capabilities, and in particular, MIRV technology. I wish to deal with the question of why we have failed to limit that technology so far, what the prospects for doing so are, and what problems may arise in the future.

There have been a number of motivations that have been important in the development of multiple warheads, and there are a number of concerns that have been expressed about this development, particularly on the American side. The Soviet Union in this area, as in all others, have been very much less forthcoming in commenting on what their concerns have been, so my remarks will be largely from an American perspective.

In the United States there has been a substantial belief that the development of highly accurate multiple warheads by the Soviet Union would be a destabilizing development: one that could result in erosion in confidence in the United States in the effectiveness of its land-based ICBMs as a retaliatory system. The argument has been that if the Soviet Union were to develop and deploy MIRVs, a missile force of any given size that it might have could conceivably destroy nearly all of an American force of similar size, or even a slightly larger one, by delivering several warheads against each American missile silo. It might have been expected that this concern about stability would have provided considerable motivation, at least on the American side, to try to inhibit the development of multiple warheads by the Russians. And if one assumes, admittedly without much basis for doing so, that similar concerns might have been felt on the Soviet side, one might have expected a reciprocal interest in preventing the development of MIRVs.

Because of these kinds of concerns, attempts were made during the last few years to limit MIRVs. However, they failed; and the United States demonstrated MIRVs for its missiles some time ago. Why did this happen? The commonly advanced argument is that limitation of MIRVs was impossible because of an asymmetry between the United States and the Soviet Union. The Soviet Union was very far behind; and could not accept any kind of an agreement that would freeze it in a position of inferiority. The United States was so far ahead that there was little interest on its side in tying its hands in an area that it was about to exploit.

The argument illustrates a more general problem relevant to the whole question of slowing the arms race, which I will comment on parenthetically here: namely, the very great difficulty of reaching agreement on any kind of limitation when one side insists on maintaining superiority in the affected area and the other insists that it cannot tolerate the other's doing so. That is the situation in which we now appear to find ourselves, because with the outcome of SALT I there have been a series of statements from the American Defense Department arguing that while the United States can perhaps tolerate parity, and perhaps even some asymmetry in the Soviet's favour in the numbers game, it is an imperative of American policy that technological superiority in the strategic area be maintained. This poses a serious problem in that I cannot conceive of the Soviet Union accepting the general principle. The hope of course is that in particular areas where the technologies are balanced, we can reach some agreements that will limit them without having to resolve the more general question.

There were doubtless other reasons for the failure to reach agreement to limit multiple warheads in SALT I besides the asymmetry in technology. One of them was simply a general interest on the part of the military in developing what they regard as a useful concept, without regard to the inter-active effects that this could have on the arms race. I shall return to this theme in my concluding remarks.

It may still be important to slow down development in this area because of the adverse reactions that one can anticipate in the event of the development of a highly accurate multiple warhead. If one believes one's land-based missiles are of doubtful utility in the retaliatory rôle, there are ways of improving the situation, but they are all unsatisfactory. They imply spending large sums trying to defend those missiles, or in buying new systems — perhaps sea-based, perhaps bombers — to get around the assumed vulnerability of the land-based missiles, or possibly adopting what we call a launch-on-warning doctrine — a doctrine that would imply launch of missiles if radar or other observations indicated their destruction was imminent, rather than waiting for a pre-emptive attack to be delivered. If these are plausible consequences of highly accurate multiple warheads being developed, there is, then, a case for trying to slow the rate of development.

Now, at this point I wish to go on record as emphatically as I can in saying that I do not subscribe to the thesis that we are in an unstable situation, or even that the development of multiple, high-accuracy warheads would make much difference. I contend that even if the Soviet Union had multiple warheads in large numbers, each of which could destroy an American ICBM with a probability of near unity, it would still not likely lead to a pre-emptive attack against the United States, or vice-versa. I say this, having in mind the fact that for an attack to be a 'success', missile-launching submarines and bombers would also have to be destroyed with virtually 100 per cent effectiveness; and that it is extremely unlikely that a responsible decision-maker could ever have sufficient confidence to make such an attack seem rational, considering the catastrophic consequences that might ensue if even a few of an adversary's missiles or bombers should escape destruction. However, having said this, I will go on and discuss the problem as if acquisition of highly accurate MIRVs would make a difference in the likelihood of pre-emptive attack. I do this because there are other people who apparently do believe that further improvements in this area would be seriously destabilizing. I might just say, parenthetically, that I go through this argument with some misgivings, because I believe that every time it is done, there is the risk of lending unwarranted and undesirable credence to the belief that stability may be in jeopardy.

The situation as regard MIRVs has changed somewhat, of course, since SALT began. The development has been completed, at least on the American side, and in sense that has made the opportunity for an agreement even smaller now than it was then. Since the Soviet Union still has some catching up to do, a pre-requisite for any agreement that would in one way or another have the effect of limiting MIRV technology would probably be that the Soviet Union demonstrate some kind of capability. In other respects, however, the prospects for an agreement are somewhat improved. The ABM Treaty has diminished, if not removed, one of the major arguments for going ahead with the development of multiple warhead technology. The major rationale for those systems was that they were desirable for penetrating massive ABM systems, and with those systems now proscribed by agreement, there is much less of a case to be made for MIRVs.

I wish now to describe the present situation as regard them, first from the American side. MIRVs have been deployed on American ICBMs and SLBMs, and the yields are large compared with the Hiroshima bomb, but small compared with some of the weapons which have since been tested. The important point, however, is that the combination of yield, accuracy, and reliability, which the Americans have demonstrated, or which it is believed can soon be demonstrated, is not such that they could be used effectively to destroy Soviet ICBM sites. The Soviet Union has not demonstrated a capability of destroying American ICBM sites either.

The issue remaining for us is whether or not further evolution in this area can be slowed by agreement, and whether it would be worth trying to do so. An argument can be made that it would be worth trying, and that it may be possible to achieve success. As I remarked, the counter-force capabilities are not yet available, and one could envisage some kinds of arrangement that would prevent their attainment.

At least three things are required if a superpower is to develop a capability to destroy its adversary's hardened missile silos in a pre-emptive attack. First, there is the attainment of high accuracy. In the past, accuracy improvements by factors of two have occurred every several years, and with one or two more generations of such improvement, probabilities of kill could be achieved that would approach 90 per cent or so with weapons of the size now being deployed. This would make them counter-force weapons. If, therefore, one could somehow prevent such improvement, that could be important. High reliability would also be useful if one sought to use these as counter-force weapons, but uncertain reliability can be compensated for at less cost than poor accuracy by allocating more than one weapon per target. Hence, reliability may be less important. The third requirement is to have high confidence that if an attack is launched, the performance of the weapons used will be within some critical limits. This is a matter of knowing how good the accuracy is and knowing how reliable the weapons are. High confidence in estimates of these parameters can only be achieved, in general, through rather large-scale test programmes. One cannot have 95 per cent confidence that missiles will perform in a given way if several failures are observed in thirty or forty launches. A much larger test programme may be required, the size depending strongly on the number of failures observed. Thus, one can envisage two possibilities of limiting technology in this area: slowing down the rate of accuracy improvement, and denying each side confidence in its weapons.

The attainment of improvements in accuracy is going to be more difficult than in the past. The improvements cited earlier, improvements by factors of two every few years, have largely involved simply improving guidance components and capabilities for turning off rocket engines at precisely the right time. We have about reached the limit, however, of what may be achieved through such developments alone. From now on, we have to take into account terminal effects, that is, re-entry phenomena; and that will be more difficult. To achieve further accuracy improvement will likely require one or both of two developments: an improvement in the design of the re-entry vehicle, so that its trajectory during re-entry will be less affected by variations in atmospheric conditions, and/or some means of sensing such deflections or perturbations during re-entry so that corrections can be made. The question is, can one observe the kind of tests that would be required in connection with such developments. If this can be done, one can conceive of writing an agreement proscribing such tests in which one can have some confidence as regards compliance. I believe this is possible, particularly if there could be included as part of the agreement, a requirement that tests be conducted only in certain specified areas where observations by the adversary power could be made. The Soviets have tested their weapons in the Pacific and the Americans have observed the re-entry from ships that have large radars. Similarly, the Russians have monitored American re-entry tests in both the Atlantic and Pacific oceans. If it were agreed that future tests would be conducted such that re-entry would occur only in these areas, it would be possible to verify whether or not there were dramatic changes in the kinds of re-entry vehicles that were being tested. One could thus envisage that if an agreement were reached that would prohibit tests of any new kinds of re-entry vehicles, major improvements in accuracy would not occur except as a result of treaty violation, which would be observable.

An alternative approach to slowing development leading to counter-force capability would be limitations on numbers of tests. I have suggested earlier that in order to have the kind of confidence that one would require for a pre-emptive attack, or for initiating nuclear war in any kind of way, one would want to have extraordinary confidence in performance estimates, and that this might require very large numbers of tests. Furthermore, even once one had established that kind of confidence, one probably would not retain it unless testing were continued at some reasonable frequency. The military, in particular, would lose confidence if they were denied this. This suggests that if one could limit the number of tests by mutual agreement to perhaps a dozen or so a year, it would be very unlikely that anyone would ever have the confidence required to initiate a pre-emptive attack.

There is in the foregoing proposal a trade-off possibility: suppose a quota of a dozen tests a year were agreed to; then one could use them to improve accuracy and reliability, to develop new kinds of missiles and re-entry vehicles, or to establish confidence in those weapons one had. However, with a modest quota, one probably could not do all of these things. The preferred kind of an agreement from the perspective of arms control would, of course, be one that both proscribed the testing of new kinds of rockets and re-entry vehicles and limited the number of tests of old ones.

For completeness, I wish to comment on some of the problems that would come up in any effort to limit MIRV development, and then make some more general remarks.

One of the problems I have identified already: we are still far from parity in multiple warhead technology. That, however, appears to be simply a matter of time.

Secondly, there is the possibility of improving the state of the art as regards MIRVs by testing them on missiles fired over such short ranges that external observation would not be feasible. I think that really need not be a serious concern. It is unlikely that technology that could later be exploited for counter-force purposes could be proved out in short-range tests. The implication is that short-range tests should be excluded from any quota or prohibition on missiles testing.

A related problem arises with respect to the question of satellite launches. Could one carry out technological improvements that would contribute to the attainment of counter-force capabilities through satellite testing and through space programmes? The answer appears to be that, to some degree, one could, but again the overlap problem need not be serious. An agreement could be worked out that would permit the exploitation of satellites for both civilian and military purposes without there necessarily being much of a problem. I have in mind particularly the fact that the characteristics of the boosters, and to an even greater degree those of the re-entry vehicles, for space purposes are different from those required for counter-force military weapons. Hence, one could, I think, reach an agreement that would permit satellites to be launched without such launches having to be included in any quota that would relate to ballistic missile testing.

A further problem is that ABM is still not dead. The treaty says one may not have a militarily significant deployment, but research and development are continuing, and based on everything observed since SALT I, one would have to conclude that there is still a fear that, the treaty notwithstanding, some day large ABM systems might be deployed. This raises the issue of how much weight should be given to the political commitment inherit in the ABM Treaty. My view is that the existing commitment is an important one, and the diminution in likelihood that ABM systems will be deployed is sufficient that it should be reflected in policies with regard to MIRV development. But there are probably other people who think otherwise — who do not believe that the rationale for developing MIRV is diminished by the ABM Treaty *per se*.

One more possible difficulty is that there are asymmetries in the concerns of the Soviet Union and the United States that are, and will be, reflected in their approach to limiting research and development. In the particular case dealt with here, one gets the impression that the Soviet Union has been troubled about the American MIRV development, no so much because of a particular concern that we might develop a so-called 'first strike' capability or counter-force capability, but rather on account of the multiplication of numbers of warheads that could be delivered. On the other hand, the American concern, at least the stated concern, has been about the specific attainment by the Soviet Union of a first strike capability. To the extent there are such differences, the motivations of the Soviet Union and the United States to achieve the kind of agreement discussed may be very different. The former may be much interested in seeing deployment of MIRVs by the United States constrained, but may not share an American interest in constraints on qualitative improvements.

Now, finally I come to the most difficult problem of all: the fact that the acceptability of limitations on development is strongly contingent on the relative weight given to the concept of sufficient or simple deterrence on the one hand, and to interest in the use of nuclear weapons for war fighting purposes on the other. As I remarked earlier, in war fighting marginal advantages have made a difference in the past; and they will in the future. This bears on the problem of qualitative constraints in two ways.

Firstly, if marginal changes make a difference, then one's verification capabilities have to be such that one can detect them, and this implies in many cases the kind of intrusive inspection that so far has eluded the Americans in every effort they have ever involved themselves in with the Soviet Union.

Secondly, to the extent that there is an interest in 'war fighting' with nuclear weapons, there is going to be a strong tendency to seek marginal advantages, and there will be serious resistance to limiting technology. In fact, limitation of technology is going to require the military to accept the kind of thing that they are taught never to accept, namely second-rate weapons instead of first-rate weapons. If, for example, one limits the number of tests of missiles severely, the generals and admirals will be asked to accept the fact that they are going to have weapons in their inventory in which they can have little confidence, and maybe confidence that diminishes with time. I think it is entirely reasonable to ask that of a military man, or to insist that he accept it, if one is concerned exclusively with deterrence and retaliation, but if one actually expects him to use the weapons in question for war fighting purposes, it is probably an unreasonable request. I do not wish to say that limiting research and development on war fighting systems is impossible, but it will pose very difficult problems.

These arguments lead me to conclude that the greatest opportunity for limiting development is going to be with respect to those kinds of weapons that are unambiguously accepted as having only a deterrent rôle. To illustrate the point, I might comment on the possibility of limiting development in anti-submarine warfare. This would be of interest as a means of minimizing concerns about the possibility of future vulnerability of SLBM forces. However, I would suggest that agreeing on limitation on ASW development would be much more difficult than in the area that I have talked about, the limiting of improvement of missile technology. This is precisely because of the war fighting problem. As regards anti-submarine warfare, whether one is concerned with the rôle of strategic weapons being limited to deterrence or not, the fact is that much of the technology certainly is relevant to fighting a conventional war in which nuclear weapons may not be involved. Thus, I am sceptical about the likelihood of agreements limiting ASW activity.

On the other hand, I would go so far as to say that SALT II is very likely to consider the issue of limitations on missile testing, if not exactly in the form that I have suggested. I would add that their approach to negotiations will provide an interesting clue as to what the real intentions of the superpowers are with respect to the rôle of nuclear weapons in the 1970s. If the Americans are really desperately concerned about stability and if that concern is absolutely overriding, one would expect that there would be tremendous pressure from the American side to reach an agreement to constrain development in this area. On the other hand, if the Americans attach considerable weight to the use of nuclear-armed missiles in a war fighting rôle, one would expect that Service pressure for improvements in capabilities would be dominant. Hence, from observing how the negotiations go, one will perhaps be able to determine the extent to which the United States and to a lesser degree the Soviet Union are interested in these aspects of nuclear strategy.

I conclude by making a few general remarks about limiting testing as a means of dealing with weapons development. First, I see it as probably the only way. There may be exceptions, but generally, unless the political climate changes, it is going to be difficult to negotiate agreements based on the kind of intrusive inspections that would permit one to limit R and D at any earlier point in the research, development, test and evaluation cycle. If intrusive inspection is not on the cards, the point to put a handle on the development problem is at the test stage where there are demonstrable effects that are easily observed.

If agreements can be reached to constrain testing, there may be a significant slowing down in the evolution of various kinds of military systems. The very large amounts of money that are spent in the research and development cycle really are spent on advanced development testing, not at the research stage. Hence an agreement on the foregoing lines would mean significant reductions in the constituency that will press for the affected R and D. And, most important, there would be less fear of future attack, and less possibility that those with a stake in the acquisition of military hardware, for whatever reasons, will be able to exploit such fears in making a case for their demands.

8. THE ROLE OF DETERRENCE IN DISARMAMENT: SOME THEORIES AND SOME DEFECTS

Joseph Kashi

Many arms controllers seem to regard 'deterrence' as an inviolable quantity, as dependable in a crisis as the sun rising every morning. In a crisis, we seem to maintain, 'deterrence' shall not fail to prevent the outbreak of war. Even a madman would be deterred. Yet there have been crises where the tactical implementation of current theories of deterrence has been frighteningly inadequate and dangerous. During the Cuban Missile Crisis, for example, Khrushchev wrote 'there is a smell of scorching in the air'; Dean Rusk remarked 'You and I have won a considerable victory: we are still alive'; and John F. Kennedy, the man who decided to embark upon an obscure and perhaps uncontrollable course, estimated the chance of war over Cuba as being between 'one-third and one-half'.

International relations is a peculiar field. The perceptions of decision-makers are, in effect, reality, since many of the subsequent actions and reactions of these decision-makers will probably be based upon these perceptions. They form self-fulfilling prophecies. If the men charged with preserving the United States and the Soviet Union felt nuclear war was near, then we must take seriously their fears that the deterrence of war by the existence of well-protected second strike nuclear forces is not an assured and automatic phenomenon.

This paper will explore some ways that deterrence can break down during a crisis; the implications of this upon future disarmament agreements; and some suggestions for broadening our nuclear policy so as to make deterrence more stable and less susceptible to factors beyond the conscious control of decision-makers.

Nuclear deterrence is commonly defined as the dissuasion by terror of an unwanted action or attack by a foreign nation through severe explicit or perceived threats of massive retaliation by the aggrieved nation's second strike nuclear forces. The operational aspects of deterrence include the need to designate against whom the threat is made, under what conditions the threat will be carried out or withdrawn, what military capabilities are available to carry out the threat, and whether the threat of nuclear attack is credible or not. Most strategies of deterrence are based upon the existence of well-protected second strike forces. Both the United States and the Soviet Union maintain and constantly upgrade these forces. Their mutual deterrence are considered stable and symmetrical, as neither side has the ability to launch a clear first strike knockout blow but each can cause extremely high retaliatory damage to the other side.

Before abstractly considering purely military methods of deterrence, let us look at how deterrence worked during the Cuban Missile Crisis. Because a variety of bureaucratic and political accidents, deterrence nearly failed during the Cuban Crisis. John Kennedy was under extreme political pressure to respond strenuously and without flinching. For several days, the main issue before 'EXCOM' was deciding the best means of hitting the missile bases with a surprise bomber attack. The option of an air attack was temporarily discarded when Kennedy was incorrectly informed by the Air Force that a small air attack could not destroy all of the missiles with confidence and prevent retaliation. The Chiefs of Staff and six of Kennedy's fourteen advisors continued, however, to press for an air attack throughout the crisis.

On October 28 an ultimatum was delivered by Robert Kennedy to the Soviet Ambassador, Anatole Dobrynin: the Soviet Union must announce the prompt withdrawal of all IRBM and MRBM missiles or they would be destroyed. Suppose Khrushchev had believed that nuclear weapons were so horrible that they would never be used? Could Kennedy have backed away from his irrevocable commitment without suffering grave strategic defeat and without being politically destroyed? How could Khrushchev back out gracefully and defuse discontent about his 'softness', especially as he seems to have fought for the emplacement of missiles in Cuba in the first place.

Organizational problems also place severe constraints upon the 'rationality' of the decisions leaders may make and upon the range of options that are quickly available. Moreover, the operating characteristics of large organizations often produce independent of any conscious decision a number of situations that may induce decision-makers to take actions which they would otherwise avoid. For example, organizations and bureaucracies often have perceptions and goals that differ from those of other organizations within a government and from those of national decision-makers. Often there are parochial interests that do not help maximize the security interests of a nation. For example, the US Air Force has constantly attempted to get scarce funds for a new, expensive manned bomber even though bombers are only marginally useful in the age of rapid ICBMs and submarine-launched missiles. Thus, if we accept organizational behaviour as a constraint upon decision-makers, we may conclude that the final action of a nation is likely to be not an optimal strategy for any set of goals, but a compromise between the goals and influences of the several different organizations or bureaucracies that comprise a government; and that, in general, such groups tend to seize upon the first apparently satisfactory response to the immediate problem rather than to seek the optimal solution, even though classical models of analysis assume that decision-makers are free to calculate how to maximize the national interest and then to carry out the optimal line.

Another factor is that problems of co-ordinating large groups or numbers of groups and of inter-group rivalry may result in unwanted actions taken independently by a single group that may vastly complicate a situation. Also, selective and distorted exchange of information and orders becomes inevitable.

Finally, we may conclude that rapid change of a bureaucracy's perceptions, goals, and methods of operation are virtually impossible. This is the result of rather rigid contingency plans and standard operating procedures; the limited number of anticipated situations that an organization is programmed to handle efficiently; and the attempts to fit novel situations into existing patterns of organizational behaviour.

Rather than consider the Cuban Missile Crisis in full from these alternative perspectives, let us briefly examine a few incidents arising from political or organizational problems that nearly resulted in armed conflict.

John Kennedy and Robert McNamara continually attempted to change the US Navy's plans for a blockade. They wanted the blockade line pulled back to within 200 miles of the Cuban coast so that Khrushchev would have time carefully to consider his response. The Navy could not or would not, change its battle plans, as they were satisfactory from a narrow military perspective, though not from a political perspective.

An Air Force U-2 air sampling plane accidentally strayed over Soviet territory because of faulty navigation. It was challenged by Soviet fighters. Help was requested from American fighters who subsequently escorted it back to Alaska. An armed clash nearly ensued here. 'There's always some SOB who doesn't get the word', said Kennedy. This incident occurred on Saturday morning, October 27, during the blackest moment of the crisis, when several other incidents beyond the control of Khrushchev or Kennedy raised tension to incredible levels. Perhaps the most dangerous of these was the communications foul-up within the Kremlin. On Friday evening, October 26, a long, personal letter from Khrushchev was received by Kennedy. Khrushchev offered to withdraw Soviet missiles if Kennedy would promise not to invade Cuba. Kennedy generally agreed to this deal. On Saturday morning, a much harsher, more formal letter was received by the United States demanding a trade of American Jupiter missiles in Turkey for Soviet missiles in Cuba. Kennedy felt that he could not make this deal under pressure. Why the change? Had Khrushchev been overruled by the Presidium? Or did he decide that Kennedy had weakened and could be bluffed? Many analysts now believe that it was neither. Instead, they think that the formal letter was drafted before Khrushchev's personal letter and had been slowed down while moving through the Soviet foreign policy bureaucracy. As a result, it was transmitted by basically unco-ordinated sub-groups at such a time as nearly to destroy Khrushchev's plan for an acceptable settlement.

While tensions were high that Saturday morning because of the switched letters, an American U-2 was destroyed by Soviet SAM-2 missiles while on a reconnaissance mission over Cuba. Kennedy and Khrushchev up until that point had done everything possible to avoid actual armed combat. Had the Soviet Union deliberately decided to provoke the situation and scare Kennedy into backing down? How should the United States reply? It is now believed that Soviet anti-aircraft crews in Cuba had been ordered to shoot down any intelligence planes flying over Cuba; the orders were received long before the crisis and had been forgotten by the Kremlin when tensions rose.

Meanwhile, the US Air Force thought it had been ordered to destroy any SAM-2 site that shot at US reconnaissance planes. By a lucky accident, a member of EXCOM remembered this just a few minutes before an unintended air strike was to have been launched and hence the strike was halted.

As for the suddenly-prominent American missiles in Turkey, Kennedy had ordered these removed twice within the preceding year. The State Department did nothing, however, as it feared Turkish political reaction. Kennedy entered the crisis confident that his weakest spot had been secured months ago. Now, it had reappeared greatly to complicate an already serious crisis and push him further into the corner.

Many people believe that the lessons we learned during the Cuban Crisis will remain with us and prevent any future dangers of this nature. But just as an organization can learn a lesson, it may also gradually unlearn the same lesson unless it is continually reinforced. Few would wish, however, to reinforce these ideas and lessons by a series of occasional serious crises. Autonomous bureaucratic behaviour may occur that complicates or initiates dangerous actions that no 'rational decision-maker' would choose. Thus, it is arguable that no matter how wise or compassionate a national leader is, the probability that deterrence will never fail cannot reach 100 per cent. We will always have to deal with apparently 'irrational' behaviour arising from systems and with severe constraints on the ability of decision-makers to choose and implement a course that national security dictates.

Turning from ideas of organizational behaviour to more traditional analysis, I would like to examine several potential defects in the 'Rational Actor' model of decision-making. Here, too, Kennedy felt events were 'approaching the point where they could have become unmanageable'.

Under the pressure of new quantitative and qualitative developments and the internal political pressures to maintain a numerical superiority over one's opponents for psychological reasons, a deterrent situation can become dynamically unstable when both sides seek to preserve an approximate balance of forces under a climate of high uncertainty about future deployments, technologies, and intentions.

Inasmuch as nuclear forces must be sufficiently destructive and invulnerable to act as a second strike force, an arms race is likely should either side begin new weapons, such as MIRV, ABM and ASW, that might eventually become destabilizing first strike weapons. Given the high uncertainty about perceptions of our opponents, and predictions of technological breakthroughs and future deployments by any adversaries, there is a tendency to overcompensate, and thus further fuel the arms race through the using of worst-case analysis and planning. Once started, it is difficult to stop the cycle, since each side further misperceives the responses and intentions of the other side. A dialectic of mutual suspicions and confirming actions can set in.

Moreover, there is implicit pressure to stay ahead of opposing force levels for bargaining purposes, since national decision-makers are still prone to analogize present nuclear forces with the balance of power international system which operated before the Second World War. This almost certainly leads to an arms race to preserve a deterrent posture, because uncertainty about opposing deployments is compounded by the need to project six to ten years in the future to compensate for the long development lead-time needed for the deployment of counter-weapons. Until that deployment is completed, a nation will become increasingly sensitive to the adequacy of its deterrent posture, and will, moreover, feel pressed by others because of the perceived vulnerability of its deterrent forces. One can easily call to mind the tremendous effect on American military plans that was caused by the Russian launching of Sputnik and the alleged 'missile gap'. Though modern deterrence is postulated upon the invulnerability of strategic forces, it is very difficult to maintain the comfortable psychological illusion of absolute and unchanging invulnerability of deterrent forces. Consequently arms races can occur following the introduction of new weapons by either side into their nuclear forces.

The problem of a spiral of fear can be traced to the use of a damage-limiting first strike strategy by a side that might pre-empt because it feared a pre-emptive, damage limiting attack upon itself as war drew seemingly near. In an increasingly tense situation, the thought of war and a first strike becomes very real as decision-makers try to find the strategy that best fits the chances of war or peace. Social psychologists now believe that the pressures of crisis seriously degrade the ability of decision-makers to find innovative strategies that might aid de-escalation. Karl Deutsch, for example, cites the mobilizations of the First World War as a case where tension and the expectation of war escalated to such a degree as to make war inevitable.

The point of this digression into the question of force structures is to illustrate both the large deterrent factors each nation would possess no matter what attack was launched and to illuminate the possible deficiencies which the prudent planner feels that he must compensate for.

Of the more obvious factors motivating the matching of enemy build-ups one is closely associated with deterrence. The need to show one's resolve and willingness to escalate in a crisis is considered necessary to prevent an opponent from thinking that he is getting a free ride and thus becoming too bold. But, where does one stop the cycle of gradually increasing escalation and turn 'chicken'? At what level, if any, does prudence force a decision-maker from escalating just a bit further in order to 'win' a battle of wills? Who would wish to see these questions answered empirically?

Deterrence is also affected by the image one presents to the opponent. Practising 'rational' moderation in response to an opposing build-up may convince adversary leaders that when the crunch of crisis comes, these reasonable and moderate men will once again act 'rationally' and will behave with restraint, backing down from a dangerous stance once the issue of nuclear use arose. Khrushchev, perhaps as a result of the American decision to allow the Berlin Wall, may have felt that he would be able to stage a similar *fait accompli* with the missiles in Cuba. When Kennedy acted in a manner quite unexpected by Khrushchev, the world came rather close to a war that might have occurred because no one was intellectually prepared for the crisis that preceded it, and because both national leaders had staked prestige on very rigid, conflicting positions.

Deterrence might seem to be enhanced on an abstract level if one nation seems reckless or automatically responsive to arms build-ups. In effect, this forces the other nation to decide whether to escalate the conflict. Yet, this sort of manipulation of fear might have the opposite

97

effect and raise tension to the point where deterrence is dangerously close to breaking down, due to a lack of confidence in its stabilizing effects.

The problem of brinksmanship and deterrence in an escalating situation is illustrated by Herman Kahn. He believes that should nations become involved in a crisis where nuclear war seems possible, confidence in one's deterrent force and in the concept of assured deterrence will become severely shaken. During such a crisis, both of international relations and of faith, pre-emptive war becomes more likely.

Military deterrence alone cannot adequately cope with an escalating crisis due to the great potential for miscalculations based upon misperception of enemy actions and intentions. We would find it very hard to bargàin with our adversaries if the actions of each signified different levels of hostility and resolve. No amount of information can completely erase these problems of intellectual and cultural asymmetry, but the gap can be narrowed by communicating often concepts of strategy adhered to by each nation.

Seen in this light, then, the usefulness of solely military deterrence would seem to be limited to preventing less serious crises from escalating into more serious ones. It does not facilitate a process of de-escalation and disengagement. Yet a crisis may erupt despite the very substantial pressures resulting from the fear of inadvertent war. The extreme destructiveness of modern weapons poses another problem: many believe that nuclear weapons will never be used because of the unimaginable destruction that would follow. If one really believes that deterrence is this stable, then the credibility of the threatened resort to nuclear weapons becomes almost nil and we shall have no actual deterrence at all. A nation may thus get caught in a crisis for which it is not prepared and in a provocative, but untenable position. Rigidity may easily follow. One may well ask how credible deterrence would be once nations have hardened their postures into irrevocably committed positions.

Kahn believes that brinksmanship-type escalations may be controlled by 'secret but definite internal firebreaks' imposed by a nation on itself as to how far it is willing to escalate. By keeping such firebreaks secret, one may avoid advertising to the other side how far they must escalate in order to prevail; unfortunately, one also risks war in this posture, since either side may have miscalculated how far it may push the other side without forcing that side to war. In this sort of situation, an insidious, gradual escalation may occur, with each side tempted to go just a little higher in order to win and justify the large chances taken so far. War may also occur because decision-makers are increasingly tempted to go to war when threats become severe.

In this light, one may question how rational the decision-making process really is, since it is prone to miscalculation and precludes gathering all of the information needed to find the optimal situation.

Thomas Schelling's suggested use of brinksmanship as a possible strategy of 'winning' and as a method of increasing deterrence may be defined as structuring a situation so that an opponent is left with only one sensible course of action: giving in. This assumes that the opposing decision-maker is 'rational' enough to be impressed by one's threat of nuclear catastrophe, and that he does not view the future consequences of giving in as being more dangerous than trying an escalatory bluff himself. Suppose, too, that he feels that the threatener is bluffing and accordingly stands fast? For example, what might have happened if Khrushchev thought John Kennedy was bluffing in his ultimatum to remove the missiles or face an air strike?

Decision-making during crisis situations also becomes questionable. In addition to men becoming less flexible and more resistant to innovative ideas, the strains of crisis are likely to overload a decision-maker's emotional and intellectual capabilities. They become less able correctly to perceive the significance of their actions and those of their opponents.

An additional argument against pre-emptive brinksmanship is that a nation forced to back down often will seek to avoid continual humiliation and automatic assumptions by its enemies that it will continue to back down in the face of future resolute actions. This can lead to the dangerous, overly rigid postures described earlier, since the nation cannot allow its image to be that of the prudent state bending before every 'irrational threat' without fail. Such a nation would have no deterrence behind its policy, no matter how large its nuclear forces were. However, if any enemy assumes that this nation will continue to back down and escalates on this basis, then the sudden change by the formerly 'rational' nation to overly rigid postures will ·not be believed. There is some evidence to indicate that Khrushchev plâced missiles in Cuba because he thought Kennedy would accede to his grand plan to upset the strategic balance. The type of escalation postulated above could accidentally provoke a very serious situation that neither side planned or desired. It would be very difficult for these nations to extricate themselves from their positions without the sort of compromise that neither side would accept at this time.

It appears that deterrence in a crisis has several potential drawbacks if it is based upon military might alone. It is susceptible to unintended behaviour produced by hard-to-control bureaucracies and to internal political pressures. The process may be distorted by misperceptions arising out of a cycle of rising hostility. It can be upset by technological breakthroughs that reduce confidence in the invulnerability of its forces. The manipulation of risk to increase deterrence can be self-defeating because such a strategy may encourage war through unnecessarily rigid postures or the perceived need to pre-empt because of apparent enemy intentions. Weapons procurements can become unstable and the victim of self-fulfilling prophecy because of the need to project six to ten years into the future when trying to offset forces someone else may employ.

What does this mean in terms of deterrence theory and disarmament? As long as national goals and interests conflict and produce political tensions, some forms of arms will be kept by nations, if only for defensive purposes. Since the knowledge and material needed to produce nuclear weapons will continue to be widely available in the future, nations will be reluctant to part with nuclear weapons if they feel that their opponents might be able to produce them and utilize them for nuclear blackmail. Delivery of covertly assembled weapons might be feasible with commercial aircraft and with spacecraft that nations will retain in the foreseeable future. Unless very reliable international controls exist, the willingness of nations to part with all of their nuclear weapons must therefore be seriously doubted.

However, partial nuclear disarmament is possible. Current weapons stocks are so high that they are absurd. However, the logic of the arms race continues to make nations fear that their deterrent forces, their actual weapons systems and their structure, may be vulnerable to new technological breakthroughs or numerical build-ups. Even if SALT II stops the arms race, political tensions will remain and may play upon fears of deterrent force inadequacy to foster new, more tension-provoking arms races that will in turn cause further tension.

But let us suppose that the arms race ceases and nations begin gradual nuclear disarmament. Research and development will certainly continue even though a ban on the testing of new weapons might reduce the confidence we place in them and thus might prevent their deployment. Nevertheless nations may very well refuse to destroy all of their nuclear weapons, since this may help forestall nuclear blackmail and the fear of it. Thus, a small, residual force may perform a stabilizing function by calming fears about whether one is defensible in the face of possible secret violations of a partial disarmament agreement. Nations are thus less likely to see themselves as potential victims of an 'arms race Prisoner's Dilemma' and feel compelled to cheat 'just in case'.

If, therefore, in the absence of international control, complete nuclear disarmament seems implausible, the problem of managing crises where deterrence may break down because of trans-cultural misperception or accidental bureaucratic behaviour remains. Hence it is appropriate to consider now the possibility that some gaps in deterrence theory may be filled through the use of a wider concept of deterrence than the purely military one. We may consider deterrence in this case as an influence process aimed at modifying the behaviour of other nations, whether by threat of force or through less violent methods.

Ithiel Pool has delineated the various mechanisms by which a nation can be deterred from taking an action. He suggested that all of the following mechanisms may be used to 'deter' an opponent:

1. One can develop 'trust'. This seems to work best in periods of low tension, where it can be a very successful reassurance mechanism. However, combined with the use of threat in nuclear situations, a fair amount of trust based upon the expectation of grave mutual harm and each side's desire to avoid this harm may be developed.
2. As noted above, one can induce fear, but this is useful only under the following relatively limited conditions when employed as the sole means of deterrence: if it is induced within a period when the danger seems imminent within a finite time and cannot be postponed or denied; if it has been in the background for some time and if the short-run tactics of the persuader is simultaneously to threaten and to offer relief; if the person to be intimidated is allowed to develop good rationalizations for backing down.
3. One can also change the perceptions of the leaders about the external environment that they face. This sort of information is accepted even from hostile sources, particularly so in the Soviet Union, with its devotion to 'pragmatism'. Needed is both a clear definition of the strategic and political environment as we see it, and a great deal of redundancy in information transfer.
4. Deterrence may also occur when the perceptions of the certainty of a particular action occurring are changed consciously by the deterring state. This may result in either greater boldness or greater caution by a nation, depending upon how certain they are of an unwanted event occurring and how credible the information transfer is.
5. Another important but little noted deterring process is that of providing an intellectual and strategic model to a potential adversary. This has the advantage of stabilizing deterrence by reducing the misperception that may arise from asymmetry of strategic doctrines. To a considerable extent, Pool maintains, the United States has provided the Soviet Union with such models. There is generally a one to three year delay before the Soviet Union begins to accept the efficacy of the doctrines that the United States has accepted, and in some cases has already abandoned. Certainly, such commitments are partial and thus selective, but American

101

actions do seem to create substantial pressure within the Soviet Union to do the same thing.

Taken from these viewpoints, deterrence can be considered to encompass many of the options open to the United States in its diplomatic interactions.

One process that might have considerable deterrent value if properly developed so as to be congruent with modern strategic theory is customary international law. We must distinguish between law in the Austinian sense of the surely enforced domestic command of the sovereign (which is the common conception of 'law') and law as a system of shared norms in international society that works primarily as a political process. We should further consider those portions of the law which arise from the customary practice of states and thus are laws of stable international behaviour, not laws for behaviour. To some degree, we are dealing with what Karl Deutsch terms 'quasi-law', a group of expectations set up by the common, but tacit, crisis management practices of the nuclear states. Such 'quasi-law' arises from the pragmatic experiences of states and from the tacit or explicit recognition of such principles by governments in their international dealings. 'Nuclear' diplomacy has shattered many traditional legal norms, but has hastened the formation of custom that will be viable, not because of any expectations of sanctions by international organizations but by the high cost of frequent non-compliance, even if this cost is calculated in narrow strategic terms. Interestingly, Deutsch maintains that the survival of deterrence crises may produce greater caution and such a class of quasi-legal rules of crisis management and of shared limits to conflict. After all, the highest goal of a nation, survival in the nuclear age, can be preserved only by some sort of co-operation. Study of the Cuban Missile Crisis and other nuclear crises suggests that some crisis management customs have been adopted by the nuclear powers and may eventually gain the force of customary international law. Examples are: prohibiting the secret development of advanced weapons systems, especially those that threaten the invulnerability of retaliatory forces; preventing any deployment of nuclear weapons beyond the absolute physical and military control of the power that owns them, and thus preventing them from possibly falling into the hands of smaller, potentially volatile allies; creating a large distinction between weapons useful only for defensive operations and weapons that have offensive capabilities; and intefering in well-defined 'spheres of influence' that contain regional security and legal organizations, such as the OAS or the Warsaw Pact.

102

Analyzed in terms of a modified deterrence theory, 'legalizing' such norms would have several important benefits to a disarming world. It would militate against some of the internal inconsistencies in the theory of purely military deterrence. Such rules would seem to be congruent with the dictates of strategic theory in such matters as more clearly defining thresholds. They could gain additional force as a mechanism to reassure jittery nations if they continue to be part of the crisis management procedure of larger powers. They could deter· destabilizing actions by establishing thresholds and by reducing the possibility of misperception of the intentions of opponents.

Expectations of co-operation or hostility can be co-ordinated with the expectations of other competing powers and thus reduce the dynamic of Prisoner's Dilemma situations. Disappointing these expectations in a crisis could be very destabilizing since it signals very clearly the willingness of an opponent to escalate very highly. For these reasons, we may say that these 'rules of crisis management' constitute a form of deterrence in addition to the military deterrence that backs them up. Moreover, such strategically-based rules of international custom can reduce the danger of independent, dangerous, bureaucratic behaviour. Incorporated into the crisis avoidance and management ideas of nations and into contingency planning, such stabilizing customs can both limit tension producing behaviour and guide the management of a crisis. Complex organizations cannot reprogramme their activities quickly; legalized strategic constraints congruent with strategic theory would play a rôle in crisis management even if decision-makers decided to be reckless and break these rules.

Should ideas of crisis management congruent with customary international law continue to gain the force of precedent, as they did during the Cuban Missile Crisis, then it seems possible to achieve partial nuclear disarmament while retaining stabilizing, residual national deterrent forces.

9.   THE OUTLOOK FOR DISARMAMENT

William Epstein

Introduction[1]

Throughout history, nations have sought to ensure or improve their security through armaments. That they failed in this quest is evidenced by the periodic wars which have afflicted mankind. Through the League of Nations after the First World War and the United Nations after the Second World War, nations sought security through an international organization and system, the main pillars of which were the peaceful settlements of disputes, collective security, and disarmament.

The United Nations and the nuclear age were both born in 1945. We *hope* that the creation of the United Nations will have changed the course of history. We *know* that the discovery of nuclear energy and the invention of nuclear weapons have done so. The first resolution adopted by the United Nations at the first session of the General Assembly early in 1946 called for the elimination of atomic weapons and the use of atomic energy for peaceful purposes only.

The first fifteen years or so of disarmament efforts in the United Nations resulted in deadlock and failure. During the ensuing years we have witnessed a number of successes in the field of arms control. During these years, 7 multilateral treaties and 7 bilateral Soviet-American treaties were signed. The multilateral treaties were as follows:

1959 *The Antartic Treaty,* which provided for free scientific investigation and co-operation in Antartica, the de-nuclearization and de-militarization of the area, and free inspection to ensure the observance of the treaty.

1963 *The Partial Test Ban Treaty,* which banned nuclear weapon tests in the atmosphere, in outer space and under water, and which stated the intention to achieve the discontinuance of all nuclear weapon tests for all time.

1967 *The Outer Space Treaty,* which banned stationing or orbiting of nuclear weapons and other weapons of mass destruction in outer space and provided for the de-militarization of the moon and other celestial bodies.

1967 *The Treaty for the Prohibition of Nuclear Weapons in Latin America* (The Treaty of Tlatelolco), which banned the testing, producing, stationing and use of nuclear weapons in Latin

America. The Treaty established a control organization and a control system, including IAEA safeguards, regular and special reports by the parties and special inspections when needed. It also contained a Protocol whereby the nuclear weapon powers would pledge themselves to respect the nuclear-free status of the zone.

1968 *The Treaty for the Non-Proliferation of Nuclear Weapons,* whereby the non-nuclear weapon states undertook not to acquire nuclear weapons or other nuclear explosive devices, and the nuclear weapon powers agreed to pursue negotiations in good faith to achieve a halt to the nuclear arms race, nuclear disarmament and a treaty on general and complete disarmament. The non-nuclear weapon states agreed to accept the IAEA safeguards to ensure their observance of the treaty. Great Britain and the United States voluntarily and unilaterally agreed to accept IAEA safeguards for their peaceful nuclear reactors.

1971 *The Seabed Treaty,* which prohibited the emplacement of nuclear weapons and other weapons of mass destruction on the sea-bed, the ocean floor and in the subsoil thereof. It also contained a provision for continuing negotiations in good faith for further measures in the field of disarmament for the prevention of an arms race on the seabed.

1972 *The Biological Convention,* which prohibited the development, production and stockpiling of biological and toxin weapons and provided for their destruction. The treaty also contained an undertaking to continue negotiations in good faith for the prohibition of the development, production and stockpiling of chemical weapons and for their destruction.

The bilateral treaties between the Soviet Union and the United States are the following:

1963 *The 'Hot Line' Agreement,* which provided for a direct communications link between Moscow and Washington.

1971 *The Agreement on Measures to Reduce the Risk of Outbreak of Nuclear War* between the United States and the Soviet Union, which contained provisions to guard against the accidental or unauthorized use of nuclear weapons and for notification to the other side.

1971 *The Agreement for Modernizing and Improving the 'Hot Line'* between Moscow and Washington.

1972 *The Agreement to Prevent Incidents by Naval Vessels or Aircraft on or Over the Sea,* whereby the two sides agreed to rules for

105

restraining shadowing and buzzing by naval vessels and aircraft, in order to avoid incidents occuring.

1972 *The SALT ABM Treaty* on the limitation of anti-ballistic missile systems. These were limited to two sites in each country with no more than 100 ABM single missile launchers in each. The development and deployment of radars or new types of ABM launchers was also restricted. National means of verification were to be used to ensure compliance with the agreement.

1972 *The SALT Interim Agreement for the Limitation of Strategic Offensive Arms.* This Agreement, which is to last 5 years, limited the number of land-based ICBMs to the existing number (1054 for the United States and 1618 for the Soviet Union) and sea-based SLBMs to no more than 710 for the United States in no more than 44 submarines and to no more than 950 SLBMs for the Soviet Union in no more than 62 submarines. National means of verification were to be used to ensure compliance with the agreement.

1973 *US-Soviet Agreement on the Prevention of Nuclear War* in which both countries undertook to act in such a manner as to prevent the development of situations capable of generating military confrontations between them, as might lead to the outbreak of nuclear war. This is subject to the right of self-defence remaining in force, and the obligations undertaken by each country towards its allies.

Despite the achievement of these fourteen arms control agreements, all of which are of very considerable political importance, the world appears to be losing the battle to halt the arms race. For example, in 1960 there were less than 100 ICBMs and in 1970 there were about 2,400. In 1960 there was only one submarine with 16 submarine-launched ballistic missiles, while in 1970 there were some 60 to 70 nuclear submarines with over 1,000 SLBMs; by 1977 the number of nuclear submarines can rise to some 110 to 115, with more than 1,500 SLBMs. In 1960, the number of strategic nuclear warheads was something over 1,000; by 1970, the number was some 8,000 and in 1977 the number might be some 14,000. In 1960, the number of supersonic fighters was about 6,000 and in 1970 about 12,000. In 1960, the number of naval fighting vessels was about 4,500 and in 1970 about 5,000. In 1960, the number of armed forces in the world was 18 to 20 million, and in 1970 it was 23 to 24 million. The world total of annual military expenditures was about $120 billion in 1960 (equal to about $150 billion in 1970 prices) and in 1970 the figure was more than $200 billion. If the same rate of increase continues, by 1977 the total will be about $300 billion at 1970 prices.

106

The $200 billion spent for military purposes in 1970 was nearly three times as much as what all government spent on health, nearly twice as much as they spent on education and nearly 30 times as much as they spent on aid to developing countries.

In an article entitled 'The Game of Disarmament', in the UNESCO publication *Impact* of July/September 1972, Mrs Alva Myrdal, the Swedish Minister in charge of disarmament, wrote that she saw the disarmament picture as, 'a history of lost opportunities' with little genuine disarmament progress, which she attributed mainly to the fact that the two superpowers have not really worked for nuclear disarmament, but rather to achieve a balance between themselves; only the non-nuclear weapon states were called upon to make sacrifices in the name of arms control.

On the other hand, William C. Foster, the former Director of the United States Arms Control and Disarmament Agency, writing in the same issue of *Impact* on 'Technological Peace', claims that appreciable progress has already been made and that he is optimistic about the future. He argues that there is no alternative to the gradual, pragmatic, step-by-step approach which could finally lead to a technological peace.

It is thus not surprising that while some people have described the history of the disarmament negotiations as a remarkable record of achievements, others have described it as a sorry spectacle of failure.

The United Nations

The United Nations does not, of course, make disarmament agreements or treaties, because only states who become parties to treaties can do so. The General Assembly, however, does conduct an annual review of the work and progress in disarmament and it lays down general principles, goals and guidelines. During its existence, the United Nations has adopted well over 100 resolutions on disarmament. In the last few years the General Assembly has adopted a dozen or more resolutions at each session. These have ranged from calling for general and complete disarmament, for a comprehensive test ban, for the non-proliferation of nuclear weapons, for a halt in the nuclear arms race, for a moratorium on the development and deployment of strategic nuclear weapons, for a comprehensive prohibition of all chemical and biological weapons, and for many other measures for controlling and reducing the arms race. The decade of the 1970s has been declared by the United Nations both as a Disarmament Decade and as a Development Decade, with a view to promoting the interrelated goals of both disarmament and development.

The Secretary-General has conducted four studies in the field of disarmament, with the assistance of groups of consultant experts.

In 1962 a report on the *Economic and Social Consequences of Disarmament* concluded that the problems and difficulties of conversion of resources from military to peaceful uses could be met by appropriate national and international measures, to the benefit of all countries. In 1967 a report on the *Effects and Implications of Nuclear Weapons* concluded that the problem of ensuring security could not be found in an increase in the number of states possessing nuclear weapons or in the retention of nuclear weapons by the nuclear powers, but only through the prevention of the spread of nuclear weapons and the elimination of all stockpiles and the banning of their use. The report also stated that the threat of the immeasurable disaster that would befall mankind if nuclear war were ever to erupt, whether by miscalculation or mad intent, was so real that informed people become impatient for measures of disarmament in addition to the few arms limitation agreements already achieved. In 1969 a report was prepared on *Chemical and Biological Weapons and the Effects of their Possible Use.* The experts unanimously concluded that if these weapons were ever used on a large scale in war, no-one could predict how they would affect the structure of society or the environment in which we live. The Secretary-General, in accepting the report of the experts, appealed to all states to accede to the Geneva Protocol of 1925, called for an affirmation that the prohibition contained in the Geneva Protocol applied to the use in war of all chemical and biological agents which now exist or which might be developed in the future, and called upon all countries to agree to stop the development, production and stockpiling of these weapons and to achieve their elimination. In 1971, in a report on the *Economic and Social Consequences of the Arms Race*, a group of experts outlined the enormous cost of the arms race in human and other resources, and stated that the solution to the economic and social problems confronting mankind was impeded by the diversion of resources to military expenditure. They concluded that the arms race must be stopped, not only because of the immediate perils it holds, but because the longer it continued, the more intractable would become the problems of economic growth, social justice, and the environment. They recommended a substantial reduction in the military expenditures of all countries, particularly those whose military expenditures were highest. At the present time, another study by a group of experts is going forward on the *Economic and Social Consequences of Disarmament* with a view to establishing a link between disarmament and development.

During recent years, despite the achievement of the fourteen multilateral and bilateral arms control agreements, there is evidence of growing impatience and frustration among the smaller and

108

non-aligned countries in the United Nations. They want faster progress towards halting the arms race in order to ensure human survival, and faster progress towards the development of the developing countries in order to improve human welfare. One of the non-aligned countries described the past disarmament negotiations as a process of 'the armed attempting to disarm the non-armed'. Not only were they concerned about the slow progress in disarmament but there was also some evidence that some smaller and medium powers in the United Nations wanted to play a more active rôle in these negotiations. On the other hand, there seemed to be some irritation on the part of the superpowers concerning the nature of the deliberations in the General Assembly. They were often out-voted by the weight of numbers of the smaller and non-aligned countries, which, they felt, were registering their views without sufficient understanding of the problems and difficulties of the great powers in attempting to halt the arms race.

The Conference of the Committee on Disarmament

The Conference of the Committee on Disarmament, or the CCD as it is commonly called, has been described by the Secretary-General as the most effective and productive organ for multilateral arms control available to the international community. The CCD consists of 26 members under the Co-Chairmanship of the Soviet Union and the United States. In addition to the two Co-Chairmen, there are six allies of the Soviet Union: Bulgaria, Czechoslovakia, Hungary, Mongolia, Poland and Romania; six allies of the United States: Canada, Great Britain, Italy, Japan, the Netherlands and France (which does not actually participate); and 12 so-called non-aligned countries: Argentina, Brazil, Burma, Egypt, Ethiopia, India, Mexico, Morocco, Nigeria, Pakistan, Sweden and Yugoslavia.

The General Assembly has given the CCD a whole range of disarmament tasks from partial or collateral measures to general and complete disarmament. But there appears to be a growing sense of frustration and impatience among the non-aligned members and even, to some extent, among some of the allies of the United States and the Soviet Union. There is a feeling that progress is too slow and that not sufficient has been done even to implement the commitments in the treaties already achieved. For example, the Partial Test Ban Treaty has not resulted in an underground test ban; Article VI of the Non-Proliferation Treaty, calling for negotiations for a halt in the nuclear arms race, seems far from fulfilment, despite the Sea-bed and SALT Treaties; the Sea-bed Treaty has not produced any serious negotiations for further disarmament measures; and the commitment in the Biological Convention has not yet brought into sight a treaty for a complete ban of chemical weapons. Morever, negotiations on nuclear disarmament have, in effect, been transferred from the CCD to SALT and only the Comprehensive Test Ban issue remains in the nuclear field for negotiation in the CCD, without much evidence of prospects for an early solution.

Efforts in the CCD are no longer directed towards general and complete disarmament but are confined mainly to a comprehensive test ban and a comprehensive ban on chemical weapons. Some members fear that the CCD is running out of ideas in the field of arms control and disarmament and losing some of its momentum. Since China has now taken its seat in the United Nations, the feeling is growing that both China and France should be associated with the disarmament negotiations, which cannot be very meaningful without them.

SALT

While the SALT Agreements were hailed as a welcome and important step towards nuclear arms control, many delegations have stressed that the Agreements established only quantitative limitations in the field of strategic nuclear weapons with ceilings higher than the existing number; they have also pointed out that there were little or no qualitative limitations on the nuclear arms race or on technological research and development to improve these strategic offensive and defensive missiles. Indeed, some have pointed out that, despite the SALT Agreements, there will be no reduction in military expenditures, but that, on the contrary, it seems likely that there will be an increase in military budgets in order to carry on the qualitative nuclear arms race. In any case, nearly all countries have stressed the importance in the further SALT negotiations of taking steps to limit the qualitative nuclear arms race and to effect actual reductions in nuclear weapons.

Some have said that the agreements have greater political than military importance. Insofar as they improve the relations between the two superpowers and lessen the chances of nuclear war, they are regarded as very useful instruments of crisis management by the two superpowers. Others, however, have pointed to the dangers of the trend towards bilateralism and want a return to multilateralism in the field of nuclear disarmament; they fear that if a trend is established for bilateral negotiations between the two superpowers, it could pose some dangers for multilateral negotiations and perhaps even for the international system itself. In the Introduction to his Annual Report on the work of the organization, the Secretary-General stated:

110

. . . the idea of maintaining peace and security in the world through a concert of great Powers, although these Powers obviously have special responsibilities in matters of peace and security, would seem to belong to the nineteenth century, where the process of technological advance and democratization is producing a new form of world society. The world order that we are striving to build in the United Nations must meet the requirements of such a society, and any other system, however effective in the past, obviously cannot be acceptable, in the long run, to the peoples of the world. The interests, the wisdom and the importance of the vast majority of medium and smaller Powers cannot, at this point in history, be ignored in any durable system of world order.

World Disarmament Conference

The idea of a World Disarmament Conference was put forward, without success, on several occasions in the past by the Soviet Union. In 1965, the United Nations adopted a resolution, sponsored by a number of non-aligned countries, in favour of the convening of a World Disarmament Conference, but since China, which at that time did not occupy its seat in the United Nations, showed no interest in participating, the conference was never held. In 1971, however, the Soviet Union renewed the idea in a formal proposal. The General Assembly approved the idea in principle and invited all states to send their views and suggestions to the Secretary-General on the relevant questions relating to the holding of such a conference. During the discussions China, which now occupied its seat in the United Nations, re-stated its basic approach which favoured the holding of a World Summit Conference to ban the use of nuclear weapons, to eliminate all nuclear stockpiles, and to eliminate foreign military bases.

In the Communiqué of the Moscow Summit Conference in May 1972, the United States and the Soviet Union stated that a World Disarmament Conference could play a rôle in the disarmament process at an 'appropriate time'. In the statement issued by the conference of non-aligned countries at Georgetown, Guyana, in August 1972, the participants felt that the convening of a World Disarmament Conference, after due preparations, which would include all the nuclear weapon states, would be a useful step and that its aim would be to exert a positive effort in achieving progress towards general and complete disarmament and primarily towards banning and eliminating nuclear and other mass destruction weapons.

It is obvious, of course, that the Soviet Union favours the holding of a World Disarmament Conference. France, which does not participate in the Geneva disarmament negotiations (CCD), also supports the idea. The United States and, to a lesser extent, Great Britain are opposed to holding the conference at the present time. Whether China will insist on the acceptance of its ideas as a pre-condition for the holding of the conference, or whether it will be content if its proposals are included together with other items on the agenda of the conference, is not yet clear.

On the other hand, it appears that the smaller powers, including the allies of the Soviet Union and some of those of the United States, as well as practically all the non-aligned countries, seem to favour the holding of a World Disarmament Conference at some early date. They obviously wish to move in the direction of faster progress towards disarmament, and the developing countries in particular are anxious to establish a link between disarmament and development. Moreover, many of them feel that the holding of a World Disarmament Conference would be the best way to get China and France to participate in both the disarmament discussions and the detailed negotiations. A WDC could also convert the tendency towards bilateral discussions to a multilateral plane.

The issues that would be dealt with in a World Disarmament Conference would first and foremost concern nuclear disarmament, but the conference could perhaps also revive interest in general and complete disarmament. It could, of course, also deal with the unfulfilled commitments for a comprehensive test ban, a complete chemical ban, further disarmament measures for the sea-bed, and the full implementation of the Non-Proliferation Treaty, namely to make the treaty universal and to prevent both the horizontal spread of nuclear weapons to non-nuclear countries, and vertical proliferation by the further sophistication and accumulation of nuclear weapons by the nuclear powers. It could also encourage the creation of additional nuclear-free zones in addition to that in Latin America. It could, of course, also deal with problems of conventional disarmament. In fact, the conference could deal with the whole range of measures and all aspects of arms control and disarmament. Several delegations have suggested that the conference could take up the comprehensive programme of disarmament put forward in 1970 by Mexico, Sweden and Yugoslavia, which the General Assembly requested the CCD to take into account in the further work and negotiations on disarmament.

In recent years a number of delegations and disarmament experts have favoured a new approach to disarmament. Since the fourteen multilateral and bilateral agreements achieved during recent years have failed even to slow down, let alone halt, the arms race or prevent the escalation of military expenditures, it had been suggested that a more meaningful approach to the problem would be a substantial reduction of military expenditures, perhaps by 25 per cent, as the best

way to stop the spiralling arms race. Such a substantial cut in military
expenditures could be implemented by each country in the way it
thought best. Supporters of this global approach, in place of the
piecemeal approach of individual measures of arms control, have
pointed out that the United States and the Soviet Union each made
unilateral reductions in their military budgets in 1963-1964, in
accordance with what was known as the 'policy of mutual example'.
While proposals in earlier years for reducing military expenditures ran
into difficult questions of verification there is a growing belief that,
with the new techniques developed in recent years by way of
satellites surveillance and a better understanding of the industrial and
budgetary policies of the main military powers, the problem of
verification might not be as intractable as it was considered to be in
the past.

The Decade of the 1970s

The main problem for the immediate years ahead is how to prevent
the proliferation of nuclear weapons, both by new states becoming
nuclear powers (horizontal proliferation) and by the further
sophistication and accumulation of nuclear weapons by the nuclear
powers in a continuing nuclear arms race (vertical proliferation).
A number of authorities have stressed the importance of making the
Non-Proliferation Treaty (NPT) universal — that is by obtaining the
adherence of all nuclear powers and by all the near-nuclear powers.
A number of the latter have signed the Treaty, but not yet ratified it
(such as the EURATOM countries, Japan, Switzerland and Australia)
and, on the other hand, a number of potential nuclear powers such as
India, Israel, Spain, South Africa, Argentina and Brazil have not signed
the Treaty. A world of ten or fifteen nuclear powers would certainly be
much more unstable and unpredictable than the present world of five
nuclear powers.

In this connection it has been argued that it is essential to stop the
vertical proliferation of nuclear weapons in order to be able to prevent
their horizontal proliferation. Countries such as Canada, Japan and
Sweden have stressed the rôle and importance of a comprehensive test
ban as an earnest of the intentions of the nuclear powers to halt the
nuclear arms race. They have also said that the cessation of
underground tests by the Soviet Union and the United States might
also have some influence or provide some inducement for China and
France to halt their tests in the atmosphere. It is feared by many that,
if underground nuclear tests are not halted and a comprehensive test
ban treaty achieved ending all tests in all environments by everyone,
then both the Partial Test Ban Treaty and the Non-Proliferation Treaty

113

could be undermined and their very existence put in jeopardy. The latter Treaty provides for the holding of a review conference by 5 March 1975, five years after the entry into force of the NPT. Fears have been expressed that, unless a comprehensive test ban and real progress towards halting the nuclear arms race is achieved by that time, the continued viability and credibility of the Non-Proliferation Treaty may be put in doubt.

Much has been learnt during the past decade about the techniques and requirements for successful disarmament negotiations. Technological advances such as satellite photography and surveillance have removed many of the problems of verifications. It is also recognized that verification and control do not need to be 'foolproof' but only sufficient to deter a party to a treaty from risking a violation. The fact that a number of arms control treaties have been achieved, that nuclear weapons have not been used for over a quarter of a century and that the risk of nuclear war has receded somewhat, also provides a better climate for accommodation. Moreover, recent developments in the world in the direction of detente and the normalization of relations between the great powers, as well as the stabilization of the balance between the two superpowers, would seem to provide improved prospects for progress in the field of disarmament.

Never before in history have so many treaties and agreements been recorded in the field of disarmament. And never before in peace-time has so much in the way of human and economic resources been devoted to fueling the spiralling arms race. The decade of the 1970s, which the United Nations has designated as the Disarmament Decade, is likely to see arms control and disarmament discussed and negotiated in more conferences and forums — multilateral, regional and bilateral — than ever before.

Whether the nations of the world will take advantage of the opportunities which arise is not yet clear. Whether, and to what extent, China will actively participate in the disarmament negotiations and discussions is also not yet clear. Once again, as so often in the past, the nations of the world face a real cross-roads. They may take the road of real progress towards the goal of nuclear disarmament and general and complete disarmament, or they may take the road of lost opportunities. Human survival and human welfare may depend upon which road they take, but the outlook at the present time is still cloudy.

NOTE

1. This paper expresses only the personal views of the author and not necessarily the views or official position of the Secretary General of the United Nations.

10. VERIFICATION AND CONTROL

Jules Moch

I wish first to make a short remark about the title of this paper, *Verification and Control*, which reminds me of a curious detail of the negotiations on disarmament. The period of greatest hope for disarmament was just after the Korean War. From 1951 there existed a Disarmament Committee of eleven Member States. This Committee had to meet publicly in the United Nations Building in New York and therefore the speeches were more for propaganda than for real effect. I then proposed, in 1953, the creation of a Sub-committee of five powers: Great Britain, Canada, France, the United States and the Soviet Union, authorized to meet not publicly and not in the United States, where we were then under pressure brought by the wave of McCartheyism. So we met and worked seriously in Lancaster House, in London, from 1953 to 1957.

In New York, I had presented in 1952 a French proposal for general and complete disarmament (GCD) under international control. In London, in 1954, the Foreign Secretary, Selwyn Lloyd, expressed the wish to study this paper and, subject to minor amendments, to sign it with us, so that it became the Anglo-French proposal of 1954.

When we prepared the common text, we misunderstood each other, when speaking of 'control', because we both translated the French word 'contrôle' with the English one, 'control', and vice-versa. But these two words do not have the same meaning. The French 'contrôle' means verification, that is inspection without any other implication. The English 'control' means supervision. So that the French 'contrôle' is to be translated by 'verification', the British 'control' being equivalent to the French word 'direction'.

So we began to speak of 'verification or contrôle'. The two words remained so associated in the special language of the peace-builders that, twenty years later, they often appear together! Remember, therefore, that they should really be rendered as follows: 'English verification or French contrôle'!

Disarmament negotiations are almost as ancient as war and, hence, as man, but have never led to very positive results. In spite of the unanimous and permanent wish for peace, wars have cost in lives and in expense much more than anyone can imagine. I wish to quote briefly five examples:
1. The two world wars — which men of my age experienced from their

116

beginning to their end, lasting for more than ten years – involved the deaths, according to varying estimates, of between 50 and 60 million, which means more than the whole population of Italy, or of Britain, or of France.

2. Total war expenses, including the pensions for the former soldiers and the wounded, the widows and orphans, and the cost of rehabilitation of the bombed regions, amounted, for France alone, to more than a $100 billion. That means that the two wars cost my country, in addition to the normal expenses during those ten years, twenty-five to thirty years of the French gross national product of those times.

3. In all the years of our century, which we call a civilized one, we notice only two years of universal peace: 1910 and 1927.

4. There are now 142 independent states, including those which are not members of the United Nations. Out of those 142 states, the 120 most important ones spent in 1970 a total of $204 billion on military expenditure, including $81 billion by the United States, $55 by the Soviet Union, $7 billion by China and $6 billion by France, which unhappily comes fourth in this race to ruin! These $204 billion are mostly used to produce armaments which are so dreadful that each government is convinced that no one will ever dare to use them. Nevertheless each human being pays $60 a year for defence and this tax rises to $396 *per capita* in the United States; to $300 in the state of Israel always threatened by her neighbours; to $169 in the Soviet Union; to $128 in Sweden, because of her enormous expenditure on civil protection; and to $121 in France, fifth on that list!

5. In cruel opposition to this horrible inflation of military expenditure, we must note the insufficient help to developing countries. That help is given by nations, whose individual national product amounts from $1,500 to $4,000, to the 2 billion people starving from hunger whose national product *per capita* does not exceed $150. This help, public or private, multilateral or bilateral, amounts to $13 billion a year: that means only 6 per cent of the total of military expenditure. It does not even compensate for the consequences of the population explosion, provoked by the spread of improved techniques of medicine and hygiene. It is in this way that the gulf each year widens between the fortunate nations and pariahs of the earth.

If we were to double in twenty years the standard of living of the one billion men earning less than $100 a year, it would be necessary to triple international aid from $13 to $40 billion a year, and, therefore, to find $27 billion more. With present military expenditure that is impossible. But, if there were a GCD treaty, to be executed over six or seven years in order to avoid unemployment and economic crises, it would be possible to increase aid to the level necessary to achieve a doubling of the standard of life of the poorest men of the world by giving 12½ per cent of military expenditure over the first two years to an International Development Fund.

We must now look to the most serious technical difficulty, we always had with the Soviet Union, precisely on the question of verification or control, which always brought the negotiations to an impasse.

We, the Western side, always asked for permanent international inspection on the spot. We said, for example, that, if the number of tanks, guns or planes from a given type existing in a country was 'E'; if, following the stipulations of the treaty, this nation had to destroy 'D' of them, and was allowed to keep the remaining number 'R', the three numbers E, D and R were bound by the relation: $E = D+R$. For complete verification the control organization has to establish the accuracy of two of these three numbers, because if two of them are known, the third can be calculated.

The Soviet Union agreed to let the inspectors verify 'D' — the destroyed weapons — but not those existing before destruction, 'E', or those remaining after destruction, 'R'. They always argued that those two quantities, E or R, could only be verified on the spot, involving all the airports, if it was a verification of aeroplanes, involving all the barracks and the factories, if it was a verification of guns, and so on. And such inspections they never accepted. They maintained that if the inspected country has to destroy 10 per cent of its tanks, and if you see 100 of them destroyed, you can calculate, without inspecting on the spot that this nations had 1,000 tanks and will keep 900.

We always answered: 'But if this country, having accepted in the treaty the destruction, as a first step, of 10 per cent of its tanks, possesses 3,000 tanks and presents, instead of 300, only 100 to be destroyed, how will we know the truth, without inspecting the existing tanks before the act of destruction, or, without inspecting the remaining tanks after this act of destruction?'

The Soviet Union then rather curiously answered that if a government promised to destroy 10 per cent of its armaments, it will do so; and that they would never accept the legalized espionage which the Western Powers would organize under the name of 'inspection on the spot'. One day, Gromyko asked me: 'Do you wish to inspect under all the beds of Russian men and women to verify whether there is not a little box of lead containing a bit of plutonium?' Another day,

118

at a plenary session of the United Nations General Assembly, he joked with the French Government: 'We will not allow your espionage in the Soviet Union and we do not want inspections on your soil: it is enough for us to read your official publications'. And he then told the General Assembly that a zone of the Sahara, delimited by two parallels and two meridians, had become inaccessible. 'It is there that you French will establish your experimental area for your atomic bomb', he declared triumphantly. The news was sensational! My answer, the next day, was of the same character. I called Paris, where our Atomic Energy Commission had monitored all the Russian explosions, and could tell Gromyko the exact position of one of the Russian experimental grounds in Siberia, near the Aral Sea. Such long-range inspections were, however, exceptional ten years ago. In the great majority of cases, inspection on the spot was necessary.

A new factor appeared in the discussions leading to the Partial Test Ban Treaty: the Americans accepted the adequacy of long-range control for all tests, except for those underground. For the latter they accepted long-range verification only provided they had the right to make twelve inspections on the spot yearly in dubious cases. To our astonishment, Krushchev's answer was not negative. He accepted 'two or three inspections', but not twelve. No agreement could be reached on a compromise of six or seven, and hence the underground tests were excluded from the Test Ban Treaty. And since then the Soviets, having dropped Krushchev, dropped also his concession: they do not accept now any inspection on the spot.

The constantly accelerating progress in technology is modifying more and more quickly the conditions of war, of diplomacy and of inspection. This is not the place to describe in detail the essential rôle played by the development in radar during the Battle of Britain in 1940, or the rôle of transistors, which appeared some time before the insurrection of French generals in Algeria in 1961 and which were the reason for their defeat. Nor can I elaborate on the announcement made by a smiling Zorin at our Sub-Committee in October 1957 of the launching of the first Sputnik, which, he added with much truth 'would change all the elements of international life'.

But I will elaborate on the changes in the matter of verification. Today, aircrafts and satellites carry sensors operating on radio frequency, infra-red, ultra-violet, and even X-ray and gamma-ray regions of the spectrum, with such high resolution that a picture taken from a U-2 flying at a height of 21 kilometres showed details on the soil as small as 1.5 metres. It was only a beginning.

Ten years ago a Satellite, Samos II, had a ground resolution of 75 centimetres (2.5 feet) only. In 1971, the ground resolution from heights of many kilometres is only 30 centimetres.

All objects radiate infra-red radiation, which have two advantages. They are seen at night and, because the wavelengths emitted depend on the temperature, this enables the sensor to detect objects through camouflage or underground.

Infra-red is now being used both in the satellite early warning system to detect missiles by the radiation emitted by the hot gas from the rockets, and in observation satellites to observe at night and through camouflage. X-ray detection is used in satellites to detect nuclear explosions. Radar has all-weather capabilities. The arms control applications of satellites are wide. They are used to monitor Soviet and Chinese deployments at their nuclear test grounds.

The SAMOS (Satellite and Missile Observation System) has developed since 1960. It was later divided in two types. First there are the Area Surveillance Satellites which, with an inclination of 80° to 90°, provide coverage of the Soviet Union and of China, and which, since 1968, have been able to provide immediate transmission of data through Communication Relay Satellites. Secondly, there are the Close-Look Satellites which are heavier than the Area Surveillance Satellites, and which carry a camera with longer focal length and wider aperture. They operate in a lower orbit.

Gradually the two types are being replaced by the Big Bird, which is much heavier (12 tons). The ground resolution is 30 centimetres from a height of 160 kilometres, which seems incredible. They have a new television camera, with a telescopic objective having a 'zoom' capability. The pictures are transmitted directly to Washington, or can be developed immediately on board and then transmitted to Washington.

The result of these technological developments is that there has been perfect knowledge in Washington since 1962 of the number of silos and missiles in the Soviet Union, and in Moscow, of the number of American silos and missiles. For example, the American Department of Defense published the fact that, in February 1969, 25 missile launchers were in place around Moscow, and 64 some months later. In 1971 new types of Russian silos were identified: 10 in February; 40 on 22 April; 60 on 18 May. Thus the characteristic of all their silos, and of the missiles in the silos were known in Washington.

Radar techniques have also similarly improved. The first radars (Radio Detection and Range) had in 1955 a range of 1,600 kilometres and detected a number of tests before the launching of the first Sputnik in November 1957. Now their range is not less than 5,000 kilometres. One exists in Greenland, one in Alaska and one in

120

England, and their echoes provide sufficient data to calculate the trajectory of a missile.

OTH radar (Over the Horizon Radar) reflects off the ionosphere and penetrates to great distances. There are now three such networks and two others in construction.

Some kinds of satellites can detect and track missiles, namely the MIDAS (Missile Defence Alarm System). Another example is the LASP (Low Altitude Space Platform) which is designed to track re-entry vehicles by infra-red sensors.

All these developments have been very significant in the SALT negotiations, since each of the two participants know exactly what the other possessed and was preparing.

Again, computers permit the collection of masses of data taken from the technical press; from the general and partial statistics relating to production, to traffic, to consumption of electrical power, and from the reports of travellers. The computers also classify this information immediately and give a good picture of military activities, if they exist. So, on-site verification is no longer such a vital question as it was ten years ago, and progress could be made on the road to disarmament if the major powers were sincerely determined to go forward along that road to impose a halt to wars wherever they are going on.

The political situation of the world should contribute to such developments. Over twenty years ago the pessimists thought a war with the Soviet Union unavoidable within three months, while the optimists hoped for six months of peace at least! Now, the probability of such a catastrophe is no longer seriously considered either in the West or in the East.

In this Decade of Disarmament, instituted by the United Nations, our most important and indeed most urgent task is to resume work on a treaty for GCD, to be carried out in progressive stages under international inspection, which should be long-range inspections everywhere it is possible.

We, pacifists of all nations, must continue to strive tirelessly for disarmament. We must contribute to this aim — the noblest in the world — by daily pressure on governments, on parliaments and on public opinion, so as to accelerate the necessary evolution towards a disarmed peace. This question, is without any doubt, the most important of our time. Paraphrasing Karl Marx, I am tempted to cry 'Pacifists of the world, unite.' Because when men are united against military expenditure, democratic governments must comply. And when one Government has complied, others will quickly follow.

If we accept that mankind is not insane and that it will survive, I am sure we shall succeed in our fight for peace and, as Leon Blum, my best friend and leader, who died in 1950 after being one of the greatest statesmen of France, said: 'I hope because I believe. I believe because I hope!'

11. MAIN ISSUES IN THE DISARMAMENT NEGOTIATIONS

Roberto Caracciolo

In recent years I have been, on behalf of Italy, one of the delegates at the Conference on Disarmament in Geneva and have had the honour during this period to negotiate three treaties on matters concerning disarmament. I purposely say treaties on matters concerning disarmament instead of treaties on disarmament, for I am well aware of the contention according to which only the last of these three treaties – the one we concluded on the prohibition of biological weapons – deserves to be called a disarmament treaty, whereas the other two – the one on non-proliferation, and the other banning the emplacement of nuclear weapons on the ocean floor – are more properly referred to as treaties on non-armament.

Be that as it may, I thought that the best contribution I could make would be to try to give some background information on the activities of the Committee, on its qualifications, and on the chances of its getting any nearer to fulfilling the task with which it has been entrusted. I hope thus to contribute, in a very modest way, to the implementation of Resolution 2825/C (XXVI) of the 1971 General Assembly, which declared that progress would be promoted towards general and complete disarmament if universities and academic institutions were to establish continuing courses and seminars to study problems of the arms race, and requested the Secretary-General of the United Nations to bring this Resolution to the notice of all educational, scientific and cultural organizations with a view to its widest publication and dissemination.

That was not the only action taken in 1971 by the United Nations in favour of encouraging a spread of knowledge of the problem with which we are dealing. For while it is true that actual disarmament is dependent on governmental decision and consequently on governmental political will – and in this matter of will they can be, and actually are, responsive to public opinion – there is the other face of the problem, to which all qualified people of the world can make their contribution, that is to say, scientific work on peace research. To encourage this activity the General Assembly in 1971 passed another Resolution 2817 (XXVI) which requested the Secretary-General to prepare every other year an informative report on scientific works produced by national and international, governmental and non-governmental, public and private institutions in the field of peace research. This is a relatively new interdisciplinary science, which is still in the developing stage and it is to be hoped that there will be closer co-ordination in respect of the many initiatives now flourishing in several countries: while referred to, by many, as polemology, that is the study of the causes of conflicts, others prefer to use, for this new science, the term of irenology, which stresses the need for a positive process modifying the structures of international and inter-individual relations.

To revert now to the Committee of the Conference on Disarmament, usually referred to as CCD, though I do not intend to emphasize its importance as the only existing multilateral negotiating body on disarmament, I would like to answer the usual criticism of it, heard in some quarters. These critics compare the rôle of the Conference to that of the chorus in a Greek tragedy which approves, comments on or deplores the deeds of the leading characters.

Nothing could be more remote from the truth. The rôle of the minor powers in CCD is really irreplaceable. They exercise the following three vital functions: acting as a spur on the superpowers, while preventing them from putting aside, once and for all, those problems that embarass their political action; acting in a mediatory capacity too obvious to necessitate any explanations; and finally helping in the crystallization – or should I say the translation into treaty language – of the understandings reached among the major powers. In support of these statements I would like to offer, as an example, the rôle that the non-nuclear powers have played in reaching a final accord on a treaty for banning biological weapons: their action is evident if one only compares the initial draft treaty prepared by the United States and Soviet Union with the final draft as negotiated with the help of the minor powers and approved by the United Nations General Assembly. A similar rôle is played by a few delegations of non-nuclear states, including that of my own country, within the field of chemical weapons, in an endeavour to bridge the gulf dividing the two superpowers.

In stressing the rôle of the smaller powers at the Disarmament Conference, I am not trying to understate the fundamental part played by the two superpowers which, in an unique institution in the international field, have reserved for themselves the title of Co-Chairmen of the Conference, a title that corresponds, more or less, to the functions of a steering committee. Needless to say, without the green light being given by the United States Government and by the Soviet Government on the general principles of a negotiation, it would be impossible to pursue any fruitful discussion in the Committee. But this is 'Realpolitik'. The same applies to all other political problems, except that sometimes the rôle of the superpowers is less visible than in a restricted conference such as ours, which even formally recognizes – though this recognition is today open to argument – a permanent 'status' of Co-Chairmen for both of them. But that leaves, as I have been trying to demonstrate, enough room for positive action by other delegations: it must not be forgotten that one of the characteristics of world politics today is the fact that parallel to the influence or pressure exerted by the leading nations and which works downwards from the top, there is also a growing pressure that works upward from the bottom to the top. That is why public opinion, when properly channelled, can produce unexpected results.

It goes without saying that the Conference on Disarmament in its unique activity as a treaty-maker, has benefitted from a favourable international conjuncture: created when the Cold War which had reached its lowest temperature in Cuba was beginning to unfreeze, the CCD has been, during these last years and until the Strategic Arms Limitation Talks were started, the main, if not the only, negotiating forum between Americans and Russians, where discussions were facilitated by the mediative and catalyzing actions of the smaller powers; the CCD has, therefore, become in recent years the most obvious manifestation, almost the show-case, of that bipolar balance that has characterized the last ten years of international politics.

Fresh prospects for our disarmament efforts were opened up by the conclusion, in Moscow, of the first round of the Strategic Arms Limitation Talks which followed closely the beginning of the international tripolar policy inaugurated by President Nixon with his trip to Peking which – it is to be hoped – will give way, in time, to a new era of multipolar diplomacy.

I shall not go into a technical analysis of the two agreements that were signed in Moscow, nor try to ascertain whether they will give the two superpowers 'equal megatonnage' or whether the result of SALT I will permit one of them to retain a 'megatonnage advantage'. I will merely underline a certain number of points that emerged in the press briefings given both by the chief American negotiator and by the President's adviser, at the moment of the signing of the two agreements in Moscow:

1. The language of Article I of the ABM Treaty may, at first glance, seem very general, but on closer examination it marks a most significant step forward in the relations between the two superpowers. In effect, it says that neither side will try for nation-wide defence of its territory. This is an admission of tremendous psychological significance for it is a recognition that the deterrent forces of both sides are not going to be challenged.

When one thinks of the concern in the last twenty-five years about first strike and counter-force, a general recognition by both countries that they are not going to build a nation-wide defensive system, seem to be of the first importance politically, psychologically and militarily.

2. In assessing the significance of the freeze provided for in the interim agreement on certain measures with respect to the limitation of strategic offensive weapons, the essential questions to consider are not whether the freeze reflects disparities between the forces that are being frozen, nor whether it perpetuates the existing situation. The important question to ask is what situation it prevents: in other words, one must try to visualize what the situation would have been, let us say in five years from now, without this freeze.

3. It is important also to note the wording used in Article V of the interim agreement in which both parties undertake not to interfere with national means of verification and not to take measures to conceal their operations so as to prevent the working of national means of verification; the psychological importance of this commitment may be felt, I hope, in future discussions on problems of verification which, up to now, have proved to be the stumbling-block in all disarmament negotiations.

4. With the Moscow agreements the two parties have begun to fulfil, of course in a very limited measure, the obligations that they has assumed under Article VI of the Non-Proliferation Treaty. By doing so, they have strengthened the credibility of the NPT and encouraged more states to accede to it.

5. Another point of a more procedural character, but of far-reaching consequence, arising from these Moscow agreements is that, during the two-and-a-half years that led up to their conclusion, both parties have by now surely developed a workable system for the conduct of their negotiations. As I understand it, this is a system to ensure good communications between able delegations at the negotiating conference and a number of expert committees at home engaged in the technical studies. A mechanism was also found so that, whenever the negotations reached deadlock, direct exchanges could take place between leaders at the summit in order to break that deadlock by means of a compromise fair to both sides. So the red or hot line has become an effective instrument in important negotiations.

6. This is a good omen for the future for one must look at the Moscow agreements not only for what they have achieved but mainly for what they may promise in the future. It would be, of course, too simplistic an interpretation to discern in the Moscow agreements the

end of a period of confrontation between the two superpowers, and infer that co-operation between them is looming on the horizon while the world is still racked by other divisions in the social and economic field.

It is fair to say that the 1972 arms limitation agreements will be judged not only for their impact on the general disarmament effort, but also in the wider and global context of their contribution to human survival, progress and prosperity, and to the security of all nations. The impact these agreements will have on world affairs and their full significance for the future of mankind will only be revealed by the follow-up action in SALT II, and by the subtle and gradual changes they will bring about in world politics.

At this stage, the Moscow arms limitation agreements can be regarded as no more than the first early results of negotiated efforts to introduce some order and mutual control in the relentless nuclear arms race, and into its inherent drive to enhance continually the over-kill capacity which is already possessed. The beginnings of a rationalization and more efficient management of the costly vertical nuclear proliferation, which was rapidly becoming uncontrollable, are therefore the main results of the Moscow Summit of May 1972.

As a consequence, the doctrines of parity, of nuclear sufficiency and balanced reduction of forces could, if given the chance, yield more significant and fruitful results. They could provide the basis for planned and balanced reductions until such time as mutual confidence and international security may render nuclear weapons altogether superfluous.

While the Moscow agreements were hailed in CCD as a first step by the two superpowers to fulfil the obligations they had assumed under Article VI of the Non-Proliferation Treaty, there have also been insistent efforts by a number of delegations to persuade them to fulfil an equally significant commitment made some five years before that, when on 5 August 1963, they stated, in the preamble of the Treaty banning nuclear tests in the atmosphere, in outer space and under water — likewise signed in Moscow — their determination to continue negotiations to achieve discontinuance of all test explosions of nuclear weapons for all time. That earlier undertaking remains unfulfilled to this day.

All the efforts of several delegations to close the gap left by the Partial Test Ban Treaty have failed because of the rigid position adopted by the two superpowers.[1] Numerous proposals have been advanced over the years, designed to stimulate action, but the deadlock remains over the contentious verification issue. I shall cite only a few of these proposals, in somewhat simplified terms: the proposal for a threshold treaty accompanied by a moratorium with the proposal for verification based on a challenge procedure; the more elaborate proposal for a gradually descending threshold; and the proposals concerning various measures of restraint to be observed while negotiations on a complete test ban (CTB) went forward.

Many delegations have also argued, at considerable length that improved techniques and equipment for seismological monitoring, resulting from extensive research, have markedly reduced the dimensions of the long-standing verification problem, and that a compromise solution should be possible in principle, if both sides were interested in a mutually satisfactory agreement.

This issue of locating and identifying underground nuclear explosions by seismological means is now being actively pursued by a small group of delegations. In fact, after the suggestion for the setting up of a world-wide network with an international centre which would process data received from all countries, which failed to receive the full support it needed to be translated into action, representatives of scientific institutions from Canada, Japan and Sweden met in Tokyo in June 1972 to exchange extensive technical reports and views on the seismological discrimination research being undertaken in their countries and to seek agreement on steps to improve the trilateral co-operation, including data exchange for future research on this subject.

At the Tokyo meeting, there was a full exchange of information on the capabilities for the detection of seismic waves by key national seismograph facilities. It was concluded that these facilities, in co-operation with the currently operating international routine programme of earthquake reporting, are sufficient for the detection and approximate location of seismic events at least as small as underground nuclear explosions of intermediate and higher yield in consolidated rock. It was also agreed to collect the tripartite data for the continuing study of the identification of underground explosions of intermediate and higher yield in consolidated rock, at the explosion yield levels where there is already a high probability of explosion identification.

The two most effective seismological earthquake-explosion discrimination criteria known to governments are: (a) the method based on the relationship between the surface wave magnitude and the body wave magnitude; (b) the short period discriminants based upon the frequency and time-domain information in the short period body wave signals. The individual national research and development programmes using these methods were examined, and it was concluded that it would now be advantageous to develop a programme of trilateral data exchange in order to evaluate tripartite capabilities in these fields. The primary requirement for this evaluation is the

128

acquisition of a common event data base in mutually compatible recording formats for earthquakes from important seismic regions and detected explosions which continue to be detonated at the present time at the principal test sites. To facilitate tripartite evaluation of seismic events of mutual interest an agreement was reached in Tokyo on the form and quantity of data exchange, such data to be exchanged between scientific institutions on request from and as available in the respective countries.

The rigid position taken on the CTB issue by the two superpowers, one side insisting on the necessity of on-site controls, the other rejecting it, may seem to indicate, at first glance, a radical difference of attitude on this problem. But, as time goes on, some fundamental analogies can be found in their positions.

One example of this seems to be reflected in Article VII of the ABM Treaty and in similar Article IV of the interim agreement on the limitation of strategic offensive arms, both of which allow for modernization and replacement of the weapons considered. This permissiveness leaves the door open for more — even if limited — underground testing.

Another indication can be found in the evaluation of the Soviet Union's approach towards the possibility of reaching a CTB. It was noted, in fact, that beside the adoption of a system of verification exclusively based on national means of control, a new precondition to the signing of a treaty has been put forward recently by the delegation of the Soviet Union, that is, the ending of all nuclear tests by all powers. A change of attitude on the part of the United States with regard to the problem of verification would, therefore, not seem to be sufficient by itself to overcome the actual stalemate.

That does not mean that we must abandon hope of getting, in the near future, an agreement on a comprehensive test ban. It is interesting to note, in that respect, the answer given by the Presidential adviser to a question that was put to him by the Press in Moscow: while stating that the obstacle had been, hitherto, the debate about inspection, his answer also indicated American willingness to re-examine the issue. We must also consider the possibility that an agreement between the two superpowers to stop nuclear testing could, at a certain moment, induce China and France to comply — at least *de facto* — with such a ban!

It is a fact that the problem of a CTB has been debated for some time in the United States, and that some schools of thought seem to visualize the possibility of establishing a system of verification not compulsorily based on on-site inspections. According to certain reports, the United States executive branch seems to consider that in approximately two years, they will have greater understanding of the

129

best design for a new network and the optimum siting and distribution of instruments, and will by then have acquired useful experience in the actual operation of a large and complicated network, including experience with the automated data processing techniques which become increasingly important as lower magnitudes are approached. It seems to be conceded by all that the capability of a seismic monitoring network can be developed to identify explosions down to somewhere in the neighbourhood of magnitude 4.0.

It remains to be seen whether a change of attitude by one or both of the two superpowers will come about, at a later stage, in CCD, or whether such a change will take place in a wider context and eventually become part of a package deal between the superpowers, following the reassumption of SALT. That will also show whether the SALT agreements, already concluded, represent a platform from which to take off towards wider negotiations designed to expand an important bilateral advance into multilateral achievements, or whether they will be no more than a ceiling to allay temporarily the smaller nations' legitimate concern about where the nuclear arms race between the superpowers is leading the world.

The CTB is now, however, a measure of tremendous importance compared with more direct approaches to disarmament. In this respect I think one could agree with an opinion that can be found in the SIPRI Yearbook of 1972 and which I would like to quote. According to this report, the reasons for the focus on the CTB appear to be institutional and historical. Since the United States and the Soviet Union have taken mainstream arms limitation negotiation away from the CCD to SALT, the only issue connected with nuclear weapons still open for discussion in Geneva is the CTB. Besides, this issue has been debated on and off for almost ten years, and many countries feel that they were deceived when they were led to believe that the Partial Test Ban Treaty would limit or stop tests.

The reaching of an agreement on a comprehensive test ban will therefore have also a symbolic and psychological effect and may allay a certain sense of frustration which is not unrelated to the increasing disquiet at the rôle of CCD and to the increasing interest in creating new forums, like the convening of a World Disarmament Conference, though the belief that the establishment of a new setting for the continuation of the same debate will suffice to overcome the resistance of the superpowers, is — at least — questionable.

The CCD has recently concentrated much of its attention on the problem of banning chemical weapons (CW). During earlier years there had been much insistence, especially on the part of the socialist delegations and also of some non-aligned ones, that chemical weapons and biological weapons (BW) should be dealt with together, and that both should be banned by the same treaty.

After very long discussions it was agreed that the two problems should be separated and by doing so we were able to negotiate and reach an agreement on a Convention for the banning of the production, development and stockpiling of bacteriological (biological) and toxic weapons and for their destruction. That Convention was approved at the XXVIth session of the United Nations General Assembly, and signed by more than eighty countries in the capitals of the three depositary States.

By insisting on dealing separately with the two types of weapons, whose use had already been banned comprehensively in the Geneva Protocol of 1925, we certainly did not mean to establish a priority between them, nor to state that one was less dangerous than the other.

Of course, potentially, biological weapons could reach the highest degree in the scale of horrors and also are, probably, the easiest to produce, even without sophisticated technical equipment. But the banning of these dreadful weapons was easier for the CCD for two fundamental reasons: because B weapons were not yet included – at least officially – in the panoply of war of the major powers, and because they were single-purpose weapons not used currently – as most chemical weapons are – in a civilian context. It was simpler, then, especially for verification purposes, to reach an agreement to ban a weapon that has not so far been used than to ban a weapon which, on several occasions, has already produced its lethal effects.

While choosing this simpler way with the intention of preventing the spread of a new danger to the human race, the CCD did not skip the more difficult task, and, therefore, we expressed in Article IX of the BW Treaty our political will to 'continue negotiations in good faith' on chemical weapons 'with a view to reaching early agreement on effective measures for the prohibition of their development, production and stockpiling and for their destruction'.

When we tackled the problem of C weapons we rapidly ran into the same obstacle that we have faced in all our previous conventions on disarmament matters: the problem of verification. The American thesis, shared by many other delegations, that there should be adequate international verification, possibly implemented by on-site inspections, was confronted with the Soviet thesis, opposed to any form of intrusive control, and in favour of national controls alone accompanied by a complaint procedure to the Security Council of the United Nations, where – as we all know – the permanent members can exercise their veto rights.

We had, then, almost come, by the end of our spring 1972 session, to another complete standstill, when a breakthrough was made possible

131

with the request, submitted both by the Swedish and by the Italian delegations, for some unofficial meetings with the participation of experts in order to discuss some fundamental and technical aspects, typical of the problem of chemical weapons, and in particular, the scope of the definition of such agents, and their control. The socialist countries at first denied any need for such technical meetings, and argued that the problem was essentially a political one and, therefore, mainly a question of political will.

Fortunately, and thanks to the insistence of the non-aligned delegations, the Soviet delegation did not persist in such a simplistic attitude, accepted the convening of experts and even participated actively in the debates that we held at the beginning of July 1972. The informal meetings we held undoubtedly gave a new and practical turn to the discussions on CW for they focused on the nature of some specific provisions to be included in a treaty to ban CW.

It was widely recognized that, whatever the legal language used for the definition of the scope of the treaty, all the categories of chemical agents to be banned should be clearly identified on the basis of criteria internationally worked out with a view to ensuring that the treaty provisions would be equally and effectively applied. As to the criteria to be used for that purpose, experts of the various countries participating in the debate indicated such requirements as the determination of an index of toxicity, the identification of groups of C agents on the basis of comprehensive structural formulae and other chemical and operational criteria which, appropriately combined, could lead to a technically exhaustive classification. Accordingly, the Italian delegation suggested that such a classification could be worked out by an international panel of experts and attached to the treaty in the form of an annex that could be periodically revised by an international committee of experts established by the convention.

The addition of such a technical interpretation of the scope of the treaty, based on internationally adopted criteria, would allow all contracting states to adopt uniform internal legislative provisions, thus assuring an equal and reliable application of the treaty.

The Soviet delegation itself, which had previously repeatedly maintained that the definition of the scope of the treaty had to be a very general one, recognized the possibility of drafting and finalizing, outside the text of the basic agreement, certain questions related to the definition of the scope of prohibition of chemical weapons. The chances of reaching an understanding on the problem of the definition of the chemical agents to be banned would seem thus to have been improved.

The informal meetings with experts at the beginning of July 1972 also resulted in some progress, though slight, being made in regard to the problem of verification which, as has previously been indicated, was the main reason why the negotiations had come to a standstill. In fact, the Soviet delegation, which up to that moment had been strictly in favour of national forms of control, showed a more flexible approach by putting forward the idea of an 'international programme' to be established by the contracting parties in order to co-ordinate the activities of national control committees charged with the implementation of the verification system in each state. Moreover, these informal meetings had the merit of clarifying several points of the complex issue of veritication. The very requirement of adopting different forms of control according to different classes of agents, owing to the practical difficulties of laying down an uniform verification method applicable to all kind of agents and to all provisions of the treaty, was in fact widely recognized. Great interest was also expressed by several delegations, including those from the Soviet bloc, in the possibilities offered by indirect forms of control based on the collection and standardized evaluation of technical, economic and statistical data relating to production and trade in raw material and chemical products.

However, considering the enormous difficulties that still confront the members of the CCD in achieving agreement on verification measures which will satisfy all contracting parties, the idea of an approach by progressive stages towards the target of a complete ban of CW, is now beginning to circulate among some delegations in the Committee. In particular, the opinion has been expressed that some intermediate and partial measures, agreed by the CCD, could be taken now if the achievement of a complete and effective convention on the banning of all chemical weapons appeared impossible at present. Of course, those who favour such an opinion have stressed the point that whichever initial stage were agreed, it should be accompanied by a commitment to proceed to a final stage at which the prohibition on CW would be made comprehensive.

Before concluding this 'exposé' on the issues of disarmament negotiations a few words on the future prospects of CCD must be added.

This body may seem sometimes too static, but as a commentator wrote recently in an article published by a Geneva newspaper: 'La Conférence du Désarmement "bouge" . . . mais par touches imperceptibles'. One proof of CCD's vitality can also be found in a movement that has, recently, taken place in our midst, in favour of an 'aggiornamento', or of an adaption of our structure in order to make it easier for China and France to join in our work.

It is doubtful, however, whether a change in our very special institution of the co-chairmanship or a limited increase in our membership — it has to be limited so as not to impair our efficiency as a negotiating body — will suffice to induce China to adopt a new policy towards the problem of disarmament. This policy was stated in 1971 at the United Nations and has been restated ever since: China has clearly demanded, as a precondition for her participation in such discussions, a renunciation by the other nuclear powers of first use of nuclear weapons. Otherwise she would build up her own nuclear arsenal in order to reach the credibility point of a deterrent.

A new problem for CCD will be posed if a World Disarmament Conference is convened, for there seems to be widespread agreement on the necessity of creating, as a first step, a preparatory negotiating body, capable of preparing the ground for such a conference. What would this preparatory body be like? It should be either a committee very similar to the existing CCD, with only some procedural changes — and this opinion is shared also by my delegation — or a completely new body, in which case it is difficult to conceive the coexistence of two separate and differently constituted negotiating bodies on matters concerning disarmament, without one of them losing some of its strength and efficiency.

It remains then to be seen whether a future General Assembly will end up by adopting a resolution convening the suggested World Disarmament Conference. Much will depend, of course, on the position of the leading nuclear powers. However, there is an understandable desire on the part of non-aligned countries to raise disarmament issues in a larger forum where, being more numerous than in a restricted body and having also the possibility of availing themselves of the support of other nuclear powers, they may hope to be in a stronger position to impose on the two superpowers their views that have met so far with nothing more than 'une fin de non reçevoir' from the American and Soviet Governments.

The task of a diplomat does not, of course, consist in making predictions but rather in trying to assess events, and possibly to facilitate them. I would nevertheless venture to look ahead and conclude, by saying perhaps obviously enough that the next General Assembly may mark yet another turning point in the history of disarmament negotiations.

NOTE

1. This paper was prepared before President Nixon's Summit meeting in Moscow in 1974.

12. THE DOCTRINE OF TACTICAL NUCLEAR WARFARE AND SOME ALTERNATIVES

David Carlton

Introduction

The doctrine of tactical nuclear warfare is at present taken seriously
only in the context of the military stalemate in Central Europe where
both NATO and the Warsaw Pact have placed so-called tactical nuclear
weapons in the hands of field commanders for possible use exclusively
in the immediate theatre. Estimates made in NATO countries suggests
that there may be 7,000 warheads on the Western side and possibly
some 3,000 warheads in the Warsaw Pact countries with a smaller
number of delivery vehicles in each case. Some of these might indeed
be used effectively in a strategic rôle, that is on the heartlands of the
superpowers. It is thus arguably misleading to talk of them as tactical
nuclear weapons. But in so far as this term is used, it should be
understood to refer to theatre-based nuclear weapons intended for
deployment against enemy theatre-based forces rather than enemy
cites.

The purpose of the present essay is to analyze the strength and
weakness of the current NATO attitude to the possible use of such
tactical nuclear weapons and to consider also a number of possible
variants and alternatives. At the outset, however, it is necessary to
state that for the purposes of the analysis three assumptions, made by
NATO Governments, are taken for granted: first, that the contingency
of a massive Soviet invasion of Federal Germany has to be taken
seriously; secondly, that NATO conventional defence would be or
might be inadequate to resist such an onslaught; and thirdly, that the
other NATO countries, including the United States, could not
tolerate the possibility of allowing Federal Germany to be permanently
conquered. Any or all of these assumptions may be inaccurate or
immoral or both. But it is not intended to explore such arguments
here. It is sufficient to state that the foregoing assumptions, rightly
or wrongly, appear to be held in most NATO capitals.

Within this framework the merits of various options will be
considered. But it is perhaps important to stress at the outset that
some of the arguments may well apply more or less forcibly in the
case of the United States as compared with her European partners.
Again, in weighing the value of particular options the reader may wish
to bear in mind that two possibly conflicting desiderata have to be
taken into account: first, how best to deter any war; and, secondly,

135

how to be in a position to wage a war, should one occur, without either defeat or utter devastation.

The Present Position

The precise number of tactical nuclear weapons on each side, to which reference has already been made, has undoubtedly been arrived at more or less accidently and could not possibly be defended in strictly logical strategic terms. But, leaving aside numbers, is it possible to defend the presence of any such weapons in Central Europe? They were originally deployed by the United States as a means of redressing conventional disparity in Central Europe at a time when the Doctrine of Massive Retaliation was rapidly losing credibility as the Soviet Union came within sight of being able to inflict unacceptable damage on the United States. Yet such weapons have not been deployed in other theatres throughout the globe where American armed forces were or are face to face with states thought to possess superior conventional force. It seems reasonable, therefore, to see the tactical nuclear weapons in Central Europe as a somewhat irrational symbol of an intense degree of involvement. It is a symbol to which Federal Germany has always attached great importance. Indeed, the West Germans have tended to believe that it is more than a symbol in that they have traditionally held that the use of tactical nuclear weapons would inevitably trigger the use of American strategic nuclear weapons. This is an assumption for which there is probably no justification. After all, if the Americans would not use their strategic nuclear forces if American armed forces in Europe were attacked, why should they do so if tactical strikes had been exchanged? The real firebreak, so far as the Americans are concerned, may therefore be not between nuclear and non-nuclear weapons but between the use of nuclear weapons on the heartlands of the superpowers and all other military actions, nuclear or non-nuclear.

Nor is it in the Federal German interest that nuclear warfare should occur in any circumstances. For their territory would be devastated even if in the end of the enemy were persuaded to cease its aggression. In short, whatever might be the case for NATO as a whole, the West Germans must surely regard the destruction of their territory as worse even than its loss intact to the enemy.

There is, moreover, a further problem concerning tactical nuclear weapons: they are likely to become increasingly vulnerable to a first strike attack. And we have no reason to suppose that the Soviets, if they decide to make a massive attack in Western Europe, would obligingly refrain from eliminating the more obvious tactical nuclear missile launchers.

136

It seems, therefore, that the present NATO doctrine of using tactical nuclear weapons in response to a massive conventional attack is and probably always has been open to severe criticism. It is thus necessary to look in detail at the merits and demerits of the alternative strategies available to NATO.

Some Alternative Policies Involving Agreement with the Soviet Union

1. General and Complete Disarmament

The most utopian alternative to the present NATO position would so to transform the world so that multilateral General and Complete Disarmament would be implemented with foolproof inspection and a reliable system of guarantees against agression. NATO Governments pay lip-service to this ideal but, whether or not it is desirable, it is obviously not a practical proposition in the immediate future. For this reason no further consideration will be given to this option in this context.

2. Large Nuclear-Free Zones

An alternative to the present military deployment in Central Europe might be a version or a variant of the several plans for military disengagement put forward by the former Polish Foreign Minister, Adam Rapacki, between 1958 and 1964. All his plans were, however, completely unacceptable to Western Governments and probably remain so. The principal NATO objection to the substantial demilitarization of the two German states was and remains that the Soviet Union, as was shown in the case of Czechoslovakia in 1968, could very rapidly return to Central Europe whereas the Americans could not possibly do so at the same speed with the same numbers. A variant on the Polish plans was supported by the British Labour Party when in opposition before 1964. This involved linking demilitarization to the neutralization, on the Austrian model, of the two German states, Hungary, Czechoslovakia and Poland. But once in office, Harold Wilson and his colleagues did not take their own plan seriously. Nor does any policy of this kind seem likely to win support in Western Europe whether today or in the future. For the plain fact is that Federal Germany is not and does not regard itself as a second Austria. Her leading role in the European Economic Community is in itself a sufficient reason why this kind of neutralization is now, if it was not always, unthinkable.

3. Small Nuclear-Free Zones

There is much to be said for the Warsaw Pact and NATO States agreeing to withdraw their tactical nuclear weapons some distance from

137

each other. This would decrease the chances of escalation to nuclear war arising out of some minor border skirmish — perhaps resulting from accident, misunderstanding or unauthorized action by a field commander — involving an assault on nuclear installations. And it is arguable that at least a strip of territory ought to be free from nuclear weapons so as to allow conventional forces the chance to see whether they could successfully repel a large-scale, deliberate, conventional attack.

The difficulty about this policy is that it is a mere modification to and not a substantial alteration of the present unsatisfactory position. It is not in itself undesirable — and may indeed already have been silently implemented to some extent — but it is in short not sufficiently radical.

Some Alternative Policies for Unilateral Implementation by the West

1. Small Nuclear-Free Zone in the West Only
There is a case for NATO ceasing unilaterally to deploy tactical nuclear weapons in the vicinity of the borders of Warsaw Pact States for the reasons previously given. But, as with the multilateral variant, this move would not sufficiently reduce the dangers inherent in the present NATO strategy.

2. Massive Retaliation to Replace Tactical Nuclear Warfare Doctrine
The Americans could recognize that the introduction of the doctrine of tactical nuclear warfare had been a mistake and could accordingly return to the doctrine which preceded it, namely that of threatening to meet Soviet conventional aggression with all-out massive nuclear retaliation. But the fact is that such a threat would be niether credible to the Soviet Union nor to the European members of NATO. The result would almost certainly be either, the vertical and horizontal proliferation of nuclear weapons among European states or even possibly the emergence of a European collective nuclear deterrent force.

3. American Abandonment of its Guarantee of Europe
It is possible that the Americans could decide that there is no way in which they can provide a credible nuclear guarantee of Western Europe and they might accordingly decide to abandon the attempt to do so before their bluff is called. It would be a belated conversion to the Gaullist view, but it need not follow that the adoption of that policy could not be accompanied by a gesture of generosity to the Europeans such as the provision of large numbers of nuclear weapons

138

and submarines in a kind of a super-Nassau Agreement. But whether or not this were done, an American withdrawal of its guarantee would provide an immediate impetus to the strengthening and possibly the pooling of European nuclear forces.

Such a development would be destablizing and dangerous from many points of view. To give just one example: it might well wreck the SALT agreement reached in 1972. But it cannot be said, from the European point of view, that it is self-evidently undesirable if no other more credible means of deterring possible Soviet aggression can be found.

4. American Deployment of Atomic Demolition Mines

One superficially attractive way of improving on the present arguably inadequate strategy for deterrence is for NATO to bury Atomic Demolition Mines (ADMs) along the whole of the Central European border. At least such weapons would be completely invulnerable to first strike attacks and insofar a contribution to stability.

On military grounds it is sometimes objected that, though invulnerable, ADMs would be irrelevant in the event of an airborne attack. But to this the effective reply is that the main conventional threat to Western Europe consists of tanks and these could not hope to penetrate a barrier of nuclear mines.

A more substantial objection is that the American President would have to agree to a greatly increased degree of pre-delegation of his authority to use nuclear weapons as compared with the present, thereby possibly increasing the risk of accidental use. Moreover, it is very difficult to see why, if such a barrier is appropriate in Central Europe, it should not be equally appropriate along every frontier where tension exists. In short, do the proponents of ADMs favour a variant on the famous Gallois thesis about the desirability of the proliferation of nuclear weapons in general? If not, how is the existence of an ADM barrier only in Central Europe, to be justified, especially as the terrain there is not particularly well suited to such a barrier? If the reply is that Central Europe is an area where some kind of nuclear presence is needed for psychological reasons, does it not follow that the same kind of 'irrational' justification is being accepted as leads supporters of the *status quo* to favour the retention of the present tactical nuclear weapons in the area? A final resource for the proponents of ADMs might be to concede that this is so, but to argue that the policy of deploying such weapons in the European theatre, though perhaps 'irrational', is less 'irrational' or less dangerous or less vulnerable than the present deployment of tactical nuclear weapons.

There may indeed be some merit in this defence of ADMs. But if the argument is placed on the psychological plane, there is the difficulty, ironically enough, that the West Germans are and always have been against them. They argue that an ADM barrier would be unacceptable to the people living in its vicinity and that its construction would be symbolically unfortunate at a time when the *Ostpolitik* is breaking down barriers of a different kind. Unless, therefore, the proponets of ADMs are able to change many minds in Federal Germany, this alternative to the *status quo* is likely to remain of merely theoretical interest.

5. American Adoption of the Doctrine of Limited Strategic Nuclear War

This alternative would involve the withdrawal of American tactical nuclear weapons from Europe accompanied by a declaration that the United States would respond to irresistable Soviet conventional aggression by limited strategic nuclear strikes on so-called counter-value targets such as individual cities in the Soviet Union or in Eastern Europe. In short, this amounts to a 'hard-liner's' version of the nuclear-free zone option.

Critics of this approach often argue that the limited use of strategic nuclear weapons is either unthinkable, because Armageddon would inevirably result, or, alternatively, that if Armageddon did not result, such limited use would not achieve the objective of forcing a Soviet withdrawal from occupied territory. Both these views probably derive from the commonplace assumption that nuclear weapons are totally unlike other weapons in that they cannot be rationally used in any circumstances. But this may well be a false assumption. It is of course obvious that a superpower cannot use nuclear weapons in an indiscriminate way against an adversary equipped with an adequate second strike capability and thus they cannot be used like weapons in the pre-nuclear age to win outright victories. Yet the disputes between superpowers have to be resolved in some fashion and it cannot be presumed that the existence of nuclear weapons will always be ignored in every such dispute.

Most serious disputes in the pre-nuclear age were ultimately resolved on the basis of the presumed or actual military power on each side. On some occasions a war was fought; on other occasions one side made concessions after having concluded, rightly or wrongly, that the other side had greater military strength at its command. Today the difficulty for the superpowers is that each possess an infinite capability *vis-à-vis* the other. In a dispute, therefore, neither superpower is obliged to or can climb down because it recognizes the superior power of the other; nor is an all-out war a rational option. But the dispute has nevertheless to be resolved and agreement may not always be attainable on what constitutes a 50-50 compromise. In such a situation there is accordingly a high, arguably an absolute, premium on resolve. But how is resolve to be demonstrated? It seems in fact to be inescapable that if one superpower is faced with defeat at the conventional level, it has no alternative but to escalate to the nuclear level in order to establish its determination not to yield. Yet the all-out use of nuclear weapons would be suicidal. Hence in such circumstances it would seem that nuclear weapons can only be used rationally in a limited fashion, and arguably without a specific military objective in view. In short, a superpower seeking to hold territory otherwise irretrievably lost to a rival in conventional conflict is most likely to succeed in its defensive aim by threatening and even, in the last resort, by delivering nuclear 'teaching strikes' on targets in the rival's heartland.

There is no doubt, however, that the use by the Americans of even one nuclear weapon on a Soviet city might have the most serious consequences. Certainly no American President would take such a decision without recognizing that the Soviet Union might well feel obliged at least to retaliate in kind, even if only as a prelude to a settlement based on the *status quo ante*. It seems safe to assume, therefore, that the initial use of a nuclear weapon would be resorted to only in a situation where the President felt that the credibility of the United States as a superpower and hence ultimately her very existence as an independent state was at stake. Indeed, only in such a situation would it be reasonable to expect the Soviet Union to respond to the use of 'nuclear teaching strikes' by in the last analysis backing down and returning to the *status quo ante*. [1]

The decisive question for Western Europeans is of course whether or not an American President would be prepared to regard the survival of the independence of NATO European states as being synonymous with the ultimate survival of an independent United States. Gaullists would no doubt argue that no state can ever be relied upon to take a guarantee of another state so seriously. But, against that view, it could be argued that both the American and Soviet leaders have come to see themselves in recent years as heading so-called 'camps' of an indivisable character.

The appeal and ultimately the viability of the option under consideration in this section depends wholly upon whether this second interpretation can be said to apply to the Americans on a permanent basis so far as Western Europe is concerned. If, on the other hand, the Gaullists are correct, Western Europeans would clearly be well advised, given the assumptions about the Soviet Union which underlie the existence of NATO, to give urgent attention to the development of their own strengthened national nuclear forces pending the possible emergence of a federal Europe with superpower status.

NOTE

1. For further reflections on this theme see the present writer's essay, 'Anti-Ballistic Missile Deployment and the Doctrine of Limited Strategic Nuclear War', in C. F. Barnaby and A. Boserup (eds.), **Implications of Anti-Ballistic Missile Systems** (London and Toronto, 1969).

This paper was prepared before Secretary of Defense James Schlesinger enunciated in March 1974 a modified American approach involving the possibility of limited so-called nuclear counter-force strikes on the Soviet Union. It is obvious from Schlesinger's statements that such strikes would be of a 'teaching' character (i.e. mere demonstrations of resolve) and would definitely not be intended to be significantly 'disarming' in the sense of depriving the Soviet Union of its capacity to inflict, if it so desired, assured destruction on the United States in a second strike. In the present writer's view this new American doctrine is an encouraging development for West Europeans: it implies that they can at least hope to be rescued from the results of successful Soviet conventional aggression without suffering any nuclear devastation. But it is doubtful whether this ray of hope, however welcome, will be sufficient in itself to overcome neo-Gaullist convictions that the Western Europeans need more and better independent nuclear forces.

13. CONTRIBUTIONS OF WESTERN EUROPE TO DISARMAMENT

Francesco Cavalletti

If we examine the history of disarmament negotiations, we realize that Western Europe has, in recent years, contributed to disarmament only in a limited and almost passive way, leaving to the United States the task of being the primary guide and driving force on the Western side. This has been particularly true during the period when negotiations have taken place at Geneva, namely on the Committee of the Eighteen and now on the Committee of Twenty-Six.

Of course before that — though I shall not deal with this aspect in detail — the rôle of Great Britain and France was important in the meetings of the Big Four after the War. But since the move to Geneva, Western Europe has played a lesser rôle for many reasons. First, the distribution of places around the negotiating table was not favourable: Western Europe was and still is under-represented. In particular, the absence of France has been regretted by many of us, including many Frenchmen. For a long period including the most decisive phase of activity, that leading up to the conclusions of the Non-Proliferation Treaty, Western Europe was represented at Geneva only by two countries, Italy and Great Britain.

But European weakness did not derive solely from the quantity of their representatives at Geneva but from many other factors: lack of cohesion, of influence, of courage and of imagination.

Of course, all European NATO members were indirectly associated with the negotiations; they were — and still are — consulted within the Atlantic Council, but, there, cautious influences made themselves felt. Substantially, taken as a whole, the European members of NATO acted more as a brake than as a spur to the disarmament negotiations; France was an absentee, Federal Germany was then committed to a rigid anti-Soviet policy, while some minor countries were frightened at every proposal.

We must admit that the attitude of the Soviet Union and of her allies at Geneva did not fail to justify and to supply arguments for reluctant or negative responses. Not only the relentless insistence of the Soviet Union on General and Complete Disarmament, to be achieved in a very few years, appeared utopian and demagogic, but most of the Soviet proposals for partial disarmament seemed aimed more at disrupting NATO than at real disarmament: witness, for instance, proposals for the withdrawal of American troops and the dismantling of foreign bases in Europe, the Rapacki Plan in its various editions, demands for the denuclearization and demilitarization of the Mediterranean and the Balkans, and so forth. To all such proposals the Western Europeans could not help making reservations. But reservations were made also to more reasonable proposals, such as observation posts against surprise attacks and a pact of non-aggression between NATO and the Warsaw Pact. Many of the Western Europeans were even reluctant to accept the two important treaties which, at long last, were successfully negotiated in Geneva, namely the Partial Test Ban Treaty and the Non-Proliferation Treaty; and France is still totally ignoring them.

In these circumstances the United States gradually arrived at the conviction that, if they wanted – as they did – to make progress towards disarmament, it would be wise not to follow her European allies nor to pay much attention to the difficulties made in the negotiations by partners who were not all quite familiar with the implications of nuclear weapons and who were too timorous or prompted by parochial motivations. Thus we witnessed a gradual loss of European influence in the disarmament talks, a closer and closer co-operation between the United States and the Soviet Union and at last the Soviet-American decision to deal with all nuclear matters through bilateral contacts. Now the Geneva Committee, always scantily attended by the Western Europeans and encumbered with the attendance of too many non-aligned countries, is confining itself to the discussion of relatively marginal matters and is no longer considering nuclear disarmament.

These developments have aroused feelings of suspicion throughout the European NATO countries which, without realizing that they share a responsibility for the creation of this situation, have become progressively afraid to be the losers in the disarmament negotiations.

With the foregoing considerations in mind, it is necessary to ask whether this state of things will continue for years to come, with Western Europe still being in tow to the American disarmament policy, or whether the Western Europeans will be able to embark upon autonomous action, aware indeed of the requirements of their security, but endowed with more imagination and courage. The problem has relevance both in the short and in the long term, in the framework of, and in relation to, the couse of integration in Western Europe.

Some favourable factors have recently emerged, which might foreshadow a revival of European involvement in the disarmament field. Federal Germany's policy, which in the 1960s was still dominated by concepts of the Cold War, is now wide open to an understanding with the countries of Eastern Europe. France, which was hitherto one of the most negative elements, might, now that General de Gaulle has gone, be more willing to co-operate. Moreover, one of the probable reasons for the original French absenteeism from Geneva is now no longer valid: namely the fear that she might be prevented from developing her own nuclear capability. In fact there have been rumours of a return of France to Geneva if the system of Soviet-American co-chairmanship could be reviewed. France might indeed find it worthwhile to seek a disarmament agreement, so as not to be required to embark on a further costly and perhaps unsustainable nuclear programme. If these difficulties were removed, more harmonious co-operation should be possible between France, Federal Germany, Great Britain, Italy and the other European NATO countries with a view to developing a more active and imaginative common attitude to match that of the Americans. This appears to be even more necessary now, after the conclusion – without the participation of the European countries – of the SALT bilateral agreements, which, although representing only a 'freeze', are an important step on the way to a nuclear understanding between the United States and the Soviet Union. The gap between the Americans and the Europeans could widen if the latter's relatively reserved attitude towards disarmament were to persist.

It is now appropriate to consider in which direction the European disarmament policy could develop, both with regard to long-range goals and immediate possibilities. In this connection, we must realize that a new factor is emerging in Europe, which sooner or later will have repercussions on the problems of European security and therefore on disarmament, namely European political integration. The Nine, having attained a certain level of economic integration, are now aiming at the target of a political union; this process, which will go on now within the enlarged community even though perhaps at a lesser speed, must inevitably raise, in the fulness of time, problems of common defence and security. As a matter of fact, it seems inconceivable that in the long run an economically and politically united Europe should not aim at an independent policy also in the field of her security. Of course, at the beginning the question will not be whether we should detach ourselves from NATO, for such disengagement will be unrealistic and in practice impossible for a long time ahead. Nevertheless, we shall have to plan European integration, even in terms of defence, with possible far-off targets of self-sufficiency in mind.

The idea of European military integration is not new. On the contrary, Europe attempted in the 1950s to reach political unity through military integration, by the so-called European Army, later called the European Defence Community. We tried then to use the military facts as a lever to attain later on a politically united Europe;

145

whereas, logically, the process should have been the other way round. Thus, after the EDC project, a plan for a European Political Community was drawn up; but it was no less destined to failure and was buried together with the EDC project.

Failure at that time was both unavoidable and understandable. In fact it was not then possible to set up either a European defence budget or integrated forces in the absence of the essential prerequisites, namely economic integration and political integration. Moreover, many suspected that some of the sponsors of EDC saw in it an expedient to prevent German rearmament and that the Germans themselves saw in it a means of escaping from the diplomatic and military ghetto in which they were confined.

Today, and still more so a few years hence, European military integration appears and will appear to be a different proposition, namely as the logical and natural outcome of a development which began with economic co-operation, which continued in the political field, and which will finally culminate in military co-operation. Moreover, two nuclear powers, France and Great Britain, will be associated with this process.

Faced with such prospects, we cannot cherish many illusions. If nothing is done to prevent it, the path to European integration, which is desirable on many grounds, may result in a stepping up of the arms race and the development of European weapons including even the nuclear variety. Therefore, Western Europeans must consider how best to act so as not to hamper a process of unification which is dear to all of us, but so as to avoid the possibility that progress towards disarmament might be disrupted or even blocked.

The problem does not relate so much to conventional armaments — although these, too, will come into play, as we shall see — as to nuclear ones. The European nuclear factor (as an autonomous or separate element to be taken into consideration in a balanced disarmament process) has not weighed much in the disarmament negotiations at Geneva. Indeed, it has been practically ignored. This has been because British nuclear weapons were considered to be one and the same thing as those of NATO (i.e. American), while the build-up of French nuclear forces has only just started. I do not know if and how much European nuclear weapons have been taken into consideration in the SALT negotiations. But facts demonstrate that the modest European nuclear potential certainly did not prevent an agreement from being reached.

However, the situation could change quickly. France, although possessing a limited nuclear force, has attained an independent second strike capability and the British nuclear forces, possibly detachable from NATO, have also reached a considerable second strike capability.

If these two forces were to be merged, the European deterrent would assume considerable weight. Moreover, in an economically and politically integrated Western Europe, it would be natural for other members of the Community, and particularly for the Federal Republic of Germany, to play a part in building up the common defence and therefore in increasing nuclear forces — if only by making contributions in the fields of technology and finance.

We cannot ignore the fact that in Western Europe — or at least in some Western European circles — there have always been aspirations for a European 'deterrent'. It has been stressed that the exclusion of Europe from effective control over the Western deterrent gave rise to serious difficulties and tensions within the Atlantic Alliance, particularly when, rightly or wrongly, doubts began about the credibility of the American deterrent as a means of defending Europe. This situation caused, on the one hand, the French secession from the NATO military organization, accompanied by the building up of French nuclear forces and, on the other hand, the debate about the well-known project for an integrated multilateral force (MLF). In fact this project was ambiguous and dangerous. Nevertheless, the abandonment of MLF was considered to be a defeat in many European circles.

Quite different from MLF — and much more risky — would be the placing of nuclear weapons in the hands of an integrated Europe. Even if European nuclear armaments were by far inferior to those of the Americans and the Soviets and even if we could fully rely on the self-control of the Europeans, such armaments would constitute in themselves a new and serious aggravation in the strategy of terror.

I do not think that the Non-Proliferation Treaty and the Partial Test Ban Treaty, accepted by some European countries but not by France, would constitute an insurmountable barrier to such dangerous new developments. In fact, it might be alleged that when a new entity, a new subject of international law, is created by the merging of sovereign states, the resulting state is free from the legal commitments previously undertaken by the members who compose it. This thesis, held by the Italian Government in the Geneva debates about non-proliferation, was not even much contested by the Soviet Union; and I believe it is a juridically sustainable thesis, according to current doctrine.

Of course, the setting up of a Federal Europe likely to aim at the right to possess and use nuclear weapons is far in the future. Apart from the very serious problems facing the Europeans themselves, who are still quite divided on the very concept of a United Europe, there are many external difficulties. These include the political and military consequences of a European disengagement from NATO; the possible opposition of the United States; and above all the attitude of the Soviet Union which would be confronted with the creation of a new nuclear power on her frontier.

But history evolves, sometimes even quickly, and it is not inconceivable that the United States, in order to get out of her commitment to the defence of Europe, might at a certain moment come to favour such a process; whilst the Soviet Union, rather than continue to have the American giant at her door in Europe, might find it convenient to have a less powerful neighbour, firmly entrenched in politically and militarily independent positions and representing a third force. This is, for example, maintained by General André Beaufre, who believes that the gradual transfer to the Europeans of responsibility for their own defence, even at a nuclear level, might be accepted by the Soviet Union in the light of the advantages that would accrue to them.

In any case, even apart from this extreme and distant assumption of the creation of a Federal Europe, endowed with her own nuclear defence organization, the disarmament negotiations face other dangers and complications which might derive from less far-reaching European developments in the military field.

The European desire to have direct and autonomous responsibility in the field of defence might be strengthened by the growing fear that they are about to be abandoned by the Americans. These worries, which have existed for several years, are now certainly more acute in various European circles. The recurrent indications of the American desire for disengagement might make some Europeans think that in fact Europe should shortly rely only and mainly on herself. This is why the development of military collaboration on a conventional level among the Western European countries, and the beginning of collaboration between the French and British in nuclear matters (with or without the indirect co-operation of other Western countries) is not a science fiction prospect. If encouraged by some progress towards political unity, it might be a target to be aimed at in a not very distant future. This prospect would be sufficient to raise new problems within the political-military framework for the disarmament negotiators.

Co-operation on a conventional level would not entail, in itself, very serious dangers. Even the setting up of a European arms agency or a kind of Common Market for armaments — as suggested by some French and English personalities — with or without an integrated General Staff, either under the aegis of NATO or not, would not make the general situation worse. Such an increase of European military effort would very probably coincide with the reduction or the withdrawal of American military forces in Europe. The scope of the new agency would doubtless be commensurate with existing dangers,

148

that is to say, in harmony with the level of conventional forces on both sides at that time, taking into account the possibly reduced size of American presence and any disarmament measures which might possibly have been agreed upon. There should not be any great imbalances.

The case of the Franco-British nuclear collaboration is quite different: it would be off the point to examine here thoroughly whether concrete political possibilities exist for the establishment of such collaboration, but we can inquire whether the necessary prerequisites exist.

From the technological angle, because of the different stages of advancement reached by the two countries in various sectors, co-operation between France and Great Britain would turn out to be very profitable to both and would integrate the capacities of the one with those of the other.

But it is mainly from the financial standpoint that such co-operation would be advantageous and even necessary. The present French and British nuclear programmes, when completed, around 1975, will involve — *rebus sic stantibus* — the existence of credible nuclear deterrents until 1980; after which, if new programmes and a new generation of nuclear weapons are not deployed, the nuclear array of the two countries will become unconvincing and outdated. These programmes are very expensive. It will be extremely hard, therefore, for the two countries to undertake them separately; whereas this would be perhaps feasible if expenses were pooled, possibly with a financial contribution from the Federal Republic of Germany and from other European countries.

I do not say that the co-operation agreement will be easy, either juridically or politically. Whilst the French forces were set up in quite an autonomous way, the British ones developed with the special technological and 'know-how' support of the United States, to which France is not entitled; moreover, the British forces are mainly integrated within NATO, whereas the French ones are independent and wish to remain so. Besides, Great Britain is subject to the limitation of the Non-Proliferation Treaty and of the Partial Test Ban Treaty, which France has not accepted. It would therefore be necessary to overcome a whole range of serious difficulties to create an osmosis of technological know-how and aids.

There is, last but not least, the problem of the operational use of nuclear forces. French theory maintains that the credibility of such forces exists only if the responsibility for their use is national and that it would disappear if the responsibility were shared with others, as would be the case if the forces of the two countries were merged, However, in my opinion, the security of France and of Great Britain, and indeed also of the other members of the enlarged Europe, is evidently so closely connected and interdependent that a formula providing for cumulative use might be found. For instance, we might follow the system, adopted in NATO, of the so-called McNamara Committee by setting up a similar European Committee, in which first the two nuclear powers and then also other countries, which had given a technological and financial contribution, might participate in the decisions to be taken about use.

In any event, the fact is that the possible co-operation of the French and the British nuclear forces, with or without the help of other European countries, by pooling resources or even by merely co-ordinating tasks and targeting, would be in itself operationally valuable up to 1980 and even beyond. It would multiply the efficacy of the deterrent which the two countries possess individually. In particular, the existence of a joint force of eight nuclear sumbarines — such would be the joint array of the two countries — would permit a minimum of four submarines to be kept in permanent operational service and hence practically invulnerable.

We may, therefore, conclude that there exist technical, financial and political bases for Franco-British co-operation in the next few years and that such a possibility, being liable to cause a spiralling of the arms race, raises a new and not negligible problem for those involved in the global disarmament negotiations.

Nor can we ignore a further danger, namely that other European countries, having adhered to the Non-Proliferation Treaty on condition that the nuclear superpowers should in their turn make progress towards nuclear disarmament, might be tempted to revise their position and resume their full freedom.

The chances of such a development turn mainly on how the general situation evolves and particularly on the extent to which progress — positive or negative — is made in the matter of disarmament in Europe and the world during the next decade. In this connection, the SALT agreements are without doubt of extraordinary value. I shall not deal in detail with these agreements; I should simply like to say that this achievement goes much beyond all expectations which I had formed on the basis of my personal experience in the Geneva talks. It means that times have greatly changed and for the better. Nevertheless, the agreements establish only a 'freeze', a very important 'freeze', but a 'freeze' and even a very partial one. Only the future will tell whether these agreements are the starting point for progressive nuclear reduction or only a partial and temporary pause.

Anyhow, if we could assume that by 1980 the nuclear armaments of the rest of the world had been abolished, it would be absurd to think that Western Europe as a whole or that France and Great Britain together should in the 1980s acquire a new generation of offensive and defensive weapons. On the other hand, if the nuclear arms race were to be resumed by the East and the West, it would be very difficult to prevent Europe, on its way to unification, from reinforcing its military array.

Without endorsing either of these extreme assumptions, I maintain that an interdependence exists between the general progress of disarmament in the next decade and the decisions which Europe will be called upon to take in terms of security. And it is on the basis of such interdependence that Europe might intervene in the disarmament negotiations. By promising various measures of self-denial, the Europeans could act as a driving force upon the other nuclear powers with regard to disarmament.

In other words, the military and particularly the nuclear potential of the Western European countries — a potential which is not an abstract assumption but a concrete possibility — already gives to the enlarged Europe a considerable negotiating influence. This should enable her by veiled threats coupled with assurances henceforth to intervene effectively in disarmament negotiations when progress is slow.

What are the concrete steps which the Western Europeans might take in the near future? Before addressing this question it is appropriate to consider in which bodies and at which time, some initiatives might be taken, because these initiatives and these occasions could be closely related. I think I must rule out the Geneva Committee of Twenty-Six, which has now lost much of its importance and prestige. Moreover, it is a forum in which Europeans are scantily represented. I think I have to rule out also the United Nations, whose debates rarely result in concrete measures. Nor could it be at SALT, from which the Europeans are excluded. In my opinion, we should select occasions and gatherings in which the Europeans might be sufficiently united and represented as to be able to give their initiatives the solidarity, the significance, the necessary weight and the autonomous character which such initiatives would require. These occasions could be either at some European summit meetings or at the East-West talks on European Security and on mututal force reduction.

As for European meetings we do not yet know whether the enlarged EEC will be able in the short term successfully to overcome problems of political unity. But in any case sooner or later these problems will come up and I believe that the first move in the direction of political European unity, even if modest, will be, politically and psychologically, of great consequences for the future. From the outset, therefore, statements on disarmament and definitions of objectives in the field of peace and security are essential.

The Western Europeans should solemnly declare the will of a United

Europe to co-operate in achieving disarmament and give assurances that progress towards European unification will not be accompanied by dangerous and unnecessary military strengthening, least of all by nuclear means, but that, on the contrary, the military effort will be restrained if in the meanwhile substantial progress is made towards disarmament. This statement might also contain a veiled threat and warnings to the superpowers, in order that these may accelerate agreements. In other words, they should state that only if the superpowers maintain substantial and dangerous nuclear armaments will Western Europe as *ultima ratio* be compelled to take the hard and painful path of the European nuclear collaboration necessary for her survival. We might go further and state that the enlarged Europe — whether federate or not — shall be non-nuclear if the others are no longer nuclear, or if, at least, the others start gradually to dismantle their nuclear armaments. By so doing, we should not compromise at all European security, either now or in the future, but we should elucidate the general purposes of a united and peaceful Europe and we should introduce an immediate element of clarification and *detente*. It is, of course, a declaration of intent, which might be open to criticism as platonic, but — in the light of the considerations I have expounded and of the real dangers connected with a European intensification of the arms race — I contend that it would be neither unreasonable nor ineffective.

I am fully aware that for many reasons an agreement among the Europeans about such a declaration will not be easily achieved. France will probably raise objections. Hitherto France has always proved that she wants to have her hands quite free in the nuclear field. France now seems, however, to be aiming at the leadership of the process of political unification, at least in the confederate sense, and she should be conscious of the disadvantages which would ensue if it should be suspected that a major *arrière-pensée* on the part of the participants was a desire to see an intensification of the arms race. Perhaps her other partners will be unable to obtain from France explicit commitments, but even modest statements and vaguer possibilities might be useful in stimulating the disarmament negotiations.

Let us now consider the diplomatic confrontation between East and West and the problem of the position of the Western European countries in this connection with regard to disarmament proposals.. There are two aspects to this confrontation: negotations for MBFR (Mutual Balanced Force Reductions) and the Conference on European Security.

MBFR is the first concrete proposal on disarmament to be advanced by Western Europe in recent years, or, if we prefer, the first NATO proposal for disarmament directly concerning the European situation.

It was formulated by the NATO Council at Reykjavik in 1968, reiterated in Brussels in 1969 and in Rome in 1970. In the Atlantic Council, held in Rome, the basic criteria of the proposal were set forth as follows:

1. Mutual force reduction should be compatible with the vital security interests of the Alliance and should not operate to the military disadvantage of either side, having regard to the differences arising from geographical and other considerations.
2. Reductions should be on a basis of reciprocity, and phased and balanced as to their scope and timing.
3. Reductions should include both stationed and indigenous forces and also their weapons systems in the area concerned.
4. There must be adequate verification and controls to ensure the observance of agreements on mutual and balanced force reductions.

Whereas the 1968 and 1969 NATO communiques had given rise to no Soviet reactions, the one of 1970 provoked an indirect reply from the Warsaw Pact in June 1970, in which it was affirmed that it was possible to consider a reduction of foreign troops on European territory and that the matter might be discussed 'in the organ which it is proposed to establish at the all-European Security Conference or in any other forum acceptable to interested States'.

We must now attempt briefly to evaluate the concrete possibilities of success. In my opinion, they are rather slight. First, to speak frankly, I wonder to what extent all the European members of NATO are really sincere in proposing a reduction of forces in Europe. We know that such forces are already dangerously unbalanced to the detriment of the Western countries, and I wonder what interest these countries have in asking for a reduction; for such a reduction, even if it were balanced, might make the situation worse. It might be thought that the proposal was devised by some European members of NATO with some *arrière-pensée* and as a move mainly prompted by fear that the Americans might unilaterally reduce or withdraw their forces from Europe.

Even stranger is the way in which the Soviet Union replied. The reduction of troops in Europe, associated with the withdrawal of foreign troops and the dismantlement of foreign bases, was several times suggested by them in the past at the Geneva talks. Therefore, once this proposal was put forward by NATO it should have been immediately welcomed by the Soviet Union. On the contrary, however, nothing of the kind happened; instead there was first silence, then a partial and reticent acceptance, with the stress on foreign troops, as if these were to be the only subject of the possible agreement. Probably, since some American political circles have often shown in this matter

153

only slight diplomatic skill, the Soviet Union hopes that what interests them most — the reduction of American troops in Europe — will occur spontaneously and without any counter-concessions by them. It may also be that the Soviet Union, after the Czechoslovakian events, have changed their opinion and that, though they previously sustained in Geneva the thesis of the reduction of troops in Central Europe, they are now no longer convinced that such measures would be convenient for them.

At all events, objective difficulties are inherent in the proposal and will be hard to overcome judging by the experience we had in the endless Geneva debates about somewhat similar proposals, on which no agreement was ever in sight.

The reduction of forces must of course be balanced. Now, the notion of balancing — which is normal and essential in any disarmament measure not aiming at weakening security on either side — is an abstract notion, always difficult if not impossible to translate into concrete reality. The Geneva debates proved useful at least in showing that to apply this criterion specifically to Europe is the most difficult task imaginable, both on account of the geo-military assessments involved and as a result of the present unbalanced basis which constitutes the starting point. Moreover, since the Geneva debates were held, the difficulties have even increased, as the situation to which the balanced reductions should apply appears now to be more unbalanced than ever to the detriment of the West. How is one to assess, for instance, in the framework of balanced reduction, the increase of Soviet maritime forces in the Mediterranean and the Baltic?

There is, moreover, the problem of the controls which were officially asked for by the Western countries (in the Rome declaration); we are acquainted with all the almost insurmountable difficulties related to controls. In fact, real and effective international inspection was never accepted by the Soviet Union in Geneva. Such inspection appears to be contrary to the very nature of Communist regimes, and hence I believe they will always be refused by the Soviet Government.

Indeed, all the measures of disarmament, which are now under consideration in SALT or elsewhere, do not involve any on-site international inspection; only controls which can be applied from outside the country concerned are envisaged. And, for example, if progress towards the conclusion of a Complete Test Ban Treaty is now slowly being made, this is due to the growing possibility of controlling such a ban without on-site inspections.

I doubt, in the case of MBFR, whether satisfactory controls could be obtained from outside and without on-site inspections, because of the extremely delicate and complex military situation in the territories concerned. In particular, it will be easy to be sure that certain

154

American troops have been withdrawn to the other side of the Atlantic, but it would be very difficult to obtain the same assurance about the removal of Soviet armaments and troops. In addition there is the fact that the Soviet troops, moving with the speed they demonstrated in the Czechoslovakian operation, could be back in a few hours. Under the best circumstances, therefore, a negotiation on inspection in Europe will involve endless discussions and take a very long time.

There is, however, a field in which Western Europe could usefully take the initiative without any danger and with prospects of success: namely the field of political and psychological disarmament. The ESC might usefully aim at such a target. To this end, the European countries might take the appropriate initiatives, making their independent and active contributions.

A first and important contribution might be a Pact of Non-Aggression between NATO and the Warsaw Pact. Several times proposed by the Soviet Union both in the Geneva talks and elsewhere, it has always been refused by the Western countries. The Americans were not, in principle, opposed to such a pact, but they followed their European allies, the majority of whom were reluctant or against.

The objections which have been raised on the Western Side to the proposed Pact of Non-Aggression were of various kinds. From the juridical point of view, it was objected:

1. that renunciation of aggression was already a part of the commitments provided for by the United Nations Charter and that it was useless to repeat it;
2. that we had never succeeded in defining aggression juridicially and that therefore the Pact would have an indefinite character;
3. that neither NATO nor the Warsaw Pact had an international legal status enabling them to conclude any agreements and that therefore the Pact would have had to be concluded among their member countries;
4. that in such a case the Eastern countries would have obtained gratuitously the legal acknowledgement of Pankow Germany.

From the political point of view, the objection was substantially only one, but very weighty: the one about mistrust. A Pact of Non-Aggression would have conferred on the Soviets an acknowledgement of good intentions. This might have caused the Western countries to diminish their military effort without any objective reasons to justify such slackening. On the one hand, the Governments of the free countries, being responsible for their military effort before their Parliaments and their public opinions, would have been in difficulty. On the other hand, the Communists Governments, exempt from such democratic ties, would have been able, in spite of the Non-Aggression Pact, to develop their armaments without difficulty. Substantially, to use an expression dear to the Communists, the pact might have been a 'smoke screen', behind which the Soviet Union would have pursued rearmament, and the Western countries would have been prevented from doing so.

In the Geneva debates the Western countries were reluctant to use this last argument, so as not to get into ideological polemics with their Eastern interlocutors, when on the contrary they wished to preserve in the conference a business-like and, as far as possible, friendly atmosphere.

The foregoing arguments were easily refuted by the Soviet Union; in particular, the delicate argument about 'acknowledgement of East Germany' was then minimized by the Soviet Union. They affirmed that such was not their objective in proposing a Pact of Non-Aggression and assured, in the lobbies, that they would accept any legal form of a pact not involving the acknowledgement of East Germany, since the Western countries did not want it.

Summing up, the Soviet proposal for a Non-Aggression Pact in Geneva was a most uncomfortable one for the Western delegations, because to oppose it was polemically unconvincing and politically delicate. To refuse a hand held out so insistently was an embarrassing and dangerous attitude, which might have made the Soviets believe that we had an aggressive *arrière-pensée* and might have aroused suspicions even in our own public opinions.

As I already mentioned, those who, at that time, were most opposed to the Non-Aggression Pact were not the Americans, but some in Western European countries, though on different grounds and in different degrees. First of all, there was Federal Germany on account of the possible acknowledgement of East Germany and secondly there was France which, under de Gaulle, pursued a bilateral policy of *detente* with the Soviet Union and aimed at disengaging herself from any NATO commitments. Also other European Governments, more exposed to Eastern dangers, were generally reluctant to support the idea of the Pact, of which, in their view, they would have been the first to bear the dangerous consequences.

I do not say that there are not in the West any grounds for mistrust of the Communist countries — there are perhaps also some reasons for the East to mistrust the West — but, on the whole, it is generally felt that the dangers of sudden aggression by the Eastern countries against NATO are remote. If this state of things were sanctioned by a treaty, we should invent nothing, we should not upset any psychological situation; we should only confirm, solemnly and legally, a situation in which everybody believes. And this would be done without suddenly creating dangerous military vacuums or

156

doubtful areas of inbalance such as would follow immediate reduction of forces.

It seems to me that nothing stands in the way of the European countries formulating a proposal for a Non-Aggression Pact now since the reasons which militated against the pact at the time of the Geneva talks do not appear any longer valid and sustainable.

Among the juridical arguments then advanced in Geneva, two were even then hardly convincing. To say, in order to criticize a proposed Pact of Non-Aggression, that non-aggression is already provided for by the United Nations Charter and that we had never succeeded in defining aggression, was to be led astray by strict juridical criteria, losing sight of political values. The solemn reaffirmation of a commitment, at a given time — even if this commitment is already legally taken in another body and if aggression is not defined in detail — can have a very high political significance, transcending by far the value of the juridical act taken in its literal meaning. We constantly witness public reaffirmation a desire for peace and peaceful coexistence by all statesmen and has anybody ever dreamt of saying that they were useless?

On the other hand, the acknowledgement of East Germany, implicit in the conclusion of a Pact, should not any longer be a serious impediment, now that the Bonn Government has changed its attitude. Such a pact, disregarding the alleged lack of international legal status of both military blocs, might bear the signature of all the countries belonging to the two alliances and the counter-signatures of the two Secretaries-General.

It might be objected, that a possible negative consequence of a Pact remains, namely the difficulty for the West in maintaining the necessary military effort afterwards. But it is just here that the operational strength of a Pact might lie; of course, there would be some elements of risk. But this is a calculated and reasonable risk and, moreover, without risk we cannot have any disarmament. The risk can now be taken.

The situation has evolved in the East since the time when in Geneva the Western countries refused the Pact of Non-Aggression. In fact we cannot exclude that political and psychological reaction may be felt not only in Western countries but also in the countries under Communist regimes. Such regimes, though keeping intact their totalitarian character, might be today less deaf to the pressure of their public opinions. It is one thing to ask people to give up consumer goods, when a government proclaims that a 'revanchist' Federal Germany and her imperialistic allies are constantly plotting aggression, and quite another thing to step up unproductive military expenditure when a Government has accepted, as valid and credible, a Pact of

157

Non-Aggression proposed by the alleged adversaries. Therefore, it might be more difficult, not only for the Western countries, but also for the Governments of the Warsaw Pact states to go on with massive increases of armaments, after concluding a Pact giving formal reassurance to their people, as regards the previous alleged aggressive purposes of both sides.

Then a bilateral disarmament process might be put in motion spontaneously, even in the absence of precise and formal juridical instruments and without setting up strict controls. In general terms, I am convinced that disarmament may be practically carried out, not so much on the basis of solemnly signed papers and inspections, but through mutual trust and the policy of mutual example. I have in mind a policy involving measures autonomously decided upon by both sides, more or less at the same time, substantially equivalent and exempt from inspections, but framed in a politically adequate and relaxed atmosphere. And the atmosphere is very important. In the 1960s, a Pact of Non-Aggression concluded in a climate of Cold or semi-Cold War might have appeared as a distortion, an anachronism, an insincere trap to damage the most honest party. Now, on the contrary, it would appear as the crowning of a psychological process already under way and as the measure liable to put into motion at last the mechanism of spontaneous and effective disarmament.

In conclusion, the European proposal for a Pact of Non-Aggression is in my opinion the best and the most concrete contribution that Western Europe could give in the short term to the disarmament process.

There are, of course, also other initiatives or moves which could be taken by the Europeans possibly in the framework of the ESC. For example, the Western European countries could suggest that NATO members accept the old proposal not to be first to use nuclear weapons. Why was such a proposal, several times advanced by the Soviet Government in the Geneva talks or at the United Nations, always refused by the Western side as a bloc? I believe it was mainly for the sake of European security. As is well known, American policy has always clearly excluded any pre-emptive nuclear attacks and in the United States all the strategic and tactical nuclear weapons are part of a second strike capability. The main reason why the Americans and their European allies in NATO have wanted to keep a free hand on the possible first use of nuclear devices, was the danger that an attack in Europe by the Warsaw Pact, with overwhelming conventional forces, might threaten Western security in such a way that recourse to nuclear defence would be unavoidable if we wanted to survive. The acceptance of a prohibition on the first use of nuclear weapons

158

would deprive the West of such a response.

Now, were a Non-Aggression Pact concluded between NATO and the Warsaw Pact an agreement not to be the first to use nuclear weapons would be its natural corollary. Of course, it could be argued that, once a Non-Aggression Pact is concluded, no other agreement on 'first use' would be logically necessary. But logic and politics are not always the same thing.

Furthermore, I believe that the two pacts — as they stand and with the natural connection between them — could be a valuable system of 'insurance' and 'counter-insurance', that could enhance European security to the particular advantage of the Western countries. What we fear is an aggression with conventional means from the East. Supposing that such an aggression starts in violation of the Non-Aggression Pact, the agreement on no first use would be automatically null and void, so that the victim of the violation could make use of any possible defensive devices.

I do not claim to have made an exhaustive list of the ways in which the European countries could achieve a better contribution to disarmament: of course, many other ideas might be studied. But what is now essential is that the European countries should not remain inert at this historic moment.

We must, of course, first of all strengthen the co-ordination of our policies, which should be perhaps less difficult now, thanks to the present more deeply-felt aspiration for political unity; and we must agree among ourselves on the best way to realize in Europe conciliation between security and disarmament. In doing so, we should start getting accustomed to taking an independent view and of making an autonomous evaluation of the requirements for our security at the present time. There is still no possibility of security for us without the political and military co-operation of the Americans, but the world is changing on both sides and we must adapt ourselves — willingly or unwillingly — to these changes.

Having this in mind, we must start without delay preparing for the possible developments in Western Europe and in East-West relations, being convinced of the necessity of Western and particularly of European solidarity, but with a better understanding of the intentions of our Eastern neighbours and placing more trust in our strength and in the value of the mutual peaceful aspirations of all peoples.

14. DISARMAMENT AND INTERNATIONAL LAW

Milan Sahovic

Introduction

International law by its nature extends today to practically all the domains of social life, not only at the international but also at the internal level. As such it cannot be viewed separately from political, economic, social, military, cultural and scientific activities. We can thus say that the substance and the content of international law is dependent both on extra-legal factors and on the balance of political forces which have had in the past and have in the present a direct bearing on the establishment of legal rules governing the behaviour of states. However, while recognizing this interrelationship between social and legal factors, I want to stress that international law has its own, independent and highly important functions. Once laid down, the legal obligations of states becomes a general framework and a legal basis for their standpoint, as well as a criterion to test the legality of their concrete actions in intergovernmental relations and in the international community as a whole. The substance of international law changes as the interdependence of states develops, and as the balance of political forces alters. But, notwithstanding all this, the basic social function of international law always and invariably remains the same.

It would take me very far if I were to continue discussing the social function of international law. As my task is to consider the concrete rôle of international law in the process of disarmament, I will limit myself to demonstrating the fundamental legal premises which we must bear in mind when considering specific aspects of disarmament. (This term is used to cover general and complete disarmament, partial and collateral measures and arms control.) I want to talk about these premises, not because of any undue reverence for the value of the legal obligations of states, for I have dealt with international law far too long to have illusions about where the limits of its power lie. I only want to draw attention to some issues which are usually overlooked, especially in a political debate or when new technical solutions are under consideration.

In view of the development of armaments and the creation of new types of weapons, and more particularly because of the terrifying consequences of the scientific and technological revolution of our time, it is clear that we must try to adopt new and more efficient legal

160

rules and obligations. However, this does not mean that we must neglect, as we often do, what has already been achieved. On the contrary, we must preserve continuity and strengthen the rôle of international law as a legal basis of the activity of states in the field of disarmament.

It is, moreover, worth talking about existing international law because it presents an opportunity to assess the legal value of the actions of states, as well as its strengths and weaknesses as a legal basis for the current moves towards disarmament.

Are States Under a Legal Obligation to Disarm?

Passing now to a concrete discussion of the relationship between disarmament and international law, the first question to be dealt with concerns the nature of the obligations of states with regard to disarmament. In answer to this question, we can state without hesitation that progress achieved during the twentieth century has been minimal since the basic idea of laying down a general imperative obligation upon states to disarm was first suggested at the First and Second Peace Conferences at The Hague in 1899 and 1907.

The present situation in international law in regard to this question is contradictory. In the meanwhile, following an evolution whose milestones were the adoption of the Covenant of the League of Nations, the Briand-Kellog Pact and finally the United Nations Charter, there have been renunciations of the threat of or the use of force. Parallel with this development, essential legal premises were laid down permitting states to assume the obligation to disarm – but this has not happened. The most that has been achieved in this direction is the consent of states, established first in Articles VIII, IX and XXIII of the Covenant and then in Articles 11, 26 and 47 of the UN Charter, to work for disarmament, that is to negotiate, but not to disarm until such time as they arrived at specific agreements. There is some difference between the Covenant and the Charter in regard to the formulation of the objectives of these negotiations. The Covenant insisted on the reduction of armaments to a level compatible with national safety and compatible with the implementation of international obligations established under joint action, whereas the Charter lays down the responsibility of the General Assembly to consider the principles of disarmament and the regulation of armaments, and to make recommendations to states and to the Security Council, and further authorizes the Security Council to draw up plans for the establishment of a system for the regulation of armaments to be presented to the members of the organization. The Covenant insisted more specifically on the exchange of information on the subject of armaments possessed by states and the control of private production of arms and of the arms trade. On the other hand, it is perhaps significant that disarmament as such is not mentioned among the main purposes of the United Nations set out in Article I of the Charter. Article I deals in fact with the obligations of states concerning the preservation of international peace and security.

In fact, today as in the past the substance of the duty of states assumed under international law has not changed at all. Not only the Charter but also agreements concluded during recent years in the field of disarmament confirm explicitly that states are ready to talk, to negotiate but not to recognize a clear obligation to disarm. Thus the formulation of Paragraph 13 of the Preamble to the Partial Nuclear Test Ban Treaty of 1963 states that the contracting parties, namely the United States, the Soviet Union and Great Britain, as the 'original parties', approved the Treaty 'seeking to achieve the discontinuance of all test explosions of nuclear weapons at all times, *determined to continue negotiations to this end'.* Similar formulae were used in the Non-Proliferation Treaty of 1968 (Article VI) and in the Treaty on the Demilitarization of the Seabed and Ocean Floor of 1971 (Article V). No further progress has been made.

Several attempts have been made in the last twenty years to give a deeper meaning to the provision on disarmament in the United Nations Charter but without success. In the resolutions of the General Assembly, adopted after 1945, and in various agreements among member states, some progress has been achieved in formulating the final objective of disarmament but the flexible character of the legal obligation of states to proceed to disarmament has not been altered. This evolution is particularly reflected in the text of the Declaration on Principles of International Law concerning Friendly Relations and Co-operation among States, adopted by consensus at the 25th session of the United Nations General Assembly, which lays down that: 'All states shall pursue in good faith negotiations for the early conclusion of a universal treaty on general and complete disarmament under effective international control . . .'.

Various conclusions may be drawn from this formulation in connection with the current participation of states in the attempt to achieve disarmament, but I must add that the precise extent of contemporary obligations of states in this field is obscured, first as a result of the existence of great number of bodies within which the negotiations for disarmament have taken place since the Second World War and, secondly, owing to the attitudes of states towards the composition of these bodies and their terms of reference. I particularly have in mind here the views of France and China but also the problem

162

of the relationship between the work of the General Assembly in this field and smaller bodies in which superpowers have predominant positions.

My intention is not to continue to discuss whether the possibility exists of more definite obligations to disarm being accepted at the contemporary stage of development of international law and international relations. I would only say that more extensive political preconditions are needed for such a development than is the case with particular agreements on conventional or nuclear disarmament. Consequently my conclusion on this point is that it would be utopian to try to ask governments to sign in advance a platonic obligation to disarm and that the existence of the obligation of states to negotiate on disarmament is sufficient and probably, for the time being, the only possible legal basis for the achievement of concrete results in this field.

International Law As the Basis of Steps Towards Disarmament

The foregoing remarks concerning the evolution of the duty of states to disarm do not mean that, during the development of modern nineteenth- and twentieth-century international law, no international legal acts have been adopted whose contents do not directly point to a definite attitude on the part of states towards the use of armaments and disarmament. In fact, it may be said that important achievements have been made in this regard although we may at the same time point to an interesting tendency to neglect the results achieved at the beginning of the century despite the fact that they cannot be regarded as obsolete.

The explanation should be sought in the fact of the existence of nuclear weapons, in their exceptional destructive force, as well as of the other weapons of mass destruction produced during the arms race since the end of the Second World War. The result has been that the need to create a new system of international legal obligations has become so strong that it has led to a neglect of the obligations assumed earlier even though, having previously become a part of the positive customary international law, they had acquired the character of *jus cogens*. The exceptionally destructive nature of the new types of armaments has enabled the countries engaged in the arms race to claim that their armaments are not subject to the legal obligations assumed previously and to the existing rules of international law in general.

In my opinion, however, we must insist on a preserving continuity in the development of previously adopted legal solutions. This should be emphasized all the more as the value and the legal force of the

163

general rules laid down in the past has been confirmed. They are bound to be improved on and completed or revised, and new rules must be made mainly because of needs arising out of recent developments in the political, military and other spheres.

If we look at the present position in the quest for disarmament, we see a clearly manifested desire to move from general prohibitions, which lay down rules of use or prohibition of armaments, to the assumption of more substantial obligations, which increasingly involve matters that have hitherto been considered to be an inviolable part of the internal jurisdiction of states. This evolution was achieved mostly in the last decade, between 1960 and 1970, following the series of agreements concluded for the purpose of restricting the armaments race such as the Demilitarization of Antarctica in 1959, the Partial Nuclear Test Ban of 1963, the Treaty on the Peaceful Use of Space and Celestial Bodies of 1967, the Non-Proliferation Treaty of 1968, the regional denuclearization of Latin America (the Treaty of Tlatelolco) of 1967, the Treaty on the Demilitarization of the Sea-bed and Ocean Floor of 1971 and the Ban on Bacteriological and Biological Weapons of 1972. Although of ambiguous character, the ABM Accord between the United States and the Soviet Union, concluded in 1972 during President Nixon's visit to Moscow, also belongs to this category of agreements, just as the negotiations now being conducted on chemical disarmament at the Disarmament Conference in Geneva should lead to a similar arrangement.

The crux of the matter is that these agreements restrict in different ways the traditional freedom of states in the domain of the manufacturing, stockpiling, testing or selling to other countries mainly of nuclear but also other weapons of mass destruction, while the idea of seeking ways of ensuring effective international control at both national and international levels is slowly but increasingly gaining support. The control systems envisaged in the arrangements approved so far, combined with the control system of the International Atomic Energy Agency in Vienna, are concrete achievements in the field of international law which are a clear indication that future developments will have to take place in this direction. This involves some extremely important obligations, whose practical implementation would restrict freedom of action of states in domains which have always been among the basic prerogatives of sovereign states. Of course, it remains to be seen whether this appraisal has real value but nevertheless we may conclude that, on the basis of the agreements already reached, a system of rules is beginning to emerge, which, while still insufficiently clear and comprehensive, is gradually regulating a number of questions of essential significance for the attainment of the

164

aim of general and complete disarmament under effective international control. How soon this system may be realized in the international juridical sphere and in international relations is quite another question. What is important for my present purpose is to establish that its elements are being gradually built up. Moreover, this new system of legal rules must be and is based on the general legal rules of existing international law.

Laid down in the early decades of the century, these rules have shown that despite, and perhaps because of the fantastic development in the technology of destruction, the basic legal premises for regulating disarmament have not yet been superseded by the international legal acts adopted in recent times.

I would advance only three points in support of this view: the rules of the Fourth Hague Convention still exist and are unchallenged. Examples are Marten's Clause from its Preamble and Articles 22 and 23(e) of the Hague Regulations which are annexed to the Convention. According to Marten's clause 'until a more complete code of laws of war has been issued . . . the inhabitants and the belligerents remain under the protection and the rule of principles of the law of nations, as they result from the usages established among civilized nations, from the laws of humanity, and the dictates of the public conscience'. This principle is supplemented by Article 22 of the Hague Regulations which states: 'The right of belligerants to adopt means of injuring the enemy is not unlimited'. Article 22(e) of the same regulation explicitly prohibits the belligerents from 'employing arms, projectiles, or material calculated to cause unnecessary suffering'.

These rules have remained to this day of decisive significance as criteria for testing the legality of and necessity for utilization of different types of weapons, and as such provide juridical grounds for the view that nuclear arms and other weapons of mass destruction are illegal. The original meaning of these rules concerns the problem of the utilization of such armaments, but it is possible also to argue that they must have some influence on the arms race and on the regulation of armaments and disarmament. It is obvious from this point of view that the manufacture of weapons whose destructiveness bring them under the rule prohibiting their utilization may be regarded, if not as completely illegal, at any rate as questionable.

It is possible to make a long list of such weapons but the problem is still to ensure the unanimity of states, and especially of large ones, in the assessment of the illegality of their use. And this is a problem not only with nuclear and other weapons of mass destruction. It is also a problem which relates to the latest achievements in destructive power of new types of conventional weapons.

This was seen at the Conference of Government Experts on the

Reaffirmation and Development of International Humanitarian Law applicable in Armed Conflicts, which was held in May 1972 in Geneva, as a continuation of a similar conference held in 1971 under the auspices of the International Red Cross Committees. New legal texts are now being prepared which have to be added to the Geneva Conventions for the Protection of Victims of Armed Conflicts of 1949, and of the Fourth Hague Convention, particularly with reference to the position of combatants and the illegality of the use of some armaments. During the discussion a proposal was made by fourteen countries (Egypt, Finland, Sweden, Mexico, Norway, Switzerland, Yugoslavia, Algeria, Austria, Saudi Arabia, Kuwait, Libya, Syria and Mali) that, in addition to Marten's Clause, the following provisions should be inserted in the Draft Protocol concerning International Armed Conflicts:

It is forbidden to use weapons and methods of warfare which are likely to affect combatants and civilians indiscriminately;
Delayed-action weapons, the dangerous and perfidious effects of which are likely to be indiscriminate and to cause suffering to the civilian population are prohibited;
Incendiary weapons, containing napalm or phosphorus, shall be prohibited;
Bombs, which for their effect depond upon fragmentation into great numbers of small-calibred pieces or the release of great numbers of small calibred pellets, shall be prohibited.'

Having in mind the possible further development of the arms race, the co-sponsors further proposed as general rules:

The constant development of new weapons and methods of warfare places an obligation upon states to determine individually whenever they do not attain international agreements whether the use of particular new weapons or methods of warfare is compatible with the principle contained in this article;
The prohibitions contained in this article are without prejudice to any prohibitions of weapons and methods of warfare which are found in other articles of the present protocol or in other instruments.

There were other interesting proposals to extend the list of proscribed weapons (in addition to nuclear arms and other weapons of mass destruction) and I would also mention a proposal by Hungary, Czechoslovakia, Poland and the German Democratic Republic for the prohibition of weapons whose effects cannot be controlled and such weapons and methods which are liable to alter the human environment. A long debate was conducted on all this and on other proposals.

Finally, it was proposed that a group of experts should meet and consider the entire question and afterwards join a group of experts which is studying napalm and other incendiary weapons in conformity with a resolution of the 26th session of the United Nations General Assembly.

A second point is linked to the problem of the validity of earlier prohibitions. This question was raised, in particular, in connection with the Geneva Protocol of 1925, about which a struggle had gone on for at least a decade. All the resolutions, repreatedly reiterated since the Second World War and put forward in the resolutions of the United Nations General Assembly, have always insisted on the binding nature of the Geneva Protocol and that it contains and proclaims the basic rules of positive international law.

I am especially emphasizing this aspect of the problem because in the discussion of the legality of the use of nuclear weapons there has been a tendency to deny the value of the prohibitions under the Fourth Hague Convention and the Geneva Protocol of 1925 insofar as their effects are identical with the effects of poisons and bacteriological weapons in general but outstripping them many times in destructive force. However, even here it is not possible to break the continuity. It is certain that a future explicit prohibition on the manufacture of nuclear weapons must be based on those general rules of international law which already makes illegal the use of nuclear weapons and other weapons liable to cause unnecessary suffering.

A third point concerns the general obligation of states to observe the territorial integrity and sovereignty of other states. Although one of the special characteristics of the agreements concluded in recent years is that they concern mostly the areas outside the direct jurisdiction of states (Antarctica, outer space and the seabed) and are regarded as a 'common heritage of mankind', some of these agreements are of direct importance with regard to sovereignty. Thus, the Partial Nuclear Test Ban Treaty established in Article I that the parties renounced the explosion of nuclear devices 'in any other environment if such explosion causes radioactive debris to be present outside the territorial limits of the state under whose jurisdiction or control such explosion is conducted'. This means that although the states are permitted to continue with underground tests on their territories, they are nevertheless not exempted from responsibility for any damage they are liable to cause on the territories of other states.

This is nothing new for general international law, where there is a rule according to which the territorial sovereignty of a state must not be exercised in a manner detrimental to other states but in good faith in compliance with international obligations and with international law. This is a rule which was generally recognized and confirmed in

1949 by the International Court of Justice in the Corfu Channel Case when it stated that it is 'every state's obligation not to allow knowingly its territory to be used for acts contrary to the rights of other states'.

I have drawn attention to this rule for two reasons. First, I wish to stress that general international law does not authorize states to use, in exercise of their sovereign rights, their territories, and consequently forces, in disregard of any damage they might do to other states and to the international community as a whole. Secondly, I wish to stress that demands for verification in the territories of states involved in measures of disarmament are justified also by the need to ensure a consistent application and respect for the rule concerning the observance of the sovereignty and territorial integrity of other states which is undoubtedly essential for the preservation of international peace and security.

Conclusion

I have dealt with the general rôle of international law in the negotiations being conducted today for the purpose of slowing down the armaments race and achieving general and complete disarmament. As I have emphasized at the beginning, this aspect of the relationship between disarmament and international law, being generally neglected in theory and practice and usually being seldom discussed, is sufficiently interesting to be worthy of attention.

PART II

CHEMICAL AND BIOLOGICAL WARFARE

15. THE BIOLOGICAL DISARMAMENT CONVENTION

Jozef Goldblat

Introduction

For many years chemical and biological (CB) weapons have been considered as repulsive means of warfare and contrary to the conscience of mankind. The customary international law banning the use of these unconventional weapons, is embodied in the Geneva Protocol of 1925, which is now the starting point of all discussions concerning chemical and biological warfare. However, the Geneva Protocol is no more than a law of war; it allows the retention of the weapons in question in the arsenals of states. To remove the danger of CB warfare or, at least, to reduce its likelihood to a minimum, the production of CB weapons should be prohibited and the existing stocks destroyed. Negotiations to this effect started almost immediately after the signing of the Geneva Protocol. The negotiating history is reviewed in detail in Volume IV of the SIPRI study on the Problem of Chemical and Biological Warfare.

In recent years the CB weapons debate has been particularly lively and specific. It has been stimulated by more public information becoming available about the nature and dangers of CB weapons as a result of some accidents which occurred with chemical weapons and as a result of the use of chemical weapons in US military operations in Vietnam. The protests of scientists against the misuse of science for military purposes have also increased.

Under this wave of pressure, a first, though only partial, result has been achieved in the form of the prohibition of biological weapons and toxins. This was due to a major turning point in disarmament negotiations in the spring of 1971. The Soviet Union and its allies, which for years had been insisting on a joint treatment of chemical and biological weapons, and had considered their prohibition an indivisable entity, revised their position. They agreed to conclude a convention providing for biological disarmament only, and thus accepted the approach advocated by Great Britain and the United States. Up to that moment the majority of nations had upheld the view that such a minimum solution would not be satisfactory. The Convention was opened for signature in April 1972.

The purpose of this paper is to examine critically the most essential provisions of the Convention and to assess its value and limitations.

The Provisions of the Biological Disarmament Convention

The Convention is concerned with biological agents and toxins (Article I). In its report of 1969, the World Health Organization defined 'biological agents' as those that depend for their effects on multiplication within the target organism, and are intended for use in war to cause disease or death in man, animals or plants (the target organisms). But neither this, nor any other definition, has been incorporated in the Convention. This is a serious defect, and not only from the point of view of drafting. The absence of a clear-cut definition of the subject of the Convention could enable a party, at some point in the future, to claim an exception to the comprehensive ban and to interpret it restrictively, for example, by relating it only to some target organisms, with the exclusion of others, even though, at present, the all-inclusive character of the biological agents prohibition is not questioned. A controversy similar to that over the 1925 Geneva Protocol, which some governments still consider as not banning the use of anti-plant agents, has not been definitely foreclosed.

The parties undertake not to develop, produce, stockpile or otherwise acquire or retain biological agents and toxins (Article I). However, research aimed at production of these agents or at development of new warfare agents is not banned. This omission is fraught with consequences because the prohibition on developing, producing, stockpiling or otherwise acquiring or retaining is not absolute. It applies only to types and quantities of biological agents and toxins 'that have no justification for prophylactic, protective or other peaceful purposes'.

The term 'protective', as explained by the authors of the Convention, covers the development of protective masks and clothing, air and water filtration systems, detection and warning devices, and decontamination equipment. Thus, research on and production of certain quantities of biological agents and toxins, over and above those needed to prevent diseases, will continue. They will be necessary to develop the protective equipment and devices. There is also bound to be some testing in the laboratories and possibly even in the field, as well as appropriate military training.

The very maintenance of defensive preparations, which at certain stages are indistinguishable from offensive preparations, may generate suspicion. The continued production of warfare agents contains a risk of infringement or of allegations of infringement of the provisions of the Convention.

The qualification that there should be 'justification' for the development, production, stockpiling or retention does not carry much weight. There are no agreed standards or criteria for the quantities of agents and toxins that may be required for different purposes, especially for military protective purposes; it is not clear who is to judge whether there exists justification for the production of any given quantity.

The Convention also prohibits the development, production, stockpiling, acquisition or retention of weapons, equipment or means of delivery designed to use biological agents and toxins (Article I). Research aimed at production of weapons is not banned. Here there can be no justification for the omission on prophylactic, protective or other grounds, as in the case of agents.

No verification of the destruction of stockpiles, or of their diversion to peaceful purposes, is envisaged. The parties are not even formally obliged to announce that they have complied with the commitment and when. The principle proclaimed many years ago by Jules Moch, in his capacity as representative of France in the disarmament talks, that there should be no disarmament without control, as there should be no control without disarmament, has not been followed.

The destruction commitment will concern only very few states. Nevertheless, it would seem opportune if, not later than nine months after the entry into force of the convention (the time prescribed for destruction), all parties formally announced that no biological warfare agents and toxins, and no prohibited weapon or equipment, was present on their territories.

The problem is more complicated when it comes to stockpiles which may be illicitly retained. It should, however, be borne in mind that, in the absence of new production and of fully effective methods of preservation, the military utility of secretly-stored agents will, with the passage of time, decrease.

It is generally recognized that verification of non-production, in the sense in which the term is normally used in disarmament negotiations, is not indispensable in the biological field, even if it were feasible. The enforcement of obligations under the Convention is to be carried out through measures under national control and through some international arrangements.

Each state assumes responsibility not only for observing the convention itself, but also for preventing the prohibited activities 'within the territory of such state under its jurisdiction or under its control anywhere' (Article IV), that is, by another state, private individual or organizations.

On the international level, the parties undertake to consult one another and to co-operate in solving problems relating to the application of the provisions of the convention. Such consultation and co-operation may also be indirect — 'through appropriate international procedures within the framework of the United Nations and in accordance with its Charter' (Article V).

A provision for direct consultation is redundant when a problem arise between friendly nations. It is inoperative when allegations of breaches are made by countries at war, or when for other reasons there is a lack of co-operation between the states concerned. An indirect international procedure is more likely to be set in motion. But the language used to cover such eventualities is rather loose: the sense of the term 'appropriate' is very vague. If it means recourse to the Security Council, then again a special clause seems unnecessary. According to the Charter, the UN members have a statutory right to bring any dispute or any situation which may endanger international peace and security to the attention of the Security Council and also of the General Assembly. A charge of violation of the biological convention, as of other disarmament agreements, would certainly fall into this category. If 'appropriate international procedures' means recourse to other UN organs, for example the Secretary-General, it is doubtful whether the latter would undertake the task of solving problems relating to the application of the convention without a well-defined mandate agreed upon in advance, and authority for immediate action.

The parties are entitled to lodge complaints of breaches of the convention with the Security Council. Any complaint should contain all possible evidence confirming its validity as well as a request for its consideration. Each party undertakes to co-operate in carrying out any investigations which the Security Council may initiate on the basis of a complaint received (Article VI).

The practical value of the complaints procedure is dubious. Since there is no regular international verification of non-production, it is not at all apparent how it may be possible through legal means to collect evidence confirming the 'validity' of a complaint as required. Even data concerning the continued production of biological agents, either qualitative or quantitative, are not to be reported. If the implication of the provision is that other, extra-legal means, i.e. espionage, may be employed to collect evidence on clandestine production of prohibited agents, it should be realized that the parties are not in equal positions in this respect; many may not even possess such means.

No special machinery is envisaged to deal with the charges prior to their submission to the Security Council. Only the Council has under the Convention a clearly expressed right to initiate investigations. Thus each allegation, whatever its importance, may immediately become a subject of political controversy. The permanent members of the Security Council would be in a position to veto even a technical

173

enquiry into the nature of suspected activities if the allegation is directed against them or their allies. This creates a manifest inequality of obligations — a dangerous precedent for future disarmament agreements. Some countries, including Sweden, have refrained from signing the Biological Convention until the discriminatory character of the procedure is attenuated by an understanding, formal or informal, that at least the initiation of investigations will not be blocked by a veto. A UN Security Council resolution containing merely a declaration of readiness to consider complaints and to take measures for their investigation, as suggested by some countries, will not make the rôle of the Security Council as the chief supervisor of the observance of the convention more tolerable.

In any event, and whatever the basis for a possible complaint, a complete separation of the fact-finding stage of the 'complaints procedure' from the stage of political consideration and judgement by the Security Council would be more sensible and more effective. This would require a standing body of technically qualified and internationally recognized experts who could be speedily despatched at the request of parties to carry out enquiries, in conformity with established criteria. Although a state guilty of encroachements would probably not co-operate and not permit its territory to be inspected, the very existence of an impartial mechanism for investigations would constitute a deterrent against possible use and clandestine possession of the banned weapons. It would also make it easier for an innocent state under suspicion of having violated its obligations to free itself from the suspicion through invitation to inspection. In no circumstances could a refusal to allow inspection of biological laboratories be justified on grounds of military secrecy.

As it stands now, the whole system of enforcement under the Convention is based on trust rather than on supervision. Even assuming that the Security Council is in a position to conclude that a breach of the Convention has occurred, it still remains unclear what action will follow the conclusion, other than informing the parties of the results of the investigations. No measures against the offender have been explicitly provided for.

A separate Article contains an undertaking to provide or support assistance to any party, in accordance with the UN Charter, if the Security Council decides that such party has been exposed to danger as a result of violation of the Convention (Article VII). The assistance is meant primarily as action of medical or other humanitarian or relief nature, taken at the request of the endangered party.

While it is recognized that it would be for the requesting party to decide, in the first place, on the form of assistance to be provided, a confusion exists with regard to the strength of the commitment to assist. It would seem that, since assistance is to be given in accordance with the UN Charter, the relevant provision of Chapter VII of the Charter should apply. Under this provision the UN members 'shall join in affording mutual assistance in carrying out the measures decided upon by the Security Council'. But in the understanding of Great Britain and the United States, it would be for each party to decide whether it could or was prepared to supply the aid requested. In other words, assistance would be optional, not obligatory: it could be refused without incurring the charge of non-compliance. If this is so, one can hardly see the purpose of including a clause on the subject in the Convention.

Another caveat was entered by the sponsors of the Convention to the effect that states should not be precluded from rendering assistance they deemed appropriate, before a decision is taken by the UN Security Council with regard to the violation of the convention, and also on the basis of other, non-UN commitments. This further impairs the force of the provision in question as far as UN involvement is concerned.

The Convention does not contain a prohibition on the use of biological and toxin weapons. The ban is included in the Geneva Protocol prohibiting the use of asphyxiating, poisonous or other gases and of bacteriological methods of warfare. Nobody contests that toxins are also covered by the prohibition of use. All states are urged to comply strictly with the principles and objectives of the Geneva Protocol (Article VIII and paragraphs 2, 3 and 4 of the preamble).

But in ratifying the Geneva Protocol, many countries reserved the right to use the banned weapons against non-parties or in retaliation. It is now agreed that the reservations will become pointless, as far as biological weapons are concerned, once the Convention, aimed at completely eliminating these weapons, comes into force. In fact, the Convention proclaims the determination of the parties 'to exclude completely the possibility of bacteriological (biological) agents and toxins being used as weapons' (paragraph 9 of the preamble). The phrase 'never in any circumstances', reinforcing the prohibition under Article I of the Convention, is also taken as allowing no exemption from the ban on the use of biological and toxin weapons. Moreover, the procedure for investigating cases of illicit production and retention of the weapons in question, whatever its effectiveness, is clearly also applicable to cases of illicit use, since use presupposes possession.

All this, however, does not change the fact that the Geneva Protocol is accompanied by reservations which form an integral part of that document. According to Article VIII of the Convention, nothing shall be interpreted as in any way limiting or detracting from the

175

obligations assumed by any state under the Geneva Protocol. This may imply that the reservations — part and parcel of the obligations — will continue to subsist. Legally, they can be nullified only through a direct act of withdrawal.

The Convention is of unlimited duration but each party has the right to denounce it, if it decides that extraordinary events, related to the subject matter of the convention, have jeopardized the supreme interests of its country (Article XIII). The clause is patterned after previous arms limitation agreements.

In the case of biological weapons, the withdrawal provision has little, if any, justification. Apart from being repulsive, biological and toxin weapons in their present form have, in the view of the military, little value, either as a means of offence or as a means of defence. Even if a biological attack occurred, a response in kind would be, in the opinion of many, irrational. As a form of sanction, withdrawal from the convention lacks credibility. Renunciation of biological warfare for ever, with no condition or escape clause attached, would not jeopardize the national security of any state.

The Convention is to enter into force after the deposit of the instruments of ratification by twenty-two governments, including those of the Soviet Union, Great Britain and the United States, as depositaries. The designation of nuclear-weapon states as depositaries of the biological convention is less substantial than in the previously concluded treaties dealing with nuclear matters. The choice of a non-nuclear-weapon and especially non-aligned country or countries as depositaries of a convention related to non-nuclear weapons would not be less equitable; if anything, it could facilitate wider adherence to the convention.

The Significance of the Biological Disarmament Convention

I have deliberately concentrated on the deficiences of the Biological Convention. But the Convention, as a whole, is not an unimportant document. Its conclusion is conducive to allaying suspicion among states. Its text reflects to a greater extent than some other arms control agreements the views and interests of smaller countries, both aligned and non-aligned, which actively participated in the drafting process.

In terms of disarmament, the Convention is a preventive measure: it will prevent the spread of biological and toxin weapons to countries which do not possess them now; it will prevent the development of biological agents militarily more attactive than the existing ones, which may result from scientific advances modifying the conditions of their production, stockpiling and use. The abolition of the means for biological warfare by those possessing them will also be the first real disarmament step taken during the whole post-war period, the only one involving any measure of military 'sacrifice'.

From the legal point of view, the Convention will strengthen the force of the unilateral renunciations of biological weapons made by a number of nations in recent years. It will impose equal and identical obligations on all.

Last, but not least, it will open new prospects for international scientific co-operation in the field of peaceful uses of microbiology; the co-operation would be enhanced if at least a portion of the savings derived from biological disarmament is directed to that end.

On the other hand, it is unfortunate that a split has occurred in the treatment of chemical and biological weapons. Since the signing of the Geneva Protocol in 1925, both categories of weaponry have been dealt with inseparably in a number of international documents, and have been associated with each other in a single taboo in the public mind. The technical difficulty of drawing a clear-cut boundary between chemical weapons and biological weapons adds to the artificiality of the division.

Even more regretable is the fact that, in bisecting the traditional chemical-biological unity, priority has been accorded to agents which, because of their uncontrollability and unpredictability, are of little utility and therefore judged to be militarily less important. Biological disarmament is a marginal disarmament measure compared to the banning of chemical weapons.

The latter are more dangerous because they are potentially attractive to the military. They are more predictable than biological weapons and can produce immediate effects — an important quality in combat. So far as is known, biological weapons have never been used. But chemical weapons have already been used on a large scale and with disastrous consequences, mostly 'downhill', i.e. against those who lack defences and have no means to retaliate in kind.

16. THE MAIN ISSUES IN THE CW DEBATE

Jozef Goldblat

Introduction

Under the Biological Convention, signed in April 1972, the parties
are committed to negotiating an agreement on effective measures for
the prohibition of possession of chemical weapons. A discussion, both
in a political and technical level, has been taking place at the
Conference of the Committee on Disarmament (CCD). A draft
convention was tabled by a group of Socialist countries, members of
the Committee, on the prohibition of the development, production
and stockpiling of chemical weapons and on their destruction, which
is almost identical to the Biological Convention. A number of working
papers were also presented and discussed at informal meetings of
experts. No progress has been recorded so far. One reason for this is
the complexity of the problem: stocks of chemical warfare agents,
of different types, as well as of basic material needed for their
production, exist in many countries; the knowledge of how to
manufacture and use them is not a monopoly of the major powers.
Another reason, more important, if not decisive, is that chemical means
of warfare, unlike biological means, are considered to be militarily
useful and certain military establishments are reluctant to give them
up. The Biological Disarmament Convention can serve as model for
chemical disarmament, but some of its weaknesses and ambiguities
would not be tolerated now, considering the nature of the weapons
to be banned under a chemical convention.

The main issue in the chemical disarmament debate has been what
should be the scope of the prohibition. This controversial question will
be examined here in the light of the opinions expressed by the
participants in the debate.

Object of the Prohibitions

Chemical agents form a basic element of chemical warfare capability,
whatever the weapons using them, and the system for the delivery
of the weapons to the target. A definition of chemical warfare agents
is therefore essential to define the ban under a disarmament
convention and to ensure uniform application of the international
obligations which would subsequently have to be translated into

178

national legislation.

According to the UN Secretary General's report of 1969, chemical agents of warfare are chemical substances, whether gaseous, liquid or solid which might be employed because of their direct toxic effects on man, animals and plants. (It is understood that chemical substances used for conventional weapons such as explosives, smoke and incendiaries that exert their primary effects through physical force, fire, air deprivation or reduced visibility, as well as fuel, are not chemical warfare agents). The definition contained in the 1925 Geneva Protocol, which prohibits the use of 'asphyxiating, poisonous or other gases' and of 'all analogous liquids, materials or devices', is covered by the formula used in the UN report.

These definitions, however, are insufficient when it comes to determining whether a particular chemical product should be classified as a warfare agent and consequently whether its possession should be prohibited. Besides, the wording of the Geneva Protocol gave rise to conflicting interpretations and it is considered risky to subject a new treaty to similar vicissitudes.

Chemical agents include three categories: single-purpose agents which have practically no other use than for warfare (only small quantities are employed for medical purposes); dual-purpose agents which are commonly used for civilian needs; and intermediates which may or may not have civilian applications. The first category, that of single-purpose agents, covers the most dangerous agents — the nerve agents, which are organo-phosphorus compounds but are more toxic than insecticides and pesticides belonging to the same class. There exists yet another type of compound, the carbamates, which could act in the same way as nerve agents by disrupting the nervous system. Some of the carbamates are among the most toxic substances produced synthetically, but their usefulness as chemical warfare agents is very limited in view of their chemical and physical properties. The last category, that of intermediates, does not have immediate military significance unless processed into an agent.

In the case of so-called binary weapons the distinction between the categories of agents becomes confused. These weapons, still in an experimental stage, generate a super-toxic agent from two separate components which possess a much lower toxicity than the resulting mixture, and cannot themselves be classified as chemical warfare agents. Production of the warfare agents takes place just prior to firing the weapons or when the weapon is already on its way to a target.

Technically speaking, the following criteria could be used to identify substances utilizable for chemical warfare: toxicity standard; identification of agents by name and specific structural formula;

and general structural formulae.

Precise technical criteria would be indispensable in an agreement prohibiting selected categories of chemical warfare agents, such as super-toxic agents, to distinguish them from those remaining outside the ban. The wider the object of the prohibition in a non-comprehensive ban, the more difficult it may be to draw an exact dividing line. None of the above criteria, taken separately, would seem satisfactory for the purpose of a chemical convention. A combination of them would most probably be required. For a general ban on chemical warfare agents a definition of a general nature is needed.

A general criterion could be based on the purpose which the agents are intended to serve, with reference to qualitative characteristics and to quantitative factors. It could describe the prohibited agents as substances of types and in quantities that have no justification for peaceful purposes, or as those destined for the production of chemical weapons.

In the former case, if doubts arose with regard to compliance, evidence would have to be provided that certain types or quantities of agents were used for peaceful purposes, which should be feasible. In the latter case, it is the absence of intent to use the agents for weapons purposes which would have to be proved, and this may not be possible. For instance, dual-purpose agents may be originally intended only for civilian industries, but once produced, they can be used both for peaceful and warlike purposes. A change of intention on the part of the producing states, which is clearly unverifiable, would be enough to convert civilian stockpiles into military stockpiles.

The purpose criterion, characterizing the prohibited agents as those which have no justification for peaceful purposes, was used in the Biological Disarmament Convention. For chemical disarmament, such a definition is too sweeping. But it could be supplemented by some technical guidelines relating at least to the most dangerous agents which require the strictest control and verification measures. To this end, a tentative delimitation of super-toxic agents has been proposed on the basis of the effects of these chemicals on living organisms. In addition, considering the size and output of the chemical industry in different countries, as well as the manifold uses its products are put to, a recognized authority would have to judge, on an *ad hoc* or current basis, whether or not the volume of substances produced, or otherwise acquired, exceeded normal industrial requirements.

Activities to be Prohibited

Among the activities which amount to building up a chemical warfare capability, production and stockpiling of agents deserve special attention.

The scope of non-production and non-stockpiling commitments would depend on the object of prohibition. Under a partial agreement, prohibiting single-purpose agents, i.e. those which have only belligerent use, relevant facilities would have to be shut down, dismantled or converted to peaceful uses, and the accumulated stocks destroyed. An exception could be made for some small amounts, militarily insignificant, which may be needed for scientific and medical purposes, and which would have to be declared.

Under a comprehensive agreement, prohibiting all chemical warfare agents, there would have to be, in addition to an absolute ban on the production of single-purpose agents, a limitation on the manufacture of dual-purpose agents, so as strictly to adjust the output and stockpiles to civilian needs. Whatever methods of verification are eventually agreed upon, and there seems to be a consensus that they should not be intrusive, there would always remain a possibility of evasion. Thus, for example, abuses in the case of dual-purpose agents, which are produced in very large quantities, cannot be excluded, even with a well-developed, internationally streamlined system of accounting and data reporting. Components of binary weapons pose even greater problems. Manufacture of items unconditionally forbidden could continue at undeclared facilities. Stocks of warfare agents could be illicitly retained, if not with the intention of eventually using them, then at least to avoid costly and hazardous operations of destruction. A possibility of lodging complaints of violations and having them investigated by an international body may give some reassurance, if necessary enquiries are initiated promptly, without discrimination. But it should be borne in mind that some countries may have no means to collect evidence about clandestine production or stockpiling by others. The matter is of particular importance to smaller and weaker nations which do not possess a wide choice of weapons available for retaliation against a possible chemical aggression.

What, then, could be done to achieve a comprehensive ban which would provide reasonable assurance of compliance?

The uncertainties could be minimized if a prohibition were imposed also on chemical warfare research conducted as part of a military programme, on the development of warfare agents, on the production of chemical ammunition and means of delivery of chemical weapons, on training in the use of these weapons, and on the very existence of special military units for chemical warfare. The methods available for verifying these activities are not fool-proof either. But while laboratory research is not subject to direct supervision, development may be detected at the stage of field testing; and although munitions containing chemical agents resemble conventional munitions, training in chemical warfare and the existence of chemical warfare units is difficult to conceal. It is the cumulative effect of the main and supplementary prohibitions which may be significant. The broader the ban on activities connected with chemical warfare, the lesser the likelihood of violations. The narrower the ban on such activities, the easier it may be to escape detection of breaches, because the permitted chemical warfare activities would be difficult to distinguish from the prohibited ones, and refusal to allow inspection could be justified on the ground of military secrecy.

In any event, if the aim of the chemical disarmament agreement is to reinforce the Geneva Protocol, an international machinery would be needed to deal with allegations of use. Collective action in defence of the attacked state would also have to be provided for. The deterring effect of such provisions may fill in the unavoidable residual gaps in the verification of non-possession of chemical weapons.

A Partial or a Comprehensive Ban?

To be comprehensive, a treaty dealing with chemical weapons would have to prohibit all chemical warfare agents and all activities related to the preparation of chemical warfare. From the disarmament point of view this is certainly the most desirable approach.

Partial agreements, covering selected categories of agents and only certain relevant activities, may have some intrinsic merit, but would be deficient in many respects. Thus, for example, a prohibition of super-toxic agents would have a limited value to many countries, if other agents remained unaffected. In a confrontation between a major military power and a less advanced nation, or between the developing countries which have inadequate defences against a chemical attack, even less toxic agents would suffice to cause mass destruction.

The central issue is the treatment of stockpiles. If a cessation of the development and production of super-toxic agents were accompanied by destruction of stocks, however lengthy the latter operation may be, the cause of disarmament would be enhanced: a weapon would be disposed of, the destructive force of which is second only to nuclear weapons.

On the other hand, if the existing arsenals were left intact, the cessation of the development and production of super-toxic agents and, for that matter, of other chemical warfare agents, would have no more than a preventive effect. The non-producing countries would be prevented from acquiring a chemical warfare capability; the producing countries would be prevented from further manufacturing known agents or developing ones, and from adding to their stockpiles,

Such an arrangement would bear close resemblance to the Treaty on the Non-Proliferation of Nuclear Weapons, with the sole but important difference that while the nuclear arms race is allowed to continue, the chemical potential would be frozen. This means that a ceiling would be established, both quantitative and qualitative, on the chemical weapon strength in the world at the level existing at the time of concluding the treaty. Such a partial agreement would not be a disarmament measure, considering that the chemical arsenals of the major powers have reached a point of saturation.

Moreover, the built-in inequality of obligations under a partial agreement may be considered discriminatory in that it would strengthen the monopolistic positions of the major powers. But it could not be more objectionable than the Non-Proliferation Treaty which has already been accepted by most countries.

Any partial disarmament measure is presumed to be a step in a gradual process of dismantling warfare capabilities. An agreement concerning chemical weapons could not be an exception. There is hardly any justification for perpetuating a situation where the superpowers possessing the most modern armaments, conventional and nuclear, would also remain the exclusive possessors of the super-toxic chemical weapons.

The debate on chemical disarmament is still in the phase of an exchange of views. Concrete negotiations will not be possible before it is decided what kind of agreement is actually being sought. Pending the conclusion of a chemical disarmament convention, however, certain measures could be taken to prevent the erosion of constraints which already exist on chemical warfare, and to reinforce them. It appears essential to ensure general adherence to the 1925 Geneva Protocol prohibiting the use of CB weapons. Though the number of parties to the Protocol has considerably increased during recent years, ratification or accession by some forty more countries would be needed to make the document universal. In most cases, the military potential of the states concerned matters less than the formal act of confirmation of the international rule of law. However, in the case of the United States, ratification is of material importance because she is the only great power not yet party to the Geneva Protocol, because it has a large arsenal of chemical weapons, and also because it interprets the scope of the Geneva Protocol restrictively and has used chemical weapons during the war in Indo-China.

The acceptance by the United States of the prevailing international opinion that the present law prohibiting the use of chemical weapons comprehensively covers all chemical agents — including irritant agents, such as tear gas, and anti-plant agents — might facilitate negotiations on the scope of a chemical disarmament convention. A reversal of the

183

present British stand on the question of legality of the use in war of the chemical irritant CS would also be helpful in this respect.

Another step which could strengthen the Geneva Protocol would be the withdrawal of the reservations limiting its applicability to other nations party to the Geneva Protocol, and to first use only. The prohibition of use would then become universal and absolute.

Chemical weapons stocked in foreign countries could be withdrawn with a concomitant undertaking not to transfer them to any recipient.

Chemical weapon-free zones could be established in different parts of the world; for example, the Treaty of Tlatelolco, prohibiting nuclear weapons in Latin America, could be expanded to include chemical weapons.

These interim or transitional steps, taken jointly or separately, could pave the way to the complete abolition of chemical weapons.

17. SOME MODERN PROBLEMS CONCERNING THE PROHIBITION OF THE DEVELOPMENT, PRODUCTION AND STOCKPILING OF CHEMICAL WARFARE AGENTS

O. A. Reutov

In this paper I should like to share certain ideas on possible ways and means of the prohibition of the development, production and stockpiling of chemical agents and weapons.[1]

The greater threat posed by chemical weapons today derives from the discovery and manufacture of new, more toxic compounds, whereas bacteriological (biological) agents already exist in nature and can be selected for use in warfare. Some of these agents, notably bacteria, have been known for several decades, but there is a vast number of other possible agents, especially viruses, which have been discovered only recently, and some of these also possess characteristics which make their use possible in war. Increases in potency of these various types of agents have been made possible by scientific and technological advances in microbial genetics, experimental pathology and aerobiology.

As is well known, the use of toxic gases in the First World War generated so powerful a sense of outrage that countries were encouraged to adopt measures prohibiting both chemical and bacteriological (biological) weapons. The result was the Geneva Protocol of 17 June 1925, which prohibits the use in war of asphyxiating, poisonous or other gases and of all analogous liquids, materials or devices, as well as bacteriological methods of warfare. This established a custom and hence a standard of international law, and in practice most states have adhered to the principle that nobody should resort to the use of such weapons. But despite the abhorrence in which they have always been held by civilized peoples, chemical weapons have none the less on occasion been used. For example, mustard gas was used in Ethiopia in 1935-1936, causing numerous casualties among troops and a civilian population which was not only completely unprotected, but which lacked even the most elementary medical services. It should also be noted that the existence of the Geneva Protocol of 1925 may have helped as a deterrent to the use of chemical or bacteriological (biological) weapons in the Second World War, even though the belligerents in that conflict had developed, produced and stockpiled chemical agents for possible use. The International Tribunal at Nuremberg brought into the open the fact that among the new agents which had been produced and stockpiled during the course of the war were such highly lethal agents as Tabun and Sarin. Since then the validity and effectiveness of the Geneva Protocol have been reinforced by the approval, on the part of the General Assembly of the United Nations, without a single dissenting voice, of resolutions 2162 B (XXI) of 5 December 1966 and 2454 A (XXIII) of 20 December 1968, calling for 'strict observance by all States of the principles and objectives' of the Geneva Protocol, and inviting all states to accede to it.

It is easy to appreciate the resurgence of interest in the problems of chemical and bacteriological (biological) warfare. Advances in chemical and biological science, while contributing to the good of mankind, have also opened up the possibility of exploiting the idea of chemical and bacteriological (biological) weapons, some of which could endanger man's future, and the situation will remain threatening so long as a number of states proceed with their development, perfection, production and stockpiling.

At its 23rd session, in resolution 2454 A (XXIII), the General Assembly requested the Secretary General of the United Nations to prepare, with assistance of qualified consultant experts, a report on chemical and bacteriological (biological) weapons in accordance with the proposal contained in the introduction to the Secretary General's annual report on the work of the organization (A/7201/Add. 1), and in accordance with the recommendation contained in the report of the Conference of the 18-Nations Committee on Disarmament of 4 September 1968 (A/7189).

According to the Secretary General, 'in a very short period of time, consultant experts have produced a study, which, in spite of the many complex aspects of the subject matter, is both concise and authoritative'. The 24th General Assembly approved this report, considering it to be a scientific-technical basis for the discussion of questions on prohibiting the development, production and stockpiling of chemical and biological weapons.

The UN General Assembly Resolution 62 (XXV) contains a passage which 'requests the Conference of the Committee on Disarmament to continue its consideration of the problem of chemical and bacteriological (biological) methods of warfare, with a view to prohibiting urgently the development, production and stockpiling of those weapons and to their elimination from the arsenals of all States'. The result was that the Convention on Prohibition of the Development, Production and Stockpiling of Bacteriological (Biological) Warfare Agents was drawn up comparatively rapidly.

Some progress has also been made during recent years in studying the problem of chemical weapons. For example, a considerable number of states have adhered to the Geneva Protocol, which in fact demonstrates the growing confidence which resides in this international instrument and also demonstrates that the prohibition of chemical weapons has been accepted by the large majority of states, constituting a permanent element in international relations and a general recognized rule of international law.

But on the question of drafting a Convention on Chemical Warfare, corresponding to that on Biological Warfare, we have had some difficulties. The negotiations on this subject currently proceeding in the Committee of Disarmament in Geneva are at present to a large degree concerned with what type of verification should be envisaged. But it seems to me that the character of verification system can only be determined after it is known which types of chemical compounds are to be put under control and which raw materials and intermediates should be controlled. Some experts pointed out that control over the development, production and accumulation of organo-phosphorus substances among which we have highly toxic chemical agents such as Sarin, Soman, and VX is very important.

While discussing the numerous aspects of the approach to control and the methods of control, one question emerges: will it be enough to confine ourselves to controlling the production and accumulation of organo-phosphorus substances? And whether there is likely to arise a possibility of uncontrolled accumulation of toxic substances belonging to other chemical classes? In my opinion these questions require a comprehensive discussion and analysis.

At present, a great number of toxic substances are known that do not contain phosphorus but the utilization of which as chemical weapons is very likely on various grounds — including tactical grounds. Among those substances are such well-known agents as mustard gas (*bis* [2-chloroethyl] sulphide) which is an example of a blistering agent, as well as other nitrogen analogues of it such as *tris* (2-chloroethyl) amine.

The production of such substances is simple and they can easily be produced in very large quantities. It is sufficient to say that the world output of ethylene oxide considerably exceeds the million ton mark at present — a quantity sufficient for the production of about 2 million tons of mustard gas or its nitrogen analogues. This quantity of mustard gas is enough to contaminate extensive areas and to cause inestimable suffering to mankind. More than that, if we take into account the fact that mustard gas can be produced not only from ethylene oxide but also from ethylene and sulphur chloride it means that mustard gas can be used for military purposes on a practically unlimited scale.

One can argue that the toxicity of mustard gas and its nitrogen analogues is several times less than that of modern organo-phosphorus compounds, but then, as is seen from the simple example above, mustard gas and its analogues can be produced in tremendous quantities. Besides, the production costs for mustard gas and its nitrogen analogues are considerbly lower than for organo-phosphorus substances. We could also add that the provision of protection from vesicants — particularly for the civil population — is complex and unwieldy. Mustard gas casualties have to undergo extensive and prolonged treatment, and the treatment is rather difficult as, up to now, there are no really effective antidotes.

It is a well-known fact that, despite the development of much more toxic agents of the organo-phosphorus group, mustard gas and its nitrogen analogues belong to the arsenals of a number of armies — among others, to the US Army in the form of the agent ND. It follows that vesicants constitute a very real danger and the problem of their production and accumulation is still topical.

When speaking about systemic poisons one should remember hydrogen cyanide and its derivatives. It is well known that the capabilities for producing hydrogen cyanide in various countries are rather high, being measured by hundreds of thousands of tons per annum. This is connected with the fact that hydrogen cyanide is very important as an intermediate product in the production of a number of industrial compounds. Hydrogen cyanide is extensively used in the chemical industry for the production of such substances as acrylonitrile, cyannric chloride and acetone cyanohydrin. The scale of their production is sufficiently considerable to create a potential possibility of their utilization in large quantities as chemical warfare agents.

The same can be said about agents such as phosgene which serve as intermediates for the production of a great variety of chemical substances, among them intermediates and dyes, herbicides and insecticides, polymers and pharmaceutical preparations — products of peacetime industry which are rather hard to control.

In the opinion of many specialists the existence of considerable production capabilities for hydrogen cyanide and phosgene means that they have a significant potential rôle as chemical warfare agents.

The last few years have seen the start of a practical application in agriculture of certain oximes and derivatives, the toxicity of which is close to the toxicity of war agents, though the utilization of elementary means of protection has made it possible for them to be used safely in agriculture without any harmful consequences. Examples of such compounds include *Temic,* the acute oral toxicity (LD_{50}) of which for laboratory animals is 0·9 mg/kg, and 2-fluoroethyl diphenylacetate (LD_{50} 0·95 mg/kg). (See Figure 1)

FIGURE 1

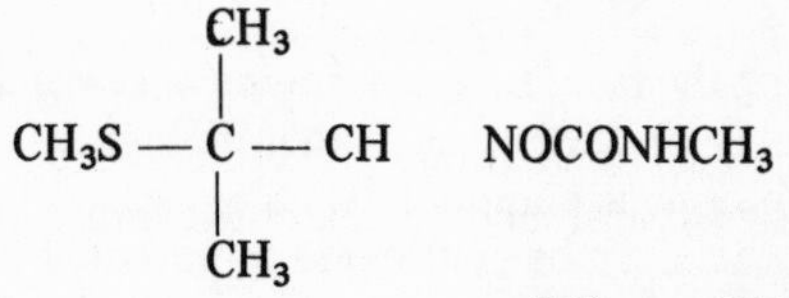

Temic

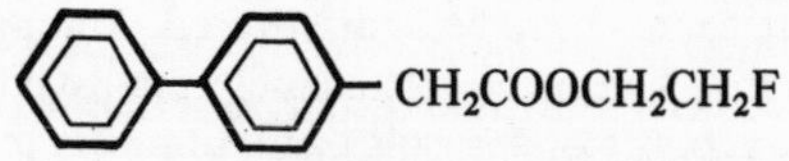

2-fluoroethyldiphenylacetate

The literature describes a large number of other compounds with a similar toxicity for warm-blooded animals, and some of these compounds can therefore be considered as potential war agents.

A large group of war agents is represented by the lachrymators and other irritants that effect the throat and interfere with breathing (sternutators); some of them are listed in the table below.

TABLE I

Agent	Minimal concentration causing irritation, in mg/m^3
α-Bromobenzyl Cyanide	0·15
ω-Chloroacetophenone	0·3
2-Chlorobenzalmalononitrile	1
Xylyl bromide	3·8
Diphenylchloroarsine	0·2
Diphenylcyanoarsine	0·05
10-Chloro-5, 10-dihydrophenarsazine (adamsite)	2

It should be noted that some of the substances listed in Table I are often relatively safe incapacitating agents, but, depending upon the concentration inhaled, their vapours or aerosols can result in serious poisoning, often of a lethal character. Thus, these types of warfare agents should be considered as dangerous agents and their production and storage should be kept under control. Particularly dangerous are arsenic compounds such as adamsite, diphenylchloroarsine and diphenylcyanoarsine; these interfere with breathing and are capable

189

of causing heavy poisoning even at low concentrations. Serious poisoning, causing harm to the central nervous system, can be achieved by certain organic compounds containing lead which, though less irritating in comparison with organic compounds of arsenic, still have a high toxicity.

It is well known that, during the last few years, intensive research has been conducted on the study of toxicity and other biological properties of various classes of organic compounds. As a result, highly dangerous substances which can be considered as potential warfare agents have been discovered. Among these, one particular group may be singled out, namely the psychotomimetics. When taken in, the vapours or aerosols of these substances cause disturbances in normal mental activities and, in a number of cases, have had serious consequences influencing the activities of the human brain. Science knows at present a number of such compounds. One of them is LSD (NN-diethyllysergamide). LSD when taken in a small quantity of 0.001 mg/kg weight results in psychosis that continues for more or less long periods, sometimes up to twenty-four hours. Many other substances have similar effects.

During the last few years, American troops have used chemical agents on a wide scale for the elimination of vegetation in South Vietnam. This results in a grave violation of eco-systems and in many instances has serious consequences for man. The wide utilization of agent Orange, the main component of which is a butylester of 2, 4, 5-T produced from technical 2, 4, 5-T, and containing considerable amounts of a tetrachlorodibenzodioxin, has resulted in a large number of mutant births. It is well known that tetrachlorodibenzodioxin has a strong teratogenic action. American troops in Indo-China have also used, as warfare herbicides, such preparations as 2, 4-D, picloram and others that are commonly employed in agriculture for fighting weeds. It would naturally be very difficult to control production and storage of such products. Even such a preparation as cacodylic acid can be used not only for military purposes for the destruction of agricultural vegetation on enemy territory but also in peaceful agriculture for the destruction of undesirable vegetation. The use of such substances in considerable amounts per area unit could result in poisoning the soil with arsenic for long periods, as well as having undesirable consequences for people eating agricultural produce from these contaminated areas. Again, the use of so-called defoliants to get rid of leaves on tropical trees causes their destruction and causes great damage to the economy of the attacked country.

It is clear from this brief review that not only organo-phosphorus compounds but also many other classes of organic compounds can be used as warfare agents. Besides being widely used in agriculture,

190

herbicides can be used as phytotoxicants.

The Stockholm International Peace Research Institute (SIPRI) arranged in September 1971 a symposium on possible techniques for verifying the nonproduction of organo-phosphorus compounds. The discussion was deliberately limited to the organo-phosphorus compounds in order to get a feasible model system. It was an advantage that thereby the most potent and dangerous chemical agents were considered. In my opinion the results of the symposium will assist the international efforts to bring about chemical disarmament especially in the United Nations and in the Conference of the Committee of Disarmament in Geneva.

Vast possibilities of utilization for military purposes of many classes of organic compounds make the task of international control over their production and storage extremely difficult as this control must embrace, practically speaking, all branches of the chemical industry, which is hardly possible. In connection with this, it would seem to me that the most rational system of control over the production and storage of chemical weapons would be one based upon national control; such control would make use of the services of specialists in those countries where the control is carried out. Such a system of control is much less expensive and more effective as the citizens of the country being checked are familiar with the industry in their country and they are in a better position to visit industrial enterprises than foreign observers. Of course, such a system would require a necessary level of trust between partners. The question of trust, for instance, would include the necessity for states to ratify existing treaties, including the Geneva Protocol prohibiting chemical and biological weapons, which most unfortunately has still not been ratified by the United States.

NOTE

1. The views expressed in this paper are only the author's personal point of view and in no way reflect either the offical position of the Soviet Government or the position of any of its departments.

PART III

THEORY OF CONFLICT AND SOME REGIONAL CASE STUDIES

18. A COMPARATIVE APPROACH TO THE STUDY OF INTERNATIONAL CONFLICT

Alan Dowty

The whole idea of comparative international politics begins with a perhaps simple-minded proposition. This proposition holds that one of the best ways to study any international phenomenon is to compare different systems of international relations in diverse historical periods, and not in the modern period alone. This can be extended to the study of international conflicts. Such an approach rests on the power of comparison as a technique that makes it possible to identify the common elements of different systems, or what is basic to any system of international relations, thus isolating what is unique to any particular system, and particularly what is genuinely unique in the modern international system.

We can think of this in terms of three levels of causation in international conflicts. The first and most basic level of conflict is that inherent to any system of interacting sovereign states, or what might be called the strategic imperative of international conflict. An example would be the simple maxim that the enemy of my enemy is my friend. In other words, these are the patterns of conflict that appear in any international system, regardless of cultural context or historical period.

The second level of causation in international conflict is behaviour specific to one kind of international system (bipolar or multipolar, for example) which is likely to recur in different historical periods. Such sources of behaviour are more particular than the very general level above, but still embrace more than one historical period. An example might be the idea that in a multipolar system alliances tend to be fluid and that defeated states have to be re-admitted to the system in order for it to operate properly.

The third, and most particular, level of causation is the level or historical variables: the forms of government that are prevalent in any particular period, the cultural-ideological atmosphere, the level of technology and, in particular, the level of weaponry and the state of economic development. One finds a stress on this level on the idea that nuclear weapons have outlawed total war in the modern period, making the modern period unique and incomparable in many respects.

Comparison of different historical systems of international relations should, therefore, be a useful method in identifying the influence of each of the above levels of causation in international conflict.

Previous research using historical material in such a broad way is rare. Research on the period since 1815 has been carried out by Singer and Small at Michigan largely as a statistical study of war since that date. Other researchers have occasionally made use of data on European history since the treaty of Westphalia, 1648 (in particular Richard Rosecrance, Michael Haas, and Quincy Wright). But every researcher has used his own methods, so that the resulting studies have hardly been comparable. In addition, hardly any of this research has taken into account pre-modern—by which I mean pre-1618—or non-Western international systems.

The first principle of my own research has been to use as widely varied cases as possible, both in time and space, and secondly, to make as few prior assumptions as possible. Even the concept of a 'system' as a starting point was rejected because it requires prior assumptions about the nature of international relations. In addition, if one looks for international systems historically there are few obvious, self-evident and self-defining 'systems' that emerge. One immediately encounters questions of definitions, i.e. of basic assumptions. So this approach begins instead with the State, defined as a political unit with a territorial base for which the use of organized violence is a viable alternative in its external relations. The idea behind this definition is that what differentiates sovereign states in their interactions is the use of organized violence as a normal, legitimate recourse.

TABLE I: Bilateral Conflicts in Four International Contexts

Context	Number of States	Direct Conflicts		Extraneous Conflicts		Total
		Tensions	Disputes	Coalition	Other*	
Classical World (280-150 B.C.)	29	45	4	0	2	51
India (1347-1526 A.D.)	23	43	1	0	0	44
Europe (1492-1559 A.D.)	34	48	9	8	8	73
Latin America (1810-1914 A.D.)	21	24	40	3	2	69
Total	107	160	54	11	12	237

* Entry of a state not directly involving either it as a demonstration of ideological solidarity with a third state, or because of financial inducements or other extraneous reasons.

194

One piece of research already carried out has surveyed the international conflicts of all states—as defined above—in four different historical and geographical contexts. Table I summarizes the contexts, the number of units in each, and the number of bilateral international conflicts among the units during the period studied.

The four contexts were chosen to represent as wide a variety as possible in time place, culture, and circumstances. The classical case covers the height of Rome-Carthage rivalry, with Hellenistic and non-Hellenistic cultures in conflict. The Indian case represents a period of multi-state Hindu and Moslem conflict, before the establishment of the Moghul Empire. Renaissance Europe covers the rise of the nation-state in a largely bipolar setting and with a strong Christian-Moslem (Ottoman) clash. The Latin American system represents Western states, in a homogeneous setting and peripheral to the central system. Two cases are modern and two pre-modern; one is entirely within the area of Western civilization, one (Europe) is largely so, one (Classical) is about half so, and one is entirely non-Western; three have a basic cultural split, and one does not; two are multipolar; two are 'central' world systems; and two are subordinate regional systems.

The next step was to classify the bilateral conflicts in these four contexts empirically by type. The first basic distinction that seems empirically obvious after looking at these conflicts was that between direct and indirect conflicts.

A direct conflict is a conflict between two states in which there is in fact a substantive issue or tension dividing the two of them. In an indirect conflict two states are brought into conflict by extraneous considerations; one or the other is induced to enter the conflict, or comes into conflict by virtue of alliance with another enemy. In the second case there is no direct issue between the disputants: the conflict is the result of external circumstances.

Direct conflicts we divided into tensions and disputes. Tensions involve a long-range, outstanding conflict between the two parties which is not dependent upon any particular issue; a dispute is connected with a particular issue and would presumably disappear if that issue were settled. In other words, in a dispute the stated issue is really the cause of the conflicts, whereas in a tension there is a more basic state of general apprehension.

It is interesting that in the 237 conflicts in these four different contexts, 214 were direct conflicts. There were relatively few indirect conflicts; even in the European case, with a high incidence of alliances, there were still only 22 per cent indirect conflicts. Nearly all of the bilateral conflicts involved a direct substantive issue between the two sides; they were not brought into conflict by extraneous forces. In addition, there was a dominance of tensions over disputes; most of the bilateral conflicts, 160 of 214, were tensions. In other words, they involved a long-term general state of apprehension between the two states, and did not revolve around one particular issue. An exception to this was Latin America; of the 54 disputes, 40 of them were in Latin America, testifying perhaps to the prevalence of minor border disputes in that area.

Not surprisingly, there was a difference between tensions and disputes regarding the incidence of war. Of the 160 tensions 108 resulted in war, while of the 54 disputes only 16 resulted in war.

As further illustration of the approach, we have investigated the question of what conditions seem to promote the emergence of 'foreign-linked factionalism', that is, the presence within a state of a faction that seeks or accepts aid from other states in order to seize power by non-ligitimized means. Obviously the current case of Vietnam furnishes an example of such factionalism, whichever faction one considers legitimate. There is here a link between internal conflict and an external conflict to which the factionalized state is a party.

In the four contexts cited, the incidence of such factionalism in bilateral disputes is surprisingly regular (see Table 2), varying from 19·6 per cent to 30·1 per cent. The regularity of the phenomenon is itself striking and significant. But one can also ask what factors seem to

TABLE 2: Bilateral Conflicts and Foreign-Linked Factionalism in Four Contexts

Contexts	Total bilateral conflicts	Conflicts with factionalism	Conflicts without factionalism	Percent conflicts with factionalism
Classical World (280-150 B.C.)	51	10	41	19.6
India (1347-1526)	44	9	35	20.5
Europe (1492-1559)	73	22	51	30.1
Latin America (1810-1914)	69	16	53	23.2
Total	237	57	180	24.1

196

account for the appearance of factionalism—in other words, to what is it correlated? A number of hypotheses are possible. Perhaps internal factionalism appears more in cases where two states are culturally similar, because it is easier to intervene in a state with a similar culture.

Secondly, perhaps it appears more in cases where the conflict is not isolated but is instead 'fused': that is, the bilateral conflict is in fact not independent but is fused with other conflicts, just as the conflict between East and West Germany is in fact fused with the conflict between the United States and the Soviet Union.

A third hypothesis posits that factionalism would appear more in cases of direct conflict: a fourth, that it would appear more often in conflicts that led to war (presumably in more severe conflicts there would be more incentive to have recourse to such techniques). The fifth hypothesis holds that factionalism would appear more in cases of tension than in dispute; the sixth, that it would appear more when the two states are contiguous, since it is easier to intervene in a neighbouring state.

None of these hypotheses was borne out. All of the hypothesized factors were shown to be unrelated to the incidence of factionalism.[1] There was, however, a connection to another factor: the relative power of the two states. Where the two states were significantly unequal in power, factionalism often appeared in the smaller of the two. There are really no two patterns here. In the first, the question of the relationship to a larger enemy state is a standing issue in the smaller state, and one internal faction is in fact in favour of 'coming to terms' with that enemy state. The debate over whether 'to fight them or join them' is not a surprising development in the case of a smaller state facing a larger enemy.

In the second pattern, the larger state acts without invitation to exploit internal unrest in the smaller state. The reverse case, in which domestic unrest in a smaller state, unrelated.to foreign issues, leads to an invitation for a second state to intervene, simply did not occur. The two outlined patterns—a pre-existing issue group and outside exploitation of domestic unrest—accounted in fact for nearly all the cases of internal factionalism.

This is again testimony in favour of the most basic level of causation, the level of strategic imperatives. Where two states are grossly unequal in power, there is a logical tendency in the smaller state for the appearance of an internal faction urging conciliation of the enemy. There is also a prominent pattern of what might be called 'double factionalism', where the smaller state is located between two larger states and is torn apart by competing factions favouring each. This pattern appeared in all four periods, with eleven cases altogether. Interestingly enough, in nine of these cases the smaller state was

197

eventually dominated or annexed by one of the two larger powers. Obviously the prognosis for a state in such a disadvantageous position is not good.

We can also examine the way in which bilateral conflicts fuse together to form larger systems of interaction. The basic pattern of fusion in all four systems, not surprisingly, is the pattern of common enmity to a third state. We find, in all four historical contexts, numerous instances in which states B and C both find themselves in conflict with state A, and form a formal or informal alliance as a result:

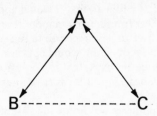

A second basic pattern simply takes the process a step further. If all three states in the preceding triangle are potentially in conflict, the state in the middle may fluctuate between alliance first with one, and then with the other:

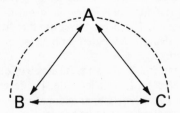

If the state in the middle is large enough it can perform the role of a balancer between the two sides. If the state in the middle is small, the situation resembles that described above in the case of 'double factionalism'.

These simple patterns of conflicts, of course, link together to form much more extended and complicated systems. This is increasingly true as the bilateral conflicts become sharper and previously unrelated conflicts become fused together in much more complex interactions. Consider the case of Europe in the 1492-1559 period which even in very simplified form (see Figure 1) is extremely complicated. Again, such composite systems occur more often in periods of sharp conflict

198

when states reach out to the periphery for allies.

FIGURE 1: Europe, 1492-1559

Composite constellation, 1494-1559: (a) Fluctuation tension triangle,
France-Habsburgs-Papacy, Papacy fluctuating between French and
Habsburg alliances; (b) Coincident tensions, Habsburgs, Papacy, and
Venice against the Ottoman Empire, (link to (a): French-Ottoman
alliance); (c) Fluctuating tension triangle, Habsburgs-Papacy-Venice,
Venice and Papacy fluctuating because of conflicting tensions (link to
constellation: Venetian and Papal alliances with France); (d) Coincident
tensions, Florence and France against Milan (link to constellation:
Milan-Habsburg alliance); (e) Local nuisance triangle, France mobiliz-
ing Scotland against England (link to constellation: English-Habsburg
alliance).

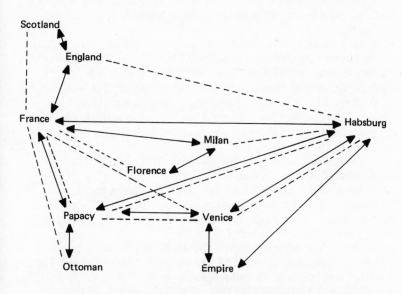

There were eight such extended composite systems, resembling what
is normally meant in discussions of 'international systems', in the survey
described. However, these systems violate some very basic ideas about
how such systems are supposed to function. In the first case most of
them are entirely explainable in terms of local direct bilateral rivalries
without reference to the system as a whole. The complex interactions,
in other words, derive more from the strategic logic of the situation
than from overall systemic conditions. States do not set out to balance

Europe, nor to accomplish any goal based on considerations of the system as a whole, but largely (in the cases surveyed) act on the basis of immediate local rivalries (though the objective and result may be to balance the system as a whole).

In the systems studied, furthermore, there are no clear patterns of behaviour associated with bipolar or multipolar systems. Common wisdom says that a bipolar system is characterized by two rigid alliance systems, while a multipolar system, by necessity, is characterized by fluid alliances. Of the eight systems in the study, two were largely 'bipolar', but both were characterized by shifting alliances. Of the five 'multipolar' systems, all were characterized by either no alliance systems, or rigid alliance systems (the eighth system was not clearly bipolar or multipolar). This again is evidence against the notion that the behaviour of nations can be studied through the structure of the overall system. The structure of the system does not seem to explain very much, at least regarding the nature of alliances in the system, and again provides testimony in favour of the dominance of direct local conflicts.

Future research will hopefully cast more light on questions such as these. In particular, we hope to study the conflict profiles of selected states over time, rather than using conflicts as the basic unit of analysis, and to pay more attention to methods of conflict resolution. In the latter case, it might be interesting to compare conflicts with violent outcomes to those with a non-violent outcome. It should also be possible to include modern cases in order to identify unique elements of the modern system.

Let us summarize very briefly the conclusions of the research reported very sketchily above.

In the first place, the overall structure of the system seems to account for very little in the conflict behaviour of states. There is no connection, for example, between the structure of the system and the types of alliances within it.

Secondly, the interplay of direct bilateral rivalries seems to account for most of the conflict patterns (alliances etc.) in these systems. This is evidence in favour of the influence of basic strategic imperatives. Incidentally, it might be noted that of the 237 conflicts, all but 46 were either between neighbouring states or between a great power expanding overseas and a small state resisting this expansion.

Thirdly, one interesting pattern of international conflict is a small state situated between two powers. This typically leads to internal splits within the smaller state and eventually loss of independence.

Finally, let us summarize what is unique to this approach: First, this is an empirical comparison over a broad domain of space and time. Secondly, we are looking for basic patterns of conflicts common to all international systems, employing as few prior assumptions as possible. Finally, we hope to compare conflicts with non-violent resolutions to those culminating in violence. (Most previous research has been directed to violent conflicts alone.)

NOTE

1. For further information on this and other research reported in this article see Alan Dowty, 'Conflict and War-Potential Politics: An Approach to Historical Macroanalysis'. **Peace Research Society (International) Papers,** XIII (1970) (The Copenhagen Conference, 1969), 85-103; and Alan Dowty, 'Foreign-Linked Factionalism as a Historical Pattern', **Journal of Conflict Resolution,** XV (1971), 429-42.

19. ARMAMENTS AND DEVELOPMENT

Peter Kodzic

In approaching the problem of arms control and disarmament in the
Third World, I shall concentrate on two different aspects. First, I shall
consider the properties of the structure and dynamics of a conflict
relationship involving armaments, and a subsequent decision-maker's
security dilemma. This discussion will challenge a common contention
that armaments intensify international tension and heighten the
probability of war in the Third World. Moreover, it will raise the
question of the feasibility of autonomous and genuine arms control
arrangements in particular regions. Secondly, I shall reflect on the
armament-versus-development controversy. This controversy appears
particularly relevant to the Third World and many attempts to resolve
it have appeared to strengthen the argument about curbing arms races
in those areas. In effect, I will be discussing here the burden of military
expenditure on a national economy. This discussion will throw doubt
on a commonly-made assertion, that the developing countries spend
much on their military programmes relative to their scarce available
resources and the immediate and urgent needs of their economic
development. In that connection, I shall refer briefly to the results of a
recent study by Emile Benoit and his associates, on the effects of
defence on growth in less developed countries.

My objective is to draw a more critical approach to the problem
of arms and arms control in the Third World and to suggest appropriate
frames of reference for guiding evaluations and judgments.

Turning now to the logic of an armaments race, let us consider
disarmament and armament as two decisional alternatives out of a
whole range of possible bilateral defence policies in the context of an
international conflict. We can assume that if both countries are armed,
a certain 'balance of power' obtains; that is, each country has
reasonable assurance that the other will not attack it. On the other
hand, if both countries are disarmed, each is likewise secure from
attack by the other. Given that the degree of safety is equal in both
situations, if we take into account the economic cost of arming, the
bilaterally-disarmed state is preferable to the bilaterally-armed state.
Unilateral disarmament, however, is highly disadvantageous to the
disarmed country while highly advantageous to the country that has
remained armed, (or, has unilaterally rearmed while the other has
remained disarmed).

The relationship reads as follows:

COUNTRY B:

		disarmament policy /1/	armament policy /2/	
	disarmament policy /1/	a_{11},b_{11}	a_{12},b_{12}	=outcomes determined by the policies applied, and the associated pay-offs to A and B, respectively.
COUNTRY A:	armament policy /2/	a_{21},b_{21}	a_{22},b_{22}	

with Country A's order of preferences given as

$$a_{21} \quad a_{11} \quad a_{22} \quad a_{12}$$

with Country B's order of preferences given as

$$b_{12} \quad b_{11} \quad b_{22} \quad b_{21}$$

Evidently, the armament policy assures each country a larger pay-off than the disarmament policy, whatever policy the other country applies. That is, if B arms, A is better off arming too, since it matches B's power. However, if B disarms, A is better off arming, since it is the only armed one and controls the situation. Likewise, if the roles are inverted.

If each country selects its best policy, namely armament, the bilaterally armed condition obtains; whereas the more preferred condition, the bilaterally disarmed state, would have obtained had each country adopted its worst policy namely the disarmament policy.

If the two countries agree to reciprocate each other's disarmament policy, an analogous analysis would apply, and sustain the argument that it is to the advantage of each country to break the agreement, regardless of whether the other country keeps it, so long, of course, as the agreement is not indiscriminately enforceable by a third party.

In such a sequence of bilateral armament moves, there arises further a problem of interpretation concerning the jointly-experienced armaments race. That is, any Country A's present armament to a higher level (a_i) may be considered a stimulus for Country B's subsequent armament to a higher level (b_i), and, simultaneously, a response to Country B's armament to the present level (b_{j-1}) which preceded it. Also, (a_j) will reinforce B's primary perception of A's previous behaviour (a_{j-1}) as accurate, and of its intermediate reaction to it, (b_{j-1}), as valid. In other words, in terms of the cause-and-effect considerations of such an on-going relationship, the armament of one country appears predicated on the armament of the other country.

communicational events
   — sequence   ...... a_{13} b_{13} a_{14} b_{14} ......

stimulus — response —
  — reinforcement
interpretation   S   R   Rf
              S   R   Rf
                   S   R   Rf
                        S   R   Rf
                             S   R   Rf

Here, each country may impose a different interpretation on the sequence of reciprocating increases in armaments. That is, what A considers its response to B's earlier stimulus, B considers a reinforcement of its previous interpretation of A's intentions and also a further stimulus to its next response, and thus, what B considers now its response to A's new stimulus and so on. Hence, one country ignores the other's interpretation while believing its own, and accordingly justifies its own position while criticizing the other other's. For example, Country A may arm to protect itself against a threat by Country B, a third country, or internal factions, whether the threat is real or imaginery. However, Country B considers this a threat, and consequently arms, justifying this move as a defensive measure necessitated by Country A's threatening armament. Country A now has further 'proof' of Country B's 'aggressive' design, and therefore, 'must' continue arming.

It is implied here that the other country's intentions are suspected, or — possibly mistakenly — equated with its capabilities. Consequently, each side undertakes defensive measures which are misperceived by the other as aggressively motivated. The hostile image of the other becomes further reinforced by a benevolent image of the self, while conversely, the belief that one's own country is peaceful is preserved by the thought that one's own armament is only a defensive reaction to the other's threat. There is inherent in the nature of this problem a self-fulfilling prophecy on the adversary's armament to an ever higher level.

The reaction pattern may be: one side heating up the military competition while the other merely follows, or the two alternating this behaviour. An inferior B may react proportionately to A's increase in capacity, whereby a given disparity remains unchanged; or over-proportionately, going for disparity reduction, while aiming at balancing A's military potential, or trying to outrun A in order to convert the whole asymmetry to its own favour.

The analysis thus far has suggested the objective and subjective difficulties implicit in the structure and dynamics of a conflict relationship involving armaments. And yet it cannot be logically inferred, nor has there been any clear empirical evidence, that armament as such, or armament races, necessarily lead to war. On the contrary, one could think of the possibility of war being avoided due to the efficient deterrence postures of the antagonists. Neither could the assumption that higher-level armaments make a war more disastrous once it breaks out be taken as necessarily valid, as the war may — precisely for that reason or another — be limited in scope and means.

Therefore, is arms control and disarmament really the issue? The issue in conflict is in fact the underlying rationale of any possession of arms and any arms race, as well as of any preventive strike against the adversary's developing and/or deployed military force, which is perceived as menacing. Also, this issue underlies any general attack prompted by a belief that one has reached a capability level that increases one's chances of victory in war, while anticipating that a future situation will not be as favourable; in turn, it underlies any pre-emptive attack launched by the other side. That is, I am suggesting that arms are a consequence of conflict and also a mere symptom of serious and unresolved differences. Moreover, as long as there are any reasons for such a conflict, it is likely that armaments will continue because the parties might wish, or feel compelled, to resort to military means. The threat is rightly inferred from both the evidence of capability and evidence of intent. Nevertheless, a reservation seems necessary: there may be instances where armament precedes conflict, in the sense that capability sometimes gives rise to new motivations and encourages arrogant behaviour. Hence a threat may be inferred only from the evidence of the capabilities of a suspected future adversary. Evidently, this strengthens the tendency to 'worst-case' thinking of national defence planners.

I wish now to complement the previous military policy alternatives by postulating some basic economic policy choices in the relations between two countries. Consider that, through time, each country has, and acquires, a certain amount of resources which it subsequently apportions between two sectors, the economic development sector and the military sector. Each country adopts a policy in either the economic development sector − co-operative or competitive policy − or the military sector − disarmament or armament policy − or both, and invests into that policy a portion of the resources allocated to the corresponding sector(s). The stakes are then determined by the amount of resources that have been allocated, while the outcomes depend on the policies pursued. The different levels of technology in each case might be accounted for by coefficients by which the resources allocated would be multiplied in the calculation of the pay-offs; and, of course, the model could be complicated further.

Economic Development Sector:

COUNTRY B:

	co-operative policy /1/	competitive policy /2/	
COUNTRY A: co-operative policy /1/	a_{11}, b_{11}	a_{12}, b_{12}	=outcomes and associated pay offs
competitive policy /2/	a_{21}, b_{21}	a_{22}, b_{22}	

Military Sector:

COUNTRY B:

	disarmament policy /1/	armament policy /2/	
COUNTRY A: disarmament policy /1/	a_{11}, b_{11}	a_{12}, b_{12}	=outcomes and associated payoffs
armament policy /2/	a_{21}, b_{21}	a_{22}, b_{22}	

The problem here is that the economic development sector and the military sector should be regarded as functionally interrelated. For instance, the efficient preservation of external security, as well as of internal order, is a prerequisite for the development of a country and a safeguard of its achievements. In our example, losing the game in the military sector may mean losing the game in the development sector altogether. Also, a country progressing at a high rate of development may possibly have larger capacities to build up its military force in the long run and thus better prospects of winning the game in the military sector.

A distinction applies, of course, between the necessary expenditures for providing the conditions of external security and internal order by military means, and the excessive costs, unnecessary for that purpose and supposedly avoidable, which may be, on the face of it at least, considered a real burden on an economy. In any case, it is a simplification to consider a military programme for preserving security and order only, while not taking into account possible aggressive projects which, as such, might be positively correlated with, and stimulating to national economic and political development.

And now, a few points about estimating what is a necessary level of arms expenditure, and about evaluating a given level of national 'defence' budget and the cost of it.

In the first place, a military budget is a base component of a military programme. The expenditure as such should be defined and evaluated in terms of its purpose, that is whether or not the allocated resources would be, or have proved to be, sufficient to enable the required realization of the military programme. This may be an efficient threat or deterrent, or may be successful in defensive or aggressive war.

Secondly, military expenditure, as against civilian investments or expenditures in other public sectors like health and education, merely means the less money allocated to the military cause, the more money could be allocated for other civilian activities (and inversely, of course). Evidently, this is a question of national priorities, where the agenda has to be, or has been, elaborated in terms of the specific and immediate needs of the estimated urgency to act. And it is conceivable that military objectives may be given an absolute priority, and not only in the sense of necessary defence.

And thirdly, the question ultimately rests with national decision-making at a relevant point in time, while taking into account the possibilities that the authority to decide effectively may also be non-rational in terms of misperceptions and miscalculations, or corruption. In particular, one should think of the possibly important influence of the military in national decision making. There are cases where a certain annual military budget is approved as a concession to the military. Some governments even decide on military operations to keep the army busy in order to preclude its intervention in domestic politics.

This means that to infer any objective criteria about what level of national military expenditure is really needed, would be largely irrelevant, except in terms of a political argument. The whole reasoning about military purpose and the contingencies of the moment, the priority assigned to the programme relative to other national needs and the resources that are available, would be likely to break down along complex structures and procedures of national decision-making. However, how a given level of national military expenditure was determined, could be subject to research.

Finally, a comment about the real economic cost of a military programme in the sense that a diversion of resources from civilian uses for military purposes precludes or retards the economic development of a country. This is evidently different from the registered nominal price of a military programme. Here, an opportunity-cost analysis applies, that is stating the cost of a given military programme in terms of an estimate of profits deriving from a hypothesized, alternative, realistic civilian investment thereby foregone.

In this connection, it is appropriate to refer to a recent study by Benoit and his associates of the effects of defence spending on the economic growth in developing countries.[1] This, so far the only and major research on the problem, may be of particular interest for some of its main conclusions; namely that defence burdens are positively correlated with civilian growth rates.[2] Hence, the implications that defence programmes tend to raise growth rates and that the favourable effects of defence expenditure on growth more than compensate for the unfavourable ones. I restrict myself here to a mere summary of that report.

The study has considered both adverse as well as positive effects of defence on economic growth, and attempted to assess the net balance between them.

As *adverse effects* there are:

'Income shift effect': when a rise in defence burdens reduces the part of total GDP that is the civilian sector and hence the apparent growth of that sector.

'Productivity effect': when more of the total product is shifted to government services which show negligible rates of productivity increase.

'Investment effect': when a rise in defence burdens absorbs resources that otherwise might have gone into civilian investment and contributed to civilian growth.

Diversion of funds from current expenditure on education,

208

health, etc...not directly included in the 'investment effect' category.

Use of vigorous manpower in defence precludes its engagement in certain civilian activities where – even in situations where unemployment and underemployment, especially in agriculture, are prevalent – its marginal productivity is considerable in seasons of peak demand; while, furthermore, the amounts invested in the transportation, subsistence and training of one soldier would usually suffice to provide general education and industrial training for a civilian.

Again, shifting governmental attention and emphasis from economic to military problems as defence programmes become relatively more important.

And, an increased danger of a takeover of political power by the army as the military becomes a relatively larger part of the governmental apparatus.

As to *positive effects,* in the first place, defence programmes provide security against external attack and help to maintain internal order and political atability, which are prerequisites for any economic progress at all. Furthermore, they possibly help to strengthen national unity and co-operation and mobilize additional energies and motivations with beneficial effects for civilian growth.

Secondly, defence programmes often provide close substitutes for civilian goods and services. Some of these are infrastructure which may be shared with civilian users. Military training for the forces, besides providing general education, gives them specific skills later utilisable in civilian jobs, as well as possibly bringing about attitudinal changes and higher productivity favourable to development. Military personnel also engage in scientific and technical specialities which are of use to the civilian economy and perform certain quasi-civilian activities which would otherwise have to be undertaken by civilians. And sometimes, the army engages in 'self-help' production projects in which the pooling of defence and civilian demand makes it possible to achieve significant economies of scale.

It appears, further, that defence programmes may in some cases stimulate economic growth through their aggregate demand and the consequent upward pressure on prices, liberalisation of monetary-fiscal policy and rise in the money supply, as well as a fuller utilisation of available resources.

And next, in cases of strategically situated countries, willingness to co-operate militarily by maintaining a larger-than-normal defence programme, or larger than could otherwise be afforded, may attract additional foreign economic aid, and thereby accelerate growth of the civilian sector. That is, potential donors, perceiving that their

209

own interests would be advanced by those countries being relatively strong militarily, may offer them sufficient aid to facilitate their maintaining large defence programmes while making sufficient economic progress to maintain high morale and internal political stability.

Because of the difficulty in measuring the particular influences of defence programmes directly, the Benoit study was based upon the statistical analysis of the relations between the defence burden and the civilian growth rate. The underlying assumption was that if heavy defence burdens are inversely (positively) correlated with growth rates (that is high defence burdens reliably accompanied by lower (higher) growth rates) and if other explanations of the correlation can be eliminated, then this would imply that large defence programmes tend to reduce (raise) growth rates, in which case there may be some presumption that unfavourable (favourable) effects of defence on growth exceed the favourable (unfavourable) effects.

With regard to Benoit's finding the defence expenditures might have a positive effect on economic growth, we must remember that the correct measure of the unfavourable effects of a given defence programme on growth is not the optimum alternative use of resources for growth, but their likely actual alternative use. And it is evident that a reduction in a developing country's defence programme would not readily or quickly translate into an equivalent rise in the civilian investment programme, as most of the resouces released in the event of defence cuts would not be of those types required to expand the investment programme – particularly the most efficient and productive sectors of it.

Finally, Benoit draws attention to the composition of defence programmes, which may be as important as the size of those programmes in determining the nature and magnitude of their impact on economic growth. In this regard, some structures and items absorb financial and physical resources which are particularly relevant to development and thereby severely restrict growth, while others make a significant contribution to the productivity of the civilian sector. By implication, we can assume that the introduction of standards of economic efficiency and cost-benefit analysis into defence planning might lead to substantial economic benefits, often with positive improvements in security as well.

It has not been my intention to engage in a critical examination and evaluation of Benoit's method and analysis. At the least, however, what this suggests is that simple and easy assertions about the effects of military spending on the economic development in the Third World should be discouraged. We need closer study, better observation and more understanding before we can make accurate and useful generalisations in this field.

NOTES

1. Emile Benoit 'Growth Effects of Defence in Developing Countries', **International Development Review**, XIV (1972), 2-10, reporting on the original study, Emile Benoit with Max F. Millikan and Everett E. Hagen, **Effect of Defence on Developing Economies,** Center for International Studies, Massachusetts Institute of Technology, January 1972, Publication No. C/71-6a).

2. Defence burden is expressed by the average annual defence expenditure as a percentage of gross domestic product, and the civilian growth rate is the compounded rate of growth in 'civilian gross domestic product', i.e. total GDP minus defence expenditure.

20. ARMS CONTROL AND DEVELOPING COUNTRIES
William Gutteridge

The real question for developing countries is not so much the possibility of disarmament or arms control in the conventional sense, but the level of armaments consonant with their defence requirements and their overall economic position. Arms races between developing countries are not common and where they occur are usually the direct product of specific political tensions: arms restraint is important to them for social and economic reasons. It may properly be asked why states have regular armed forces at all — in other words, are armed forces essential to the viability of a new state? This cannot be answered in strictly military terms. Essential needs for frontier control and internal security could well be met by armed, mobile police units, but the fact is that in Africa, for example, only the Gambia, Lesotho, Swaziland and Botswana have decided to dispense altogether with regular defences forces. In each of these cases there were specific local reasons contributing to the decision.

In almost all other countries in the world — Costa Rica is one exception — special circumstances have, however, been used to justify the opposite conclusion. Some countries, such as India, have felt themselves to be heirs to a strategic responsibility for the security of an area from which a major imperial power has withdrawn. Others such as Kenya and Somalia have found themselves involved in tension, itself largely a legacy of colonial rule. Many other countries have come by one route or another to the view that efficient security forces are a prerequisite for stability in that they provide a framework of order in which a stable social and political system can evolve. The disintegration of the *Force Publique* in the Congo in 1960 and the consequent chaos was an important illustration of the validity of this argument. In some senses new states in Africa and Asia are faced with the kind of political and religious tensions experienced acutely by Europe in earlier centuries. Generally the advantages of the armed forces in helping to encourage nation-building and consolidation are seen as off-setting their inclination (realized in many countries) to become a political force in their own right. Leaders like Julius Nyerere in Tanzania and one or two in Sierra Leone have been with reluctance persuaded to accept armed forces on the grounds that they help to consolidate a nation's prestige and may enable it, as in the U N force in Congo, to contribute to the solution of international problems. The recurrent decision of the OAU to take all means possible to eliminate 'colonialism' in Southern Africa may conceivably lead African states, for example, to expand their armed forces.

There is no doubt, however, that military defence expenditure bears particularly heavily on developing countries and that, therefore, they should in their own interest have a particular commitment to arms control and restraint. Little of such expenditure feeds back to stimulate a less well developed economy. In absolute terms a defence expenditure of three or four pounds per capita is likely to be much more significant in a developing country than thirty or forty pounds per capita in an advanced industrial country even though the proportion of the GNP spent for this purpose may appear to be comparable. In addition, the acquisition of sophisticated military equipment involves a disproportionate drain on the limited resources of technically trained manpower which are likely to be available. Even if the relevant equipment is a gift this will apply, because the stimulation of local training in technical skills will still be minimal and involve an overall loss of manpower. There is, therefore, a strong case for developing countries—and indeed for all countries—confining their military forces and equipments to the minimum for the maintenance of law and order and the integrity of the state. The question is how to ascertain the desirable level, given the particular political interests and national requirements of each country. It should be clear that this level cannot be effectively prescribed by, for example, the major developed powers through a boycott on transfers of sophisticated equipment to developing countries. Only a gradually evolved and widely accepted set of conventions for interstate political behaviour can in the end be effective, whereby each country will make its own reasonable assessment of its defence needs in relation to clearly identifiable functions, for which it necessarily requires armed forces. Such conventions as that in the OAU Charter related to the non-utility of military measures for the solution of boundary problems inherited from the colonial period will be increasingly important in this respect, and this example may account for the relatively low level of military rivalry between African states.

The evident natural vested interest of developing countries in disarmament and arms control must be seen in the context of the military superiority of the major powers. Though the Afro-Asian non-aligned states, for example, normally support arms control and disarmament resolutions in the UN General Assembly, they sometimes do not do so partly because they may see the whole question as largely one for the superpowers, or to display their concern over unrelated issues coincidentally under discussion, or out of regard for their own particular national interest as when, Zambia wanted a guarantee of her security against Rhodesia and South Africa in the Non-Proliferation Treaty.

In short, the developing countries are concerned to limit the level of armed forces ultimately in their own economic interest. Their military needs are, however, at a very low level compared with the major powers who are, therefore, in no moral position to impose standards on others. The current evidence is that developing countries, for example in Africa, in many cases display a realistic appreciation of minimum defence needs which by the standards of developed countries appears more than reasonable, but however small their military establishments they are still exposed to the risk of military intervention in politics.

21. INTERNATIONAL GUARANTEES WITH SPECIAL REFERENCE TO THE MIDDLE EAST

Alan Dowty

Introduction

One problem in any settlement of the Arab-Israeli conflict is the low credibility of signed undertakings. Various schemes have been proffered to make agreements as self-enforcing as possible, but any settlement still assumes a minimal amount of good faith and trust that simply do not exist. On the Israeli-Egypt front this problem is critical because the weight of credibility is chiefly on one side; most posited settlements call for Israeli withdrawal from some or all of the territories accupied in 1967, in return for Egyptian acceptance of the pre-1967 situation — which was previously deemed unsatisfactory.

There seems to be little an Egyptian government can do to break this 'circle of mutual disbelief', assuming its good faith. There appear no obvious ways of including, in a bilateral treaty, ironclad safeguards which bind Egypt so convincingly that Israeli can ignore the strategic-geographic dimension; the problem of the unenforceability of the promise would remain. Neither side could bind itself as it might like to, against future contingencies, such as changes in government, changes of circumstances and unpredicted crises, over which it has no control, even under the most sanguine assumptions of good will. As Thomas Schelling has pointed out, along the same lines, 'enforcible promises cannot be taken for granted...even if both sides should desperately desire to reach an enforcible agreement or find a persuasive means of enforecement'.[1]

Among states in the modern period one principal means of enforcing promises has been the injection of an outside party who guarantees one ot both sides in order to add a measure of credibility that the disputants by themselves could not achieve. In Vattel's classic formulation; 'Taught by sad experience that the sacred and inviolable duty of fidelity to treaties is not always a safe assurance that they will be observed, men have sought to obtain securities against perfidy, means for enforcing observance independently of the good faith of the contracting parties. A *guaranty* is one of these means.'[2]

Guarantees are, obviously, not a substitute for a satisfactory peace agreement, but rather a means of bolstering such an agreement by adding assurance that its terms will be respected. It is clear that outside guarantees cannot bridge the gap between irreconcilable positions. It should not, however, be beyond human ingenuity to devise improvements on the 1957-67 model. In the sections that follow, the types of guarantees that have been operative in the recent past will be examined, and an attempt will be made to determine the factors that have governed their effectiveness. The conclusions will then be applied to proposals for guarantees as part of a settlement of the Egypt-Israel conflict.

Patterns of Guarantees

Most modern definitions of guarantees have identified three basic elements: (1) help is to be given by a stronger power to a weak state unable to stand alone; (2) a specified purpose or object is to be covered; and (3) specified means, including usually force if necessary, are employed.[3] It should be stressed that in studying the *act* of guarantee (rather than only formal treaties of guarantees) we are in fact studying the act of protection of a smaller state, a much more central phenomenon of international politics than the word 'guarantee' would suggest. In addition, guarantee may cover the terms of a specific treaty to which the guaranteed state is a party, or its form of government, or a particular dynasty or regime, or its neutrality, or (as in most modern cases) simply its independence and territorial integrity.

The phenomenon that we are studying might be defined, therefore, as the acceptance of an obligation by a state to protect, by force unless otherwise specified, another and weaker state in its independence, territorial integrity, or other specified attributes. It follows from this that we are concerned primarily with the actions of great powers, and that we are not limited to formal treaties of guarantee nor to the corollary distinctions that have concerned students of international law (the principal writers on guarantees to date).

A survey of international guarantees since 1815, as part of a general study of the subject, reveals at least 115 acts of guarantee by this definition, covering at least 219 guaranteed states.[4]Included in this count are guarantees in the form of declarations, actions, general treaties, and unequal treaties of alliance as well as outright treaties of guarantee. Excluded by definition are guarantees of 'great powers' by other 'great powers' (rare in any case); mutual 'guarantees' among minor powers; formal universal guarantees such as those embodied in the League Covenant, the Geneva Protocol of 1924 or the U N Charter; declarations of abstention which call on signatories to 'respect the integrity' of a state but not to guarantee it (such as the Laos Declaration of 1962); and general doctrines of guarantee (Holy Alliance; Monroe, Truman, or Eisenhower Doctrines) which become real only as applied. As a consequence of the focus on the actual relations behind each guarantee, rather than its legal form, a guarantee was considered multilateral only if based on true unity of the guarantors, otherwise it was analysed in terms of the underlying rivalry and essentially unilateral protection which gave it force, even

216

if formalised as a general treaty.

The effectiveness of a guarantee was judged on two counts: does the guarantor make a reasonable effort to meet this obligation, and are his means sufficient to the task?[5] These can be referred to as the tests of *reliability* and *adequacy*; to be effective, a guarantee must be executed reliably and with adequate power. Many guarantees were of course not tested during their period of operation, and thus judgment of effectiveness could not be made. It may of course be argued that such guarantees were effective as deterrents, but this is in most cases unprovable.

In brief summary, the 115 guarantees since 1815 fall into two major patterns, unilateral and multilateral, with unilateral guarantees classifiable into five sub-patterns. The effectiveness of guarantees varied greatly from pattern to pattern:

A. Unilateral Guarantees

1. Protected buffer or zone. The guarantor protects adjacent territory without dominating it, either because of intrinsic interest in the territory (the Soviet guarantee of Finland since 1948) or because of this reason combined with fear of a rival's expansion (French 'alliance' with Belgium, 1919-1938). The latter cases (buffers) numbered sixteen, of which only two were effective, largely because of insufficient power. The former cases (zones) numbered nine, of which seven were effective.

2. Classic containment. The guarantor protects distant territory, of little or no intrinsic interest, without dominating it, because of fear of a rival. British guarantees against Russia in the nineteenth century, and most American Cold War alliances, fit this pattern. The remoteness of the guarantor, however, undercuts his effectiveness: only five of thirty cases were fully effective.

3. Dominant protection. The guarantor protects his predominant or exclusive position in adjacent or distant territories. This includes dominated buffers (Soviet guarantee of Mongolia), and overseas influence in both its colonial and post-colonial (e.g. French-Chad) forms. Thirty-five cases, twenty-four of them judged effective.

4. True buffers. Two powers simultaneously protect an intervening territory which neither wants the other to dominate. Such cases proved infrequent, since either true balance did not exist, or rapprochement between the guarantors led to an agreement to divide the territory. In some cases — such as the British-French guarantee of Siam after 1896 — the buffer divides colonial territory, and in others (Belgium before the

217

First World War being the classic example) a third and more 'neutral' guarantor (Great Britain) attempts to prevent imblance. Of the eleven cases, only one was judged effective.

5. Benevolent guarantees. The guarantor acts out of good will, sentiment, ideology, a desire for order, bargaining for a *quid pro quo,* or some motive other than containment of a rival or intrinsic interest. French support of Papal Rome against Italian annexation (1850-1870) is an example. Only four cases were observed, none of them effective.

B. Multilateral Guarantees

6. Aside from those essentially unilateral guarantees (e.g. Belgium and Locarno) which are multilateral in form, there are a relative handful (seven of 115) of guarantees which are truly multilateral in the sense that they transcend particular interests or rivalries, being based on the unity, at least temporarily, of all or nearly all of the great powers involved. Five of these cases derive from the 'Concert of Europe' period when there was a greater degree of great power consensus, which makes their relevance today doubtful, and in any event all of them proved very sensitive to disruptions of great power unity. The two modern cases (Tripartite Declaration of 1950; Congo, 1960-1964) proved no more durable. The entrance of Soviet power into the Middle East soon undercut the guarantors' monopoly of power in the first case, and the guarantee quickly became moribund. The multilateral guarantee of the Congo by direct action, in 1960-1964, was temporarily effective despite oppisition by the Soviet Union and other states in its latter phases, and it was truly multilateral in that a policy transcending the particular interests of any participating states was formulated and executed towards the foreign and domestic threats to the central Congolese government. This one 'success' (of seven cases) might be tempting as a model, were it not for the atypical conditions that made it possible. The Congolese case will be further discussed below.

The general conclusions drawn from this survey can be summarised as follows:

1. Only 39 per cent of the guarantees surveyed (44 of 115) were clearly both reliable and adequate throughout the period in which they were operative, despite the fact that all but a few of them were motivated by great power rivalries or interests in specific territories.

2. The form of the guarantee, whether treaty, unilateral declaration of policy, or simply implicit in steps taken, has nothing to do with effectiveness.[6]

3. Where guarantees were effective they were usually linked to a

power's protection of its own predominant or exclusive position, or to protection of adjacent areas of great strategic interests. (Nearly three-quarters of the effective guarantees can be so described, although such situations constitute only 38 per cent of all guarantees).7

4. As a result of the above, the relationship between the protector and the protected and the terms under which protection is accepted are key dimensions of any guarantee. A less powerful or more distant guarantor is less threatening to the guaranteed state, but may be inadequate to the task at hand; the difficulty in balancing the two considerations is the reason why theoreticians give different accounts of the typical strategy of a small state faced by a great power threat.8

5. All international guarantees are very sensitive to changes in the international order, and first of all to changes in alignments among the great powers, since great power rivalries are the chief dynamic of guarantees and great power accords one of the prime mechanisms. Changes in relative power may also doom a once-effective guarantee, as can be seen in the history of most buffer states. Another reason for the temporary nature of guarantees is change of government, which was at least a contributing cause to the failure of many guarantees.9

6. Multilateral guarantees based on unified great power steward-ship have practically disappeared from the international scene, testifying to the decline in great power consensus. Guarantees have appeared increasingly as unilateral ties to one great power (or bloc), typically as an alliance or defence pact.

7. Guarantees have appeared increasingly in some guise other than that of guarantees, and have become increasingly less specific and more ambiguous. This is not to say, however, that they became less effective; statistically the alliance-oriented guarantees since 1945, despite greater ambiguity, are somewhat more dependable than earlier guarantees.10

8. The changed scale of world politics has practically eliminated local buffers; the reach of the superpowers is such that guarantees come primarily from one or the other, and not from their mutual cancellation. Even states bordering a great power can sometimes be effectively guaranteed by the distant rival (consider Cuba or South Korea). A country seeking a meaningful guarantee must choose sides, must be either for or against its great power neighbour; there are no protected neutrals (save perhaps Finland) in the contemporary world.

9. The greater rigidity of world politics today also mean that the great powers assume no additional risks in attacking a small state; there are no 'balancing' states or blocs to add their might in

defence of a threatened guarantee. On the other hand it also means that fewer guarantees will be undercut by rapprochement between mutually checking guarantors or by the break-up of a guaranteeing coalition.

Special Problems of Middle Eastern Guarantees

Special attention should be paid to conclusions regarding particular guarantee problems relevant to the Arab-Israel conflict. These include guarantees against local threats rather than against other great powers, guarantees of both sides to a conflict, and the stationing of outside forces in areas of conflict in order to back up guarantees.

In the first case, great powers have typically guaranteed states against other great powers, rather than against local rivals of the guaranteed state, with whom the guarantor may have no quarrel. However effective the great powers may be checking each other, they are considerably less dependable as a source of protection against local threats. Insofar as the guarantor's main motive is simply keeping the protected state from being added to the power base of another great power, conquest of the state by another local power may be not only tolerated but even welcomed by the presumed protector.[11]

A solid base of emnity, it must be remembered, underlies most successful guarantees; rapprochement between guarantor and threatener is often fatal to the state being protected. Where a great power guarantor enjoys, or hopes to enjoy, good relations with its ward's local rival, its protection is likely to be untrustworthy. Fear of disrupting American relations with Arab states was obviously a factor in the American decision in 1967 not to force open the Straits of Tiran to Israeli ships (after the United States had promised in 1957 to 'exercise the right of free and innocent passage and to join with others to secure general recognition of this right').

Some of the cases of great powers acting in concert involve a guarantee of a state against local threats, as in, to some extent, the UN Congo operation. Such stewardship can be effective so long as the powers remain united, but as in all cases of genuine multilateral guarantees this unity is generally fragile and with its collapse the guarantee is worthless.

Guarantees against local threats seem to be effective only under special conditions. First of all, the local threatener may be a proxy, in the mind of the guarantor, for a great power rival who must be contained; American 'containment' of North Korea in 1950 can only be explained with reference to the Soviet Union and China. Secondly, a threat, though local, may nevertheless be viewed by a great power as a genuine challenge to its own position, as in the case of American opposition to Nasserist influence in the Lebanon. Finally, great powers protecting a predominant or exclusive position in protectorates or former colonies will of course usually act against any threat, including local enemies, as Britain did in 1961 by defending Kuwait against the Iraqi threat of annexation (though Britain, a formal ally, did not come to the aid of either Egypt or Jordan in their wars with Israel).

The difficulties of guaranteeing against local powers, with whom the guarantor may desire good relations, is compounded in the case of guarantees of both parties to a local conflict. The great powers may have the motivation to act against one of the two rivals; it is unlikely that it will be equally willing to act against either. This was one of the fatal weaknesses of the Tripartite Declaration of 1950 guaranteeing arms balance and boundaries in the Middle East: not only did it assume unity among the three powers (Great Britain, France and the United States), essential control by them of the situation (quickly challenged by the Soviet Union), and intervention by them in local conflicts in which they had no direct interest, but it also made the unrealistic assumption of willingness to use force against both sides, The result of such an 'impartial' posture is usually, of course, the use of force against neither, as the experience of the British as guarantors of the Cypriot constitution of 1960 against both Greek and Turks bears out. Even guarantors enjoying a predominant influence with both guaranteed disputants may be ineffective, as are the French in conflicts among their African 'allies'.

The deployment of forces on the guaranteed territory, as an earnest of commitment in a guarantee, is a device used increasingly in recent times, though it was of course employed as a means of raising 'credibility' long before the concept of 'trip-wire' troops was invented to describe the role of American forces in countries around the Soviet periphery. Such force deployment in *unilateral* guarantees are generally associated with effective guarantees or at least with the effective periods of such guarantees.

Deployment of forces cannot, however, make workable an essentially unworkable guarantee, as the Cypriot case demonstrates. Though all three guarantors were to deploy forces in support of the 1960 constitution, the Greek and Turkish contingents could at best stalemate one another, while the British sought to transform their presence into a neutral 'international' force with more limited aims and for which they bore less responsibility.*

Force deployment of a *multilateral* nature has, to be sure, a different set of problems. The UN force in Cyprus, established in 1964, though then composed predominantly of British and Canadian troops, was a true 'international' force in that it presented a generalized

*Written before the Turkish invasion of Cyprus, July 1974.

consensus rather than the policies or interests of particular states, but it was not a guaranteeing force in that its role was limited to 'peace-keeping' in the passive sense of maintaining—largely by its presence rather than by fighting—a tenuous *status quo* established by the course of events. UNEF in the Middle East, 1957-1967, and the UN forces in West Irian, 1962-1963, are similar cases; broadening a force's base to a truly international level clearly reduces its policy mandate to the lowest common denominator.[12] Rather than acting to guarantee a specified state of affairs, such passive forces are limited to interposing their presence in order (hopefully) to discourage deterioration of a situation. The UN Command in Korea, on the other hand, was not an 'international' force but rather a great power intervention in international dress, effective as a gurantee but essentially unilateral in substance.

Only in the Congo does a multilateral force seem to be both a true guaranteeing force and truly international. Both the UN policy in the Congo and the force itself were supported by states with no interests at stake, and under Hammerskjold's direction the UN force in the Congo followed an independent course of action not strictly parallel to or limited by the policies of individual states. But even here great power rivalry exerted some influence: the consonance of the operation with American aims made possible vital American support, and the subsequent alienation of the Soviet Union made it unlikely that more operations of this type could be carried out in the future. The force was also disrupted by the abrupt withdrawal of the states disapproving of Hammerskjold's policy. Finally, the unique circumstances that made the Congolese intervention successful—the ambiguous internal situation, the temporary unity against Belgian intervention, an activist Secretary General and universal opposition to Katangan secession—are unlikely to be duplicated again. True multilateral guarantees, and true multilateral guaranteeing forces, are in sum both rare and fragile. The possibility of fashioning an effective multilateral force to police Egypt-Israel agreements is discussed further below.

Applications

Generally, it must be stressed that the prognosis for international guarantees as part of an Egyptian-Israel settlement is poor. Effective guarantees are usually associated with conditions, especially great power domination, that are inapplicable to the Middle East and in any event might be worse than the disease. Discussion of past experience in relation to current problems may, however, help to eliminate totally unrealistic proposals and turn thinking along lines of guarantees more nearly suited to the situation. Specification of what an effective guarantee might look like, and what its limits would be, is in any event potentially useful in the formulation of policy and in determining to what extent guarantees can be considered in place of other safeguards for the maintenance of a settlement.

The modern rebirth of the word 'guarantee' with reference to the Middle East, and to the Egypt-Israel border in particular, is in itself of little significance, since, as we have seen, form and substance are not synonymous. There is a danger that 'guarantees' may be regarded as a concession made by one state in order to induce another state to accept a particular bargain, rather than as a relationship growing out of the real needs and interests of both. Only guarantees of the latter type, needless to say, survive historical scrutiny.

A.   Unilateral Guarantees

General guarantees based on the unity of great powers, always a weak reed, seem inconceivable in a modern context. The scope and intensity of the Cold War, even in its detente phases, make it highly unlikely that the major rivals could agree on the common stewardship of a violent local conflict in a strategically crucial area (though there was a time in a multipolar world, when powers could compete in one theatre while co-operating in another). Since Cold War rivalries cannot be transcended, the obvious course is to exploit their very inescapability and profundity as a dependable base of commitment. The enmity that collapses a general guarantee is the driving force of a unilateral great power guarantee. Moreover, two of the chronic problems of such guarantees, the danger of rapprochement between the rivals and inadequate power over distance, hardly seem worrisome today.

One great power can never guarantee both sides of a local conflict successfully; some alignment and choosing of sides is essential. This means an American guarantee of Israel and a Soviet guarantee of Egypt. As has been pointed out, however, the situation is not symmetrical; it is guarantees proffered to Israel that constitute the key to the bargaining situation, since Israel is being asked to surrender concrete advantages. Egypt, whose military position would anyway improve as a result of any Israeli withdrawal, might seek parallel guarantees as a matter of balance and as an additional security, but such guarantees would not be an integral *quid pro quo* to bargains reached. The focus is therefore on guarantees to Israel, though for the most part guarantees to Egypt involve identical logic, limitations, and likelihoods.

A unilateral American guarantee of Israel seems to have the support of of history—as far as it is supported by the structures of the Cold War. Opposition to the Soviet Union, a feared rival, is predictable without regard to Israel, but the same cannot be said of opposition to Egypt.

Although the United States in at least one case (Lebanon) did view Egypt's influence as a threat in itself, this furnishes no base for a blanket guarantee of Israel. It is not realistic to view Egypt as a Soviet proxy to be contained just as the Soviet Union itself; it is more realistic, in view of the widespread American interests in the Arab world, to view Egypt as an object of contention in United States-Soviet Union rivalry toward which the carrot is potentially as important as (or more important than) the stick. As always great powers, with multiple interests and calculations, cannot be expected to shoulder the burden of containing local powers toward whom they have no intrinsic enmity, unless they are protecting their own position in the threatened state (and there are no grounds for believing that the United States wants Israel as a client state in the Panamanian sense). Guarantees in general, and against local threats in particular, are effective when the guarantor has an intrinsic interest in the guaranteed territory itself, either because of its predominant position there or because the territory is adjacent and strategically important. An American guarantee of Israel against Egypt would be inherently unbelievable; the vague wording of all past American commitments to Israel, made by various Presidents on ceremonial occasions, is itself an indication of the limits of American involvement. In order to be credible, such a guarantee would have to specify exactly what steps would be taken under what circumstances, including the required use of force, and no such detailed commitments have been or seem likely to be offered (nor have they been to America's closest allies).

Finally, one must remember the presence of the rival superpower. Soviet backing of Egypt, rather than making it more likely that the United States would intervene against Egypt, means that no action against that state can be taken with impunity. The great powers, in their nulcear deadlock, can be effective in blocking each other, but the very totality of this stalemate means that they have less freedom to challenge untenable local situations (as the case of Cuba demonstrates). The same logic applies, of course, to Soviet guarantees of Egypt against Israel; consider the speed with which the Soviet Union dissociated itself from Egyptian moves in May 1967, in order to avoid a risky direct confrontation with the United States. The great powers counteract each other in the Middle East, but their success in doing so leads to a very limited control over local forces and conflicts in the area.

Although there are no grounds for making Israel a fully-fledged Cold War ally until and unless the Arab states became fully-fledged Soviet allies and the United States accepts that situation, there are certainly grounds for believing that the United States will counteract Soviet involvement in Egypt with an almost exactly matching counter-involvement. An American guarantee of Israel against Soviet activity is

224

in this sense based directly on American opposition to expansion of Soviet influence, and is not even dependent on action against the Soviets in Egypt itself, since the Soviet-American front is world-wide. Furthermore, the commitment need not be either formalized nor specified in detailed terms, since such formality or detail would be either superfluous (if the United States continues to fear the Soviet Union) or futile (if she did not). American *de facto* guarantees against the Soviet Union are of course matched by Soviet guarantees against American influence (the 1955 Egyptian-Czech arms deal was instigated in part by the establishment of the Baghdad Pact), making a system of reciprocal unilateral guarantees an expression of the basic great power paralysis.

The limitation of this should be clear. It is based on a bilateral stand-off; there are no floating balancers or 'neutral' or 'impartial' states among the next rank of powers whose presence is anything but superfluous in such a system of guarantees. The addition of Britain and France to round out an illusory Big Four could at best only dilute existing commitments by spreading them among a greater number of powers, but in actuality could not even accomplish this since neither additional power could divorce itself from Soviet-American rivalries nor force these rivalries aside.

Nor is such a guarantee best put into effect by the deployment of great power 'police forces' to the troubled area, despite recurrent mention of negotiations on a 'Big Four' force to enforce peace. As stated, guaranteeing forces are effective only when in support of a guarantee that is itself believable and workable. Generally, these cases involve alliances with great powers in which the proximity of a clear and present danger from another great power gives the force a *raison d'etre* and brings the host country to consider foreign troops on its territory as the lesser of two evils. Such forces are expressions of a great power rivalry wherever located, for they owe their efficiency to this rivalry. To deploy such a force, of one or more great power rivals, in support of local guarantees, would simple reduce the local arena to a theatre of their world-wide conflict. Soviet-American rivalry, to cite the relevant case, is far too dependable to imagine Soviet or American guaranteeing forces in the Middle East divorced from the Cold War. The age of true buffers is past; such a situation would either develop into another Cyprus, or lead to a face-to-face stand-off between the two superpowers and their increasingly submissive clients, or catalyze an even more tragic outcome.

The limits of great power rôles in guaranteeing Middle Eastern settlements do not appear, in sum, to be far from what both the United States and the Soviet Union are in fact doing at present without treaties or explicit agreement: consistently if sometimes fitfully blocking each other from excessive gaines as a function of the world balance of power. It is doubtful that either superpower, or either local power, can reasonably expect more than that or in all sincerity want more than that.

B. Multilateral Guarantees

Since true multilateral great power guarantees are, in modern circumstances, illusory, any "neutral" international guarantees would have to be as distant as possible from the superpowers. Since it would be composed of medium- or smaller-sized states whose interests in Middle Eastern quarrels are at best indirect, and whose power to intervene quickly even more doubtful, the deployment of an 'international' force is usually considered central to such a guarantee. In fact it might be said that the military force is the very substance of the guarantee, unlike the situation with unilateral great power guarantees where the basic commitment is vital but the deployment of forces unwise. (Needless to say, both the unilateral superpower guarantees and an international force, within their respective limits, could be employed simultaneously.)

A 'neutral' guaranteeing force charged only with the maintenance of specified elements of a local settlement, would theoretically be free of the dangers of great power forces. But such a force must also have a clear duty and adequate means to uphold guarantees of a positive and clearly defined nature, not a passive, "peace-keeping" or observation force, but a force with a clear mandate for enforcement. Generally as a force becomes more nearly 'international' or 'neutral', its mandate is progressively whittled down, and in the squeeze only special conditions, such as those in the Congo case, make possible the establishment of a force that is both 'guaranteeing' and 'international'.

The United Nations Emergency Force of 1957-1967 was not, as indicated, a guaranteeing force, nor was it a genuine 'international' force. The first point has been emphasized repeatedly by U Thant in response to criticism of his rapid withdrawal of UNEF in May of 1967; as he points out, UNEF was 'a peace-keeping and not an enforcement operation . . . which had no right to use force and which, from the beginning, had operated entirely on the basis of the consent of Egypt to its presence'.[13] Any international force regarded as a true guarantor of a particular settlement would, of course, have to have a mandate to enforce it by effective means and be able to act without the permission of the affected parties.

That UNEF was not truly international is also made clear by U Thant's reminder that the national policies of participating states had, in any event, prejudiced UNEF's future: 'Furthermore, the governments

226

which supplied the two largest contingents in UNEF had made it known that they had been approached by the United Arab Republic government and would immediately comply with its request for withdrawal of their troops'.[14] These two states, Yugoslavia and India, both enjoyed close relations with Egypt (one reason the presence of their troops had been acceptable), and could not have been expected to oppose this or any similar Egyptian request. Since the Canadian contingent was withdrawn abruptly under Egyptian demands because of certain Canadian policy statements, U Thant was in fact left with a disintegrating force which would have been totally ineffectual even had its legal base and functions been different.

It would seem that complete insulation of a military force so composed from the national policies of the donor states is an unrealistic goal. Only in the Congo operation could an international force have been said to transcend the lowest common denominator of its contributors' policies, and for reasons outlined a repeat of this episode seems unlikely even though it, too, was seriously troubled by the withdrawal of participating contingents. It might be better to design a force of contingents from states whose national orientations might lend some credibility to the effectiveness of the force, rather than to attempt a foredoomed separation of national interests from the force's operation. In this way the force, though not truly international, might at least partly enjoy a real motivation for effective enforcement rather than being completely dependent on the goodwill of its contributors.

Remembering the limitations of any 'neutral' multilateral guarantee, the following recommendations might nevertheless be made regarding the composition and mandate of any future "international" police force in the Middle East:

1. The force should be tied to the specific terms of a specific arrangement, leaving no doubt regarding the situation it is mandated to maintain. This is especially important in a 'neutral' guarantee in which several states are involved and in which their most vital interests are not at stake, since the extent of the guarantee in this case is *not* defined by the interests of the guarantor. It is interesting to note that before the nineteenth century it was customary for guarantors and allies to specify *precisely* the number of troops that would be committed, on what fronts, and under what conditions (and sometimes for what duration); it might be well to revive this practice in the new circumstances above.[15] It might also be pointed out that tying such a force to a peace settlement will make it more difficult for small defaults and violations to pass without upsetting the overall stability, a fact that will ensure greater confidence in the enforcement of the parts (just as states hesitated to revise parts of the Treaty of Vienna, for fear of upsetting the entire new order).

227

2. The force should be composed of contingents from a broad variety of guaranteeing states, excluding the superpowers, and include insofar as possible states with some interest in the maintenance of the peace treaty. In the first place such arrangements free the force from dependence on one state or bloc of states, should policies shift and enforcement of the treaty become inconvenient. The Congo force was fortunately left with enough contingents to accomplish its mission despite the withdrawal of some; the Pope in 1870 was left undefended when one state (France) changed its policy; and, as stated, UNEF was extraordinarily dependent on states very friendly to Egypt. Obviously, in order to have any credibility with Israel the force would have to include some states without extensive interests in the Arab world, perhaps some of the smaller Western European states (Denmark, the Netherlands) with a traditional friendship to Israel based on the memories of the Second World War. There are also other categories of states that might have an interest, if indirectly, in Middle East stability, such as maritime and trading nations that would be heavy users of a reopened canal (Japan, Australia, Norway, Greece, etc.). Eastern European states, such as Poland or Rumania, have sometimes feared tension in the Middle East because of apprehension that it will lead to tightened bloc discipline; again, the broader the spectrum of contributing states, the more confidence it might instil both with Israel and Egypt.

3. Needless to say, any guaranteeing force should have a clear mandate for military action, under circumstances carefully specified in advance and explicitly accepted by all sides including the guarantors. It would have to be of size to be effective militarily, with all the adequate equipment, and financed by more secure arrangements than in the past.

4. Since such a force would not be truly international, the commitments involved should be reinforced by direct bilateral understandings between each guarantor and the guaranteed state or states, covering the force to be deployed (possibly their financing as well), their commitment to battle, and the conditions under which they may be recalled. Such agreements need not be formal treaties in order to be effective, but again greater specificity, like the treaties of old, would increase credibility.

5. The recall of national contingents should be dependent on the agreement of both local parties (as well as the Security Council and other appropriate bodies), perhaps with provision made for replacement of one state by another if agreeable to all concerned. The changeability of international politics, and the nature of the local conflict, make this point crucial to the confidence that can be placed in any outside guaranteeing forces.

It should be clear, in the end, that outside guarantees are no substitute for peace agreements that are workable in their own terms, nor are they short-cuts to such agreements. When their basic limitations are understood and taken into account, they can be a useful additional tool in stabilizing a workable agreement by creating greater confidence in its maintenance. But underneath remains the inevitable question: Who will guarantee the guarantors? One of the leading students of guarantees ends his discussion of the subject with the following reminder: 'But the inescapable conclusion is this: however effective a State's guarantee may be, it will never be better protected than by the care and energy which it devotes to its own defence of its essential rights'.[16]

NOTES

1. Thomas C. Schelling, **The Strategy of Conflict** (Cambridge, Mass., 1963), 43-4.

2. Emmerich de Vattel, **Le Droit de Gens** (Washington, D.C., 1916), vol. III, 193.

3. J.W.Headlam-Morley, 'Treaties of Guarantee', **Cambridge Historical Journal,** II (1927), 152-3.

4. A full description of the survey, with a list of cases, justification of criteria, and elaboration of conclusions will be published later. Interested parties are invited to contact the author. The survey is intended to be as inclusive as possible; it includes all political entities in the period since 1815 which meet Singer and Small's criterion for population size (500,000), whether or not they met the legitimacy requirement (recognition by Britain and France), and it also includes true protectorates (those retaining internal autonomy) and units below the population threshold guaranteed by a major power.
J.D. Singer and M. Small, 'The Composition and Status Ordering of the International System, 1815-1940', **World Politics,** XVIII (1966), 236-82; and J.D. Singer and M. Small, 'Formal Alliances, 1815-1939', **Journal of Peace Research,** II (1966), 1-32.

5. This is roughly parallel to Morgenthau's analysis when he states that, in order to fulfil their function, both unilateral and multilateral treaties of guarantee 'must meet two prerequisites: they must be effective in their execution, and the execution must be automatic'. Morgenthau also points out that 'the effectiveness of the execution . . . depends upon the distribution of power between the guarantor nations and the lawbreaker'; in other words, it is important to remember that the test of adequacy depends greatly on the nature of the threat as well as the absolute strength of the guarantor.
Hans Morgenthau, **Politics among Nations,** (4th ed., New York, 1967), 284.

6. 11 of the 44 effective guarantees, and 17 of the 71 ineffective or untested guarantees, were not formalized in treaties but were either declared or implicit.

7. Adding pattern 3 (dominant protection) and protected strategic zones of pattern 1 together, there are 44 guarantees of which 31 are effective. Only 13 of the remaining 71 guarantees are effective.

8.Rothstein points out that 'neutrality of nonalignment is a dangerous security policy for small powers which are exposed to a great power threat', but warns a few pages later that 'alliance with a superior power is inherently dangerous for a small power.' Both alternatives are indeed risky, which illustrates the dilemma of a state in such a position. Robert Rothstein, Alliances and Small Powers (New York and London, 1968), 34, 61.

9. Israeli scenarios of future American guarantees of a settlement, which almost always end badly, usually assume an unfriendly change of government in Washington.

10. Of the 46 post-1945 guarantees exactly half were judged effective, while only 21 of the 69 earlier guarantees were so rated.

11. British opposition to the incursions of Egypt's Mohammed Ali in Ethiopia was punctuated by announced willingness to tolerate Belgian occupation of the same area. (Mohammed Ali was viewed by the British as the equivalent of a major rival.)
Mordechai Abir, Ethiopia: The Era of the Princes (New York and Washington, 1968), 137.

12. D. Wainhouse et al., International Peace Observation: A History and Forecast (Baltimore, 1966).

13. U. Thant, 'The United Nations as Scapegoat', War/Peace Report, March 1971, 8-11.

14. Ibid., 9.

15. Headlam-Morley criticizes the imprecision of the guarantee of Belgium (1839) by restating it as earlier generations would have phrased it: 'If, however, what God avert, any Prince or Potentate should be so neglectful of his duties as to infringe and violate the said Peace and to bring injury, violence and invasion against the territories of His Majesty the King of the Belgians, then the King of England, the King of France, etc. shall make together a league and confederation for the defence of His said Majesty and before coming to arms they shall summon the aggressor to desist from his iniquitous endeavours. And if he refuse, then they shall in arms come to the help of His said Majesty the King of the Belgians, and the King of England shall get together a gallant and strong army of not less than 50,000 men with ships properly equipped for battle, and they shall protect the territories of His said Majesty the King of the Belgians, and not desist until by force of arms they have expelled the invader and have compelled him to make reparations'.
Headlam-Morley, loc. cit., 166.

16. George Petimermet, Le Traite de Guarantie en Droit International Public (Lausanne, 1940), 108, (Translation supplied).

22. SOUTHERN AFRICA : A STUDY IN CONFLICT

William Gutteridge

The selection of Southern Africa for an empirical case study in conflict is made on the basis of the possibility of the development of the situation there into an actual rather than a potential threat to world peace. At the present time the so-called superpowers – the United States, the Soviet Union and China – have adopted relatively low-key policies in the area and have so far certainly not assigned it any high strategic priority. Nevertheless there is a widely held view that the continuance of white minority supremacy, particularly by the methods adopted in the Republic of South Africa, is objectionable in moral and human terms. In accordance with this view, a violent conflict of a kind already exists and an escalation of it is probably an essential prerequisite to its solution. Certainly the current levels of peace and stability, if these terms can appropriately be used, on the whole favour the maintenance of the *status quo*. In this situation the interaction of internal and external factors tending to lead to change would seem to involve a particular risk of the escalation of violence.

Conflict is inherent in the Southern African situation and has its roots deep in the past. To understand its origins it is necessary to go back to the Dutch colonization of the Cape of Good Hope which began with a group of settlers from Europe in 1652. At that time the southern tip of Africa appeared to be a largely empty land. The virtual elimination of the Bushmen and the Hottentots, the importation of labour from the East Indies and the southward surge of the Bantu African peoples were important factors contributing to the development of the complex contemporary situation. The consolidation of the Portuguese in Angola and Mozambique, the arrival of the British during the Napoleonic Wars, their subsequent acquisition of Cape Colony and eventual expansion northwards into Rhodesia compounded the complexity, as did the German annexation of South West Africa (Namibia) at the end of the nineteenth century.

The Southern African problem could never have been described as a simple confrontation between black and white, nor can it be so described today. Such a confrontation is the core of the matter but there are many other interests involved which are likely to have a profound effect on the development of the situation and may lead to an escalation of violent conflict. There are already some forces at work actually promoting a more violent conflict and there would undoubtedly be others if the outcome could be reliably foreseen: this is largely because of the generation of frustration and reaction by the blocking of peaceful routes to political progress on the part of the African peoples, and significantly a working party of the Department of International Affairs of the British Council of Churches and the Conference of British Missionary Societies in 1970 published a report entitled *Violence in Southern Africa: a Christian Assessment* which asserted that the logic of the Christian standpoint was to give support to armed revolution. The uniqueness of the Southern African situation lies in the uncompromising adoption by the Government of the Republic of South Africa of a policy of racial superiority. As a case study in the development of a conflict situation, its usefulness is heightened by its relative geographical isolation which serves to highlight the contributory factors. Subordinate to the main theme of black-white confrontation there is the tension, apparent in the recent student protests, between the two white groups, the English-speaking and the Afrikaner, in South Africa which is itself a legacy from the period which the 'liberal' imperialism of Britain was in direct conflict with Boer nationalism and in competition with Portuguese and German modes of colonial expansion. The object of this paper is to take in turn each aspect of the current situation and to analyze its potentialiality to effect change whether by peaceful or violent means.

Since 1948, when the Nationalist Government came to power, pressures from the United Nations on South Africa have been continuous. The situation of Indians in South Africa was the first important issue to arise from the heavy emphasis on human rights in the UN Charter. The Cold War, leading to a more sympathetic view of the grievances of subject peoples, the recognition of African nationalism elsewhere on the continent as a legitimate force combined with rigorous racial legislation in South Africa to raise the level of international criticism. The growth in Afro-Asian influence and voice in the United Nations was directly connected with South Africa's withdrawal from the Commonwealth in 1961. For a time during the 1960s attention focused on the status and administration of South West Africa (Namibia) but soon switched to the more general application of 'apartheid' in the heartland of the Republic. An embargo on the sale of arms to South Africa was proposed and there were calls for a trade boycott. Neither of these has ever been effective to the point of inducing a modification of the domestic policies at which they were aimed. The establishment of the Organization of African Unity (OAU) in 1963 and its setting up of a Liberation Committee to finance and support liberation movements waging guerilla war in Southern Africa have likewise apparently failed to produce the hoped-for results. The assertion of the moral rejection of 'apartheid' and energetic attempts to mobilize world opinion have not led to sufficient economic, political or military pressures to cause the white leaders of the Republic to modify their racial policies. There has always been among the developing as well as the developed nations enough cynical concern for their own self-interest to sustain the white supremacist regime.

The position, however, is not static. On the one hand, African nationalist leaders such as Kaunda and Nyerere adhere, at any rate in principle, to the terms of the Lusaka Manifesto of May 1969: 'we still prefer to achieve it (independence), without physical violence . . . we do not advocate violence, we advocate an end to the violence against human dignity which is now being perpetrated by the oppressors of Africa'. President Nyerere has advocated such pressures on the Southern African Governments through the United Nations that change would have to come: '. . . it is a question of whether preservation of peace by the removal of injustice is sufficiently important to us. If it is, we shall exert all pressures short of war. If it is not the war will grow.' These statements apparently allow for the possibility of peaceful change and leave the door, at least in theory, open to a peaceful transfer of power, for example in the Portuguese territories. On the other hand, the Nationalist Government of South Africa is firmly in control of the internal security of that country and strengthening its grip and at the same time claiming success for its Bantustan policy. There has, nevertheless, been some debate within the governing party between the 'verligtes' and the 'verkramptes' — the doves and hawks of apartheid — and events in the Transkei and Zululand suggest that the logic of separate development — self-governing Bantustans increasingly asserting their separate existence — has not escaped the African leadership there. The decision to establish the Bantustans may yet be seen to have played a similar role to concessions of representation and self-government in colonies elsewhere. Similarly, during 1970-1971 South African attempts to promote dialogue with African states to the north seemed to be having some success and to portend a consolidation of her position as a potential economic master in parts of the continent. The change of government following the second military coup in Ghana, the shifting situations in Uganda and the Malagasy Republic have shown this to be largely an illusion and the OAU has reaffirmed that organisation's intention of working towards the elm.iniation of the white supremacist regimes in the south. Similarly in Rhodesia the attempted Anglo-Rhodesian settlement served through the Pearce Commission's activities to inject new life into African political activity and to destroy in most people's mind the delusion of a contented Rhodesia African population. Malawi, however, remains an example of South Africa's desired relationships with African states: 100,000 Malawians work as migrant labour in the Republic, the Republic is building a new Malawian capital at Lilongwe and has provided loans for financing a sugar mill, a hotel, a fertilizer plant and other enterprises. The possibility of military usage, perhaps for reconaissance flights over neighbouring African countries, by South Africa of a new airport is in a sense incidental: there is no doubt of South Africa's intention to use her economic weight to further her influence and domination of African states wherever the opportunity offers. 'We are,' as the Prime Minister Vorster said in 1968, 'of Africa, we understand Africa and nothing is going to prevent us from becoming the leaders of Africa in every field.' The consolidation of the Republic's economic position is seen as the surest route to security, for the relationship of those African countries which become involved with South Africa is likely to be one of a quasi-colonial economic dependence because of their state of development. In this connection the role of the Chinese-built Tanzani railway and the corresponding road route may have been underestimated in that the dependence of Zambia on trade links to the south will be substantially weakened by them.

Economic factors are also important in considering the Portuguese position. On the one hand, the defence of the 'overseas provinces' of Angola, Mozambique and Guinea-Bissau is a heavy drain on Portugal's resources of manpower and money — nearly 45 per cent of the national budget is being spent in this way and labour shortages result from long-term conscription. On the other hand, the territories are closely integrated into the Portuguese economy with typically colonialist restrictions on the development of rival production and deliberate depression of the prices of African cotton and sugar below the world average. The apparently liberal policy of 'assimilation' is Portugal's strength and weakness: it has allowed her to use armed African levies without great risk and enabled her on occasions to exploit rifts in the African liberation movements, but any relaxation of the determination of the Lisbon government in the face of radical movements at home and resulting large-scale evasion of 'call-up' would lead to a rapid escalation of opposition of one kind or another.

The extent of South Africa's dependence on the maintenance of the Portuguese position on either flank is hard to estimate, but there are growing signs of concern where such long frontiers and coastlines are involved.[1] There are signs that South Africa, already tentatively involved in the Rhodesian security situation with the deployment of armed police units in the Zambesi Valley, is becoming more involved in the Portuguese territories. Apart from meetings between security chiefs there have been unconfirmed reports of aerial reconnaisance over Angola and specifically of assistance with the spraying of defoliants in FRELIMO-controlled areas of northern Mozambique. This may reflect the growing economic commitment of South Africa in the financing of,

234

for example, the Cabora Bassa dam in Mozambique and the Cunene hydro-electric scheme in Angola: for both the African nationalists and the white regimes these schemes are key aspects of the struggle in the sense that because their success might benefit Africans over wide areas they would also lead to the consolidation of Portuguese control.

The extent of South Africa's willingness to come to the defence of her northern neighbours is probably the key to the whole conflict situation in Southern Afirca in that a deterioration of the position in several areas simultaneously might cause her to spread her military resources very thinly and to overreach her strength, thus providing the opportunity which the liberation movements have been waiting for.

In this connection the possible influence of the Soviet Union and China must be taken into account. So far rivalry between these two powers has tended to weaken the 'freedom fighters' by the support given to different factions and this has apparently created some resistance on the part of African leaders in Zambia and Tanzania to the possibility of the 'carve-up' of Africa into new spheres of influence. On the whole Chinese influence has been more significant and exercised with more conviction than the Soviet partly because China needed the support of the African states to gain admission to the United Nations, and the tangible evidence of this lies in the Tanzani railway and the assistance given to Tanzania in the training and equipping of defence forces. It is likely that these external influences will be used to foster more militant attitudes towards South Africa with its important mineral resources or at least to prevent any decline in the priority given to the overthrow of white supremacist regimes. This could be achieved by the strengthening of the 'liberation' groups based, for example, in Zambia and Tanzania which would then be in a position to exert pressures on the host governments.

In compiling a balance sheet of power and influence in this part of the world it is important to appreciate that by comparison with the Western capitalist countries the stake of the Communist powers in the development and security of Africa is as yet minute. The conflict in Southern Africa cannot be seen in isolation from, for example, the economic development of parts of East and Central Africa. In some countries, notably Kenya and Zaire, more importance is attached to this than to the violent resolution of the Southern African situation. Their self-interest will help to maintain British, American and other influence in the area. Indeed, the importance of the debate in Britain about arms for South Africa lay more in the difficulties which such a policy would put in the way of British military and other assistance to such states as Zambia and Kenya than in the more dramatic aspects emphasized at the time. Again, British economic interest in Nigeria, with which country trade is rapidly growing, and other black African

235

countries are not without bearing on South Africa's situation, which, whether it is admitted or not, is more dependent on British markets and capital than Britain is upon her. As far as the military situation is concerned Britain's preparedness to supply arms for South Africa would be more important for its psychological effects on the confidence of the South African Government than in practical military terms.

With the reservations already mentioned about the possibility of South Africa overreaching her strength, the regular, as opposed to the irregular or guerilla, military situation is clear-cut. South Africa's strength is overwhelming, as compared with any forces which the OAU could deploy against her. It is not simply a matter of overall strength – in theory the member states of OAU have more than 700,000 men at their disposal, 400,000 being in sub-Saharan Africa – but a question of logistics. Minimal air forces, a small capacity for airlift and lack of storage facilities and supply bases within reach of the white-dominated states constitute an overwhelming handicap. The problems of servicing an expeditionary force of 50,000 men, which would not in any case be enough, are at present and for the foreseeable future insuperable. The question of an African High Command has never been satisfactorily resolved and there would be difficulties over language, command procedures and standardisation of equipment, weapons and ammunition. Advocacy of direct military confrontation will continue but it is unlikely to eventuate in any form until internal upheavals in Southern Africa have simplified the task. South Africa has a fairly small regular defence force with the latest aircraft and weapons but could quickly mobilise a force of more than 100,000 white men. Her strength in armoured cars and tanks make her a considerable land power, capable because of careful stockpiling of spares and ammunition, as well as of an indigenous armaments industry, of sustained effort over a reasonable period of time. The manufacture on licence of French and Italian equipment has played an important part in establishing a locally formidable position. Nevertheless the ability of any force to resist widespread and continuous uprisings including those beyond the boundaries of the Republic itself must be doubted.

The strength of the Rhodesian position on its own is certainly open to question. The white population is so small in proportion to the total population of the country that without external assistance the number of able-bodied men available to resist persistent guerilla attacks could well prove inadequate in a matter of weeks, quite apart from the fact that the economy would be at risk if they were long withdrawn from their civilian occupations. Portugal has over the last decade, in the face of armed African opposition, assembled in Angola and Mozambique armed forces totalling about 100,000 men and though the 'freedom' fighters have been contained they are still a force to reckon with, at

236

least in the Moxico province of Angola and the Tete province around
the Cabora Bassa dam in Mozambique. Indeed, there is evidence of
revival of activity in both areas, though overall the Portuguese emphasis
on economic and social weapons in attempting to maintain her African
position has been successful. This is largely because the activities of the
OAU Liberation Committee have not yet brought the guerilla
movements to the point of take-off. The infiltration of raiding parties
into Rhodesia has led to heavy casualties which have not helped to win
support from the local African population and have at the same time
deprived the 'freedom fighters' of the advantages of experienced
leadership.

Nationalist liberation organisations have been divided against each
other, partly on ideological grounds, in Angola, in Mozambique and in
the Rhodesian groups between which fighting actually broke out in the
Zambian capital, Lusaka, until President Kaunda actually enforced an
artificial unity on them. A diversity of training instructors from, for
example, Cuba, Algeria, Eastern Europe, the UAR and China and a
shortage of manpower, deriving from the failure to generate a
revolutionary climate based on a real sense of grievance, have contribted
to the present position. The terrain of Southern Africa, lacking
mountain refuges and close forest cover, and the enormous distances
involved are also factors in a situation where in any case the African
countries closest to the 'front line' are nervous about the effect on their
own stability of training camps on their territories and about the
possibility of retaliation or pre-emptive strikes from the south.

Militarily the position of the white-dominated territories of the
Republic, Mozambique, Angola and Rhodesia seems secure, and in
Rhodesia and South Africa the African populations appear quiescent,
whether through apathy or intimidation and repression. This is, then,
the position to which a balance sheet of factors apparently leads. On
the one hand, white military and economic strength, established police
security systems, the tacit support of much of the capitalist world and
some success in seducing external African cooperation by playing on
the needs of economic self-interest combine to produce an impression
of impregnability. Against this, a majority of the populations by far are
black African, who have not only the strong moral support of the vast
majority of African states but the interested involvement of external
forces, principally the Communist superpowers. The fact that so far
they have failed to mobilize and coordinate their efforts is a factor
operating at the moment in favour of the white *status quo* but this
could be reversed either gradually by determination or more abruptly
by an event which crystallized grievances, raised morale and created a
truly revolutionary situation in some part of Southern Africa. Similarly
the weakening of resolve on the part of the white regimes due to

237

problems in European Portugal or pressures on Portugal from NATO allies in the face of the shifting balance of their own self-interest in their relations with the African states, or due to new trends in South African opinion, for example, through universities affected by the internationalism of young intellectuals, could change the situation.

Even the 'stability' or 'balance' which arises from the impotent frustration of one party in the face of apparently overwhelming strength of the other party is rarely static and usually conceals a hidden dynamism leading to the possibility of 'imbalance'. In Southern Africa on a number of levels conflict already exists: it is liable to escalate because of the tipping of the scales in one way or the other which might be the product of an intangible change of mood or even of a physical intervention from outside. At the moment the significant factors on either side seem to be as follows:

THE SITUATION IN SOUTHERN AFRICA : A 'BALANCE' SHEET

A *For the status quo*	B *Tending to undermine the status quo*
1. Geographical situation and terrain.	Long frontiers and coastline-extension of the Republic's military commitment.
2. Strong military and police systems in white-dominated territories.	Gradually increasing military strength and experience of black African countries.
3. Support by many developed countries for economic and strategic reasons.	Possible changes in economic self-interest of some developed countries leading to improved relations with developing African countries.
4. Rivalry between the Soviet Union and China.	Support by the Soviet Union and China.
5. Economic self-interest of some developing African countries.	Reassertion of Pan-African pressures and influences.
6. Economic and social policies aimed at winning African support inside and outside Southern Africa.	Adverse effects of such policies especially population transfer in the Republic which might lead to increased African political awareness and activity.
7. Low morale and relative ineffectiveness of 'liberation' movements.	Rise in 'freedom movements' morale due either to repression or emergence political opportunities, e.g. Pearce Commission in Rhodesia or separate development in Bantustans.
8. Reaction of Portuguese settlers in Africa to 'liberal' policies emerging in Lisbon.	Changes in Portuguese policy towards Africa.

At present the weight appears to be emphatically on the side of column A. But no consideration of this kind can be complete without listing factors, existing or speculative, tending to affect the sum. Recently there have been the unprecedented strike of Ovambo labour in South West Africa, the riotous reaction to the Pearce Commission's visit to Rhodesia, the rise of Chief Butulezi in the Zululand Bantustan paralleling events in the Transkei, white university student resistance unique in South Africa, and intensified guerilla activity, involving some interruption of communication and undermining of white morale, at the Cabora Bassa dam site in Mozambique. Already the tendency since 1970 of British and American spokesmen to play down African criticism of their actions has been modified. In fact, the effect of any new factor in the situation could be incalculable. The more obvious possibilities are an accidental or deliberate Sharpeville-type incident in Rhodesia or South Africa, a settlement between Britain and Rhodesia, a further upsurge of political activity in the Bantustans, a change of policy in Portugal, a more determined and unified Communist strategy, or a guerrilla success, for example, in a Rhodesian city. These are eventualities or contingencies, of which the outcomes are not certainly predictable, but for which the world community needs to be prepared.

NOTE

1. This paper was prepared before the dramatic developments which occurred in Portugal during the course of 1974 (eds.).

NOTES ON CONTRIBUTORS

CARACCIOLO di San Vito, Roberto is a retired Italian ambassador who has represented his country at the Geneva Disarmament Conference. He is author of *Discorsi sul disarmo* and of articles on disarmament problems. He is the President of the Italian Committee for Peace Research.

CARLTON, David (Co-Editor) is Senior Lecturer in Diplomatic History at the Polytechnic of North London. He is author of *Macdonald versus Henderson: The Foreign Policy of the Second Labour Government 1929-1931* and of numerous articles on international problems of the present century.

CAVALLETTI, Francesco is a retired Italian ambassador who has represented his country in Luxembourg, Belgrade, Madrid and at the Geneva Disarmament Conference. He is contributor to *Politica e Strategia*.

DOWTY, Alan is Senior Lecturer in International Relations and Director of the Institute for Research in International Relations at the Hebrew University, Jerusalem. Formerly a Fellow at the Adlai Stevenson Institute of International Affairs, Chicago.

EPSTEIN, William is chief of the Disarmament Affairs Division of the United Nations Organization, New York.

GOLDBLAT, Jozef is on the staff of the Stockholm International Peace Research Institute (SIPRI). He has contributed to several SIPRI publications.

GUTTERIDGE, William is Head of the Department of Complementary Studies, University of Aston in Birmingham. He has written extensively on African problems with special reference to military considerations.

KASHI, Joseph is engaged in research in the Defense Program of the Political Science Department of the Massachusetts Institute of Technology.

KODŽIĆ, Peter is engaged in research at the Institute of Social Studies, The Hague.

LEURDIJK, J. Henk, who teaches International Relations at the University of Amersterdam, is a specialist in general theories of international politics, in strategic analysis, and in arms control and disarmament policies.

MOCH, Jules is a former French Minister of Defence. He also served as French delegate to various international disarmament conferences. He is author of *Human Folly: To Disarm or Perish?* and many other books.

MORGENTHAU, Hans is Albert A. Michelson Distinguished Service Professor Emeritus of Political Science and Modern History, University of Chicago; Leonard Davis Distinguished Professor Emeritus of Political Science, City College of the City University of New York; University Professor of Political Science, New School for Social Research, New York. He has published innumerable books and articles. He is a Consultant to the U.S. Department of State.

RATHJENS, George is Professor of Political Science at the Massachusetts Ins Institute of Technology. He was previously associated with the US Arms Control and Disarmament Agency; and the US Department of Defence. He is author of *The Future of the Strategic Arms Race*.

REUTOV, Academician Oleg is a member of the Department of Chemistry at the the University of Moscow.

RUINA, Jack is a Professor of Electrical Engineering at the Massachusetts In Institute of Technology. He has been associated with the US Arms Control and Disarmament Agency and with various other government agencies.

SAHOVIC, Milan is a member of the Institute of International Politics and Economics, Belgrade.

SCHAERF, Carlo (Co-Editor) is Professor of Physics at the University of Rome. Born in Italy, he obtained his doctoral degree from the University of Rome in 1958. He then worked as a research associate at the Instituto Nazionale di Fisica Nucleare in Rome until 1960. After being a Research Associate from 1960 till 1963 at the High Energy Physics Laboratory at the University of Stanford, he returned to Italy to work for the Atomic Energy Commission where he reained until 1973 when he left to take the chair of Physics in the Faculty of Science of the University of Rome. Founder in 1966 with Professor Edoardo Amaldi of the International School on Disarmament and Research on Conflicts (ISODARCO) he became Director in 1970.

SCHELLING, Thomas is based at the John Fitzgerald Kennedy School of Government, Harvard University. He has written widely on arms control and strategy in the nuclear age. His best-known works include *The Strategy of Conflict* and *Arms and Influence*.

TSIPIS, Kosta is a physicist engaged in research at the Center for International Studies at the Massachusetts Institute of Technology. He has also been associated with the Stockholm Peace International Research Institute.

YORK, Herbert is Professor of Physics and a former Chancellor and Dean of the University of California at San Diego. He was one of the nuclear physicists who developed the atomic bomb; was Director of the Livermore Radiation Laboratory; was in the US Defense Department under Presidents Eisenhower and Kennedy; and was an adviser to President Johnson. He is the author of *Race to Oblivion: A Participant's View of the Arms Race*.

LIST OF COURSE PARTICIPANTS

Name	Nationality	Present Address
AEBI, Alfred	Swiss – US	Graduate Inst. of International Affairs, 130 rue de Lausanne, Geneva, Switzerland
AITKEN, Martin P.	British	63 Holbrook Road, Cambridge, Great Britain
AL-MULLA, Nabila	Kuwaiti	American University of Beirut, P O Box 236, Beirut, Lebanon
BEN-DAK, Joseph D.	Israeli	(Visiting) Dept. of History, University of Lund, Lund, Sweden.
BONELLI, Adriano	Italian	International Fellowship of Reconciliation, D 3321 Gross-Heere n.60, Federal German Republic
BRAUN, Steven N.	US	Harvard College, Cambridge, United States
BRUNI, Alessio	Italian	Via Mantellini 8F, 50016, S. Domenico di Fiesole, Fiernze, Italy
CALOGERO, Francesco	Italian	Dept. of Physics, Universita di Roma, P. le delle Scienze, Roma, Italy
CARACCIOLO, Roberto	Italian	10, ch de l'Imperatrice, Geneva, Switzerland
CARLTON, David	British	Polytechnic of North London, Prince of Wales Rd, London NW5, Great Britain
CAVALLETTI, Francesco	Italian	Via degli Orsini 34, Roma, Italy
CHAMMAH, Albert	US	University of Texas at Austin, Dept. of Management B.E.B. 511, Austin, Texas, 78712, United States
CREMER, Pierre	Belgian	École de Guerre, 18, Avenue de Cortemberg, 1040, Bruxelles, Belgium
DONÀ DALLE ROSE, Luigi Filippo	Italian	Ist. di Fisica dell'Univ., Via Marzolo 8, 35100 Padova, Italy
DOWTY, Alan	US-Israeli	Hebrew University, Jerusalem, Israel
EATON, William B.	US	Univ. of Maryland, College Park, Maryland, United States
EPSTEIN, William	Canadian	Disarmament Affairs Division, United Nations, New York, United States
FISCHER, Mechtild	West German	DSFK, D-53 Bonn -Bad Godesberg, Theaterstr. 4, Federal German Republic
FLAPAN, Simha	Israeli	Jewish Arab Inst. Givat Haviva, Givat Haviva, Doar Shomron, Israel
FOGARTY, Thomas	US	Dept. of Regional Science, Univ. of Pennsylvania, Philadelphia, Pennsylvania, United States

GOLDBLAT, Jozef	stateless	SIPRI, Sveavagen 166, 11346 Stockholm Sweden
GUTTERIDGE, William	British	Univer. of Aston, Gosta Green, Birmingham, B4, JET, Great Britain
HAGELIN, Biorn E.	Swedish	Research Inst. of Swedish National Defence, Linnegatan 89, S-10450, Stockholm 80, Sweden
KASHI, Joseph	US	M.I.T. Dept. of Political Science, Cambridge, Mass., United States
KODZIC, Peter	Yugoslav	Inst. of Social Studies, 27 Molenstraat, The Hague, The Netherlands
KUBBA, Muhammad	Iraqi	American Univer. of Beirut, P O Box 236, Beirut, Lebanon
LEURDJK, Henk J.	Dutch	Univ. of Amsterdam, Herengracht 508, Amsterdam, the Netherlands
LILIC, Stevan	Yugoslav	Univ. of Belgrade, Faculty of Law, Bulevar Revolucije 67, Belgrade, Yugoslavia
LOPATKIEWICZ, Stefan M.	US	Harvard Law School, Cambridge, Mass. 02138, United States
MARLING, Mats R.	Swedish	Forsvarsstaben, Ostermalmsgatan 87, Stockholm, Sweden
MERCIECA, Charles	US	Alabama A&M Univ. Huntsville, Alabama 35762, United States
MOCH, Jules	French	97 B^d Murat, Paris 16^e, France
MOHANDESSAN, Mehrdad	Iranian	Univ. College London, 3-6 Endsleigh Gardens, London WC1, Great Britain
MORGENTHAU, Hans	US	33 West 42nd St., New York City, United States
MUSALLAM, Sami	Jordanian	78 Freiburg/Breisgau, Wilhelmstr. 17, Federal German Republic
NAKAI, Yoko	Japanese	3-27, 4-Chome, Shibuya – Ku, Tokyo Japan
NEYTCHEFF, Slautcho	Bulgarian	Bulgarian Academy of Medicine, Sofia 31, Bulgaria
PASCOLINI, Alessandro	Italian	Ist. di Fisica dell'Univer. Via Marzolo, 8, 35100 Padova, Italy
PRATT, Simcha	Israeli	Ministry of Foreign Affairs, Jerusalem Israel
REUTOV, Oleg	Soviet	Dept. of Chemistry, Univ. of Moscow, Moscow B-234, Soviet Union
RUTHERFORD, Evan L.	British	Derby College of Art and Technology, Kedleston Rd, Derby, Great Britain
SAFFOURY, Lamia	Lebanese	Univer. College, London, Dept. of International Relations. Faculty of Laws, 4-8 Endsleigh Gardens, London WC1H OEG, Great Britain
SAHOVIC, Milan	Yugoslav	Inst. of International Politics and Economics, Makedonska 25, P.B. 750, Belgrade, Yugoslavia
SANDOLE, Dennis J.D.	US	Univ. College London, Faculty of Laws, 4-8 Endsleigh Gardens, London, WC1H OEG, Great Britain

SCHAERF, Carlo	Italian	L.N.F. Casella Postale 70, 00044 Frascati, Italy
SCHUTZ, Hans J.	Austrian	Dept. for International Economic Law, A-5020 Salzburg, Weiser Str. 22, Austria
SIRRIYYEH, Hussein	Jordanian	American Univer. of Beirut, Inst. for Palestine Studies, P O Box 7164, Beirut, Lebanon
SOLMS, Friedhelm	West German	FEST, Schmeilweg, 5, Heidelberg, Federal German Republic
SOKOYA, James D.O.	Nigerian	Permanent Mission of Nigeria, 44, rue de Lausanne, 1201, Geneva, Switzerland
TSIPIS, Kosta	US	M.I.T., 77 Massachusetts Ave, Cambridge Mass., United States
UKAYLI, Mustafa	Saudi Arabian	c/o Foreign Student Advisor, Ohio State Univer. Columbus, Ohio 43210, United States
VARI, Stefano	Italian	Via della Selva n.5, 00034, Colleferro (Roma) Italy
VUKAS, Budislav	Yugoslav	Univer. of Zagreb, Law School, 41000 Zagreb, Trg. M.Tita 14, Yugoslavia
YORK, Herbert	US	Univ. of California, San Diego, La Jolla, Ca, 92037, United States
ZIAI, Iradj	Iranian	Maison du Liban, 9^E Bd Jourdan, 75690 Paris, Cedex 14, France
RATHJENS, George	US	M.I.T., Cambridge, Mass., United States
RUINA, Jack	US	M.I.T., Cambridge, Mass., United States
SCHELLING, Thomas	US	Harvard University, Cambridge, Mass., United States
SCOVILLE Herbert	US	–